COLEMAN, (Female)

	Mother's Maiden Surname.	District.	Vol.	Page.
COLEMAN, Philippa J.	OATES	Westmorland S.1 b		860
— Rebecca J.	HAYNS	Amersham	6 a	528
— Richard C.	LOWE	Norwich	4 b	1150
— Richard N.G.	HOWE	Harrow	5 f	612
/— Robert J.	HEMSLEY	Paddington	5 d	270
— Rochelle M.	LAMBERT	Edmonton	5 e	379
— Roger	HALL	Penrith	1 a	223
— Ross	MANN	Cheltenham	7 b	534
— Roy K.	BARRERO	Chelsea	5 c	322
— Roy L.	WEBSTER	Manchester	10 e	298
— Royston D.	CARTER	Bristol	7 b	467
— Sarah E.	BARNES	Trowbridge	7 c	909
— Saverio F.L.	DORIA	Chatham	5 b	614
— Sharon	KERRIGAN	Hackney	5 c	880
— Sharon Y.	GOULDEN	Basingstoke	6 b	238
— Sian E.	FAULKNER	Surrey S.W.	5 g	1362
2.— Sonia H.	HALL	Stamford	3 b	221
— Steven R.	WRIGHT	Dartford	5 b	777
— Stuart T.	KING	Cuckfield	5 h	204
— Susan	CULLEN	Islington	5 c	1670
— Susan	ROBINSON	Northampton	3 b	966
— Suzanne H.	COLLEY	Warwick	9 c	2259
— Terence A.	BYERS	Coventry	9 c	1291
— Terence A.	NORTHMORE	Plympton	7 a	889
— Thomas J.	DELAFUENTE	Surrey N.E.	5 g	679
— Timothy J.	JONES	Pontypool	8 c	333
— Timothy M.	TURRELL	Yarmouth	4 b	956
— Tony A.	BUTLER	Wednesbury	9 b	1329
— Trevor	OLIVER	Barton	10 b	355
— Trevor M.E.	COLLINS	Cardiff	8 b	346
— Valerie	HARDING	Basford	3 c	56
— Vanessa J.	GRANT	Hammersmith	5 c	1244
— Vincent	WILKINSON	Whittlesey	4 a	702
— Walter G.	MOUTINHO	Bootle	10 b	931
— Wendy	STOKES	Poole	7 c	987
— William F.	WARD	Sheffield	2 d	120
— (Female)	HENNESSY	Hackney	5 c	830
COLEMERE, Michael	GRIFFITHS	Shrewsbury	9 a	320
COLE-MORGAN, Tina J.	ROWLAND	Northampton	3 b	949
COLENSO, Jane M.	PARISH	Kingswood	7 b	839
COLENUTT, Martin	MILLS	Dartford	5 b	700
COLERIDGE, Keith	BASHFORD	Croydon	5 g	45
COLES, Adam F.	SCRIVENER	Eton	6 a	907

Detail of page from the Register of Births, showing my entry, seventh from the bottom

COLEMAN, (Female)

A Remarkable Story
of Adoption

by

Karen Lesley

ISBN: 978-1-9569859-0-3 hardback
978-1-9569859-1-0 paperback

First published in the UK by
Abbotsbury Press
www.abbotsburypress.com
info@abbotsburypress.com

Publishing Consultancy: Zoesbooks: www.zoesbooks.co.uk

Typeset in Avant Garde & Baskerville by Helm Information
amandahelm@helm-information.co.uk
www.helm-information.co.uk

Cover Design by Helm Information

Inside Cover by DNA Vision® image courtesy of DNA Art UK
Limited – Weybridge – Surrey – U.K

Printed and bound in Great Britain by Berforts Group,
Stevenage, Herts SG1 2BH

For my three beautiful daughters:
Rosemary, Annie and Nancy.
With all my love
xxx

Acknowledgements

My sincere and deepest heartfelt thank you goes to the following special individuals:

Maggie – Without her I really wouldn't have had a story to write. She has been crucial in helping me to decipher and rebuild my troubled life. Her support, patience and guidance have pulled me through some harrowing times. She is a very special individual with a great expertise – I remain indebted to her.

David, or Mr Trill as he will be forever known – an exceedingly amiable personality with a wonderful sense of humour, whose company at what were undoubtedly the bleakest of times, was greatly appreciated. His methodical and thorough approach to my onerous search also proved to be invaluable. In addition to all of the above, I would like to thank him for all the advice, help and kindness that he has shown me and my family over the years.

Paul – For loving me irrevocably and enabling me to feel truly loved for the first time in my life.

I would also like to include a handful of very good friends that have stood unwaveringly by me – some in more recent times, and others for a great deal longer. In particular: *Joy* – for her thoughtfulness, words of wisdom, and generous spirit; *Marian* – for her life-long friendship; *Victoria* – for her tireless, emotional and practical support during my most traumatic years; *Eric* – for his very sensitive intervention during the early writing process and for having the courage to show me some basic writing skills and daring to suggest one or two amendments along the way; *Joanna* – who, armed simply with a pencil, was a much-welcomed asset during the final stages of my book; and *Brenda* who proved invaluable during the later stages of producing this book.

Finally, my great thanks go to *Zoë*, without whom this book would never have materialised. Her support, empathy, understanding and, most importantly, her total belief in me, has made something miraculously come to fruition which had been, for me, truly inconceivable.

Contents

Foreword

So, your Aunt Pimrose sports a beard. You notice with dismay that your mother's hairy mole is making an appearance on your own chin. After reading this book, you will view your family, with its embarrassments, in a different light, and appreciate anew the fascination and wonder of blood ties and family resemblance. You are linked, you share a heritage, you are 'family'.

For Karen, the unthinkable familiarity of belonging has always been absent. She has been unable to share family traits, and had no one with whom she recognised a family likeness. As an adopted child, from her earliest years she has felt set apart, struggling with a deep loneliness, and with a desperate and overwhelming longing to find the mother, or parents, who felt they had to give her away, and to ask them why. With the advent of motherhood for herself, and the all-encompassing, fiercely protective love she immediately felt for her own three daughters, Karen knew she could no longer bury the feelings of deep loss and sadness that had always been the dark cloud in the background, and she started on her long journey to find her birth mother.

There will be tears as you read. Some laughs too! The overriding emotion will be that of admiration and respect for a remarkable and courageous woman, someone generous with love without having received much in the way of example along the way. This difficult and painful journey has been cathartic and healing. She has emerged as a new person, stronger and with a renewed energy and enthusiasm for life. Her love and immense pride in her own daughters shines out.

I hope the remaining knots in the tangle of her life will continue to unravel, and I wish her unexpected joy around the corner....

Brenda Smith

1. Jim Donovan

January 2006

'Paddy Coleman wasn't dead in March '62,' declared James Donovan after only a moment's thought.

This strange and completely unexpected response to my enquiry baffled me. Somewhat bemused, I knew his alarming statement had to be incorrect, as my birth certificate clearly stated that my father, Patrick Coleman, was deceased. In fact, his sudden death prior to my birth was key to my subsequent adoption. This elderly Irishman's recollection of events forty-four years ago must be muddled and confused. I realised then that any hope of gaining information that might help to further the search for my birth mother, Margaret Coleman, was going to be thwarted.

The previous day had ended on a high note. Together with Paul, my new partner, I had spent hours trawling through the electoral roll at Ilford library in East London. We had discovered that a James and Mary Donovan had resided for many years at the same address as that given on my birth certificate for Margaret Coleman. Looking down the list of names in the street and surrounding area, a strong Irish community was evident. With no sign of my parents' name, we quickly came to the conclusion they may well have been lodgers. Although the Donovan name no longer appeared at number 13, a search on 192.com revealed a James Donovan living alone just a few streets away. Could

3

this be the same man? His ex-directory status prevented me from telephoning him to verify this, but it didn't deter me. We lost no time and with excitement and trepidation drove back to Ilford the following morning possibly to meet someone who had actually known my birth mother all those years ago.

After ringing the doorbell, I watched and waited as a tall, stooped figure moved slowly along the passageway towards the opaque glazed, inner door. Paul and I stood on the doorstep, anxious and unsure as to what kind of reaction we would meet with, if he was indeed our man. As he opened the first door and then leaned forward to open the outer one, we had the opportunity to take a good look at this elderly character before introducing ourselves. A little dishevelled, he was wearing an open neck shirt revealing a white T-shirt underneath, a buttoned-up cardigan and grey trousers, all of which had seen better days.

'That's him,' whispered Paul confidently. As soon as I heard his distinct Irish accent, I, too, was convinced we'd struck lucky and his cheerful welcoming manner immediately dispelled any reticence.

'I wonder if you could help me? Are you the same James Donovan that used to live at 13 Herbert Road?' I asked.

'Yes, that's me,' he nodded, breaking out into a broad smile and revealing his few remaining teeth.

After explaining my reason for calling on him unexpectedly and my intention to trace my birth mother, he chatted with us both as if we were old friends. He spoke fondly of his late wife Mary and recalled what a great help Margaret had been to her, helping to look after their daughter Eileen and often returning from work with groceries for her.

However, he expressed total surprise that I could possibly be the daughter of Margaret Coleman. To my astonishment, he had no recollection of her ever being pregnant during the time she and her husband rented the small flat upstairs, in the house where he lived with his wife and young family. As he recalled

4

Margaret's very pleasant, kind manner and her obvious love of children, he was at a loss to understand how the Margaret Coleman he remembered could ever give up her own child.

'Are you sure you're Margaret Coleman's?' he asked, stressing yet again that she was never pregnant whilst living under his roof.

'I wish Mary was still alive,' he said, shaking his head in a bewildered fashion. 'She would have known more.'

Despite his jumbled account, it struck me how remarkable it was to find myself already talking to somebody who had actually known my mother. From the scant information on my birth certificate I knew that my father had worked as a bus conductor and Jim, as he called himself, informed me that my mother had the same occupation. They both worked at Seven Kings Bus Depot, choosing the same early shift, which then gave them time together later in the day. Also, Jim's endearing reference to my father as Paddy and not Patrick, was something that had never occurred to me. There was no doubt now – my parents were certainly Irish.

Despite his apparent fading memory, Jim was a very amiable man who quite clearly enjoyed the opportunity to indulge in relating past times. Living alone, our unexpected visit had been a welcome break from the monotony of his daily routine. Although there was little more to be gained from a man whose dates appeared muddled, it seemed cruel to cut Jim short and deprive him of a chance to dwell on past memories. Perhaps it had been unreasonable for us to call unannounced, expecting more information than he was able to give us and, with hindsight, a letter might have been more appropriate.

As Jim continued to reminisce, Paul and I made several unsuccessful attempts to pin-point specific dates, in the hope that we could discover more about the events surrounding Paddy Coleman's death. How could such a tragic event have passed Jim by? However, he remained adamant that Paddy Coleman was alive in March 1962 and asked me how I could be so sure he wasn't. When I showed him the information on my birth certificate, his face contorted. Intent on reassuring me once and for all that my information was incorrect, he disclosed a most surprising fact.

'Paddy Coleman was not dead in March 1962,' he announced slowly and articulately. 'Because I was talking to him in Fine Fare's supermarket the day Kennedy was shot!' he added vehemently.

My history wasn't great, but I was pretty sure John F. Kennedy was assassinated in November 1963. Back home later that morning, I checked the date and this was confirmed.

Far from being confused and muddled, Jim Donovan had amazingly accurate recall. It was important that we visit him again, but this time we would pay more serious attention to what he had to say.

The following weekend, armed with a large tin of chocolate biscuits, our thank-you gift for Jim, we were standing on his doorstep once again, hoping to find him home. As he opened the inner door and recognised us, he beamed excitedly whilst shaking his head vigorously. He was clearly delighted to see us.

'I've been thinking about you all week,' he said loudly, grinning even more broadly and wagging his finger at me. 'Come in, come in,' he said eagerly. As he beckoned us to follow him down the long passageway towards his lounge at the rear of his bungalow, the sound from the television was growing ever louder.

He quickly moved a pile of newspapers and magazines from the dark blue leather sofa and invited us both to sit down. As Jim approached his own chair, he reached for the television remote controls and immediately brought an end to the very loud background noise. He was clearly delighted by our arrival and the gift. After making us a cup of tea he proudly shared pictures of his family, his late wife Mary and their six children, three girls and three boys. As well as the many family photographs adorning the room, I noticed a large black and white image of John F. Kennedy hanging on the wall close to Jim's chair. He talked fondly of his late wife, pointing out the pretty blue and yellow curtains with the matching valance and tiebacks she had made soon after they moved into the bungalow from Herbert Road in the early 90s. Although a little dated, the coordinating wallpaper and its pretty border certainly showed a woman's touch. Jim also wanted to know more about Paul and myself, interested to discover that Paul worked in the building industry. Jim had been a bricklayer and hearing we had travelled from Sevenoaks in Kent, recalled working on the bridges over the bypass there many years earlier. We had stirred many memories for him.

I showed him a recent photo of myself with my three daughters. He studied it carefully.

'My goodness, you're all proper Paddies!' he exclaimed confirming our origins. 'There's no doubt about that,' he said, throwing his head back and laughing loudly. He was certainly enjoying our visit.

When at last the subject turned to Margaret Coleman, he was clearly perturbed that not only had he been unaware of her pregnancy, but also that she could give away her child.

'She threw you to the feckin' lions!' he roared angrily, using an expression that was unknown to me but seemingly familiar in the Irish vernacular. Clearly riled by the realisation of Margaret's actions, throughout our conversation he would break off and bellow the same phrase at me, alternating his choice of menacing animals to include wolves and dogs.

Jim's account of that time did appear to be very accurate. He told us that Margaret and Paddy had left Herbert Road in the autumn of 1962, remaining in the area but at an address unknown to him. He certainly had no knowledge of their current whereabouts, but remembered that Paddy was originally from Tipperary and Margaret from Kilkenny.

'Now that,' he announced triumphantly, 'makes you a Kilkenny Cat.' Once again he was pointing directly at me and throwing his head back chuckling to himself, fully aware that he was providing me with my new-found heritage. 'Oh, and you look like her,' he added. 'You're the stamp of her.'

For me, this in itself was a remarkable comment. Whilst I recognise that my own daughters and I are strikingly similar in looks, I've never had the benefit of knowing with whom else I share a resemblance.

We remained in contact with Jim in the months that followed, keeping him informed as the search unfolded. He had become very supportive and somewhat protective towards me, reminding me at every opportunity how I'd been fed to the feckin' lions, wolves and dogs. It was a surprise call from him in the late summer of that year when we were still no nearer to locating Margaret, that sent us hotfooting it back to Ilford.

'I've found a photograph of your mother,' said the easily recognisable voice on the end of the line. 'I knew I'd have one here somewhere, I've been through hundreds of snaps. It's not that good and it's only black and white, but you're welcome to it.'

It was impossible to hide my excitement and emotion as he handed me the small photo. I tried hard to fight back the tears as I studied the image. It was out of focus and hard to see any detail, but Margaret was posing and holding the hand of a young child.

My birth mother was slim, dressed in a dark pencil skirt, pale coloured jumper and high-heeled court shoes. Her thick, dark hair was styled into a beehive.

'Now that would have been taken in the late summer of '62,' explained Jim. 'That's in our garden and the little girl is my daughter Eileen, our eldest, born on 23rd March 1961. She must have been about eighteen months old in that snap,' he said after careful thought. 'Your mother was always very good with her,' he added.

I was taken aback by such a strange coincidence, Eileen was born exactly one year before me; we shared the same birthday. I studied the photograph again. Margaret had given birth just six months earlier and here she was holding the hand of a child who shared the very same birthday as the child that she had given away.

2. The Bear Hug

'Hello, it's Karen,' I said to the anxious sounding woman on the end of the line. I was fulfilling a promise I'd made to her earlier in the week, to call and alert her to our whereabouts and imminent arrival.

'We're driving through Carlow now,' I told her. Although it was past 9 p.m., she'd been insistent that I call her, whatever the time.

For her, preparations for our fleeting visit had been under way for days. Those closest to her had taken great delight in reporting to me her frenzy of spring-cleaning, baking and that morning an unscheduled visit to the hairdressers. 'Like a cat on hot bricks,' was how she'd been described.

'Will you be stopping, it's getting quite late?' she asked. I could sense the desperate tone to her voice. Confirmation of our intention to call in, albeit briefly, was a great relief to her, but clearly did nothing to allay her stress levels.

'Yes but only for ten, fifteen minutes or so. The plane was a little delayed and we've still got to drive to Waterford. They're all waiting up for us and the children are very tired,' I explained.

'Yes, yes.' she said with false nonchalance, brushing aside my concerns and insisting that there was surely time for a cup of tea.

Her invitation to call in had certainly surprised me; we hadn't spoken for many months and my actions during that time had enraged her. Her anger and fury as I took matters into my own hands had been relayed to me at regular intervals by those around her, and her frequent reference to me as 'that woman' amongst her close family had done nothing to ease my painful situation. Paul was adamant that we should accept this invitation, believing that introducing my three daughters to her would be a very positive step. Hearing about her anxiety somehow gave me an added advantage. This time, unlike our first meeting just six months earlier, I felt far more resilient. Nonetheless, she puzzled me immensely. It was difficult to understand her actions.

With our arrival now just moments away, I switched off my mobile phone, bringing an end to the flurry of texts and phone calls that had bombarded me throughout the day. The frequent messages and enquiries from the several interested parties all curious and impatient for news of my extraordinary visit had been silenced.

The afternoon had been frantic as Paul and I raced around to collect Rosemary, Annie and Nancy from their respective schools, before setting off for the airport, desperately hoping for a clear run on the motorway. We had checked in online and were travelling with cabin luggage only, in a desperate effort to arrive at our destination before midnight. Collecting the hire-car from Dublin airport had been a slow process, but eventually we were on the two-and-a-half hour journey south.

Although the three girls sat quietly in the back, nibbling a picnic hurriedly purchased at the airport, I had little appetite but passed the occasional snack to Paul as he drove the unfamiliar route in the darkness.

'You must never come to Thomastown,' she had stressed vehemently, during one of our earlier conversations. With those words still ringing in my ears, the signpost for Thomastown was now in sight. Perhaps such a brief visit late into the night on a cold November evening would go unnoticed and allow her to contain her highly guarded secret. As we approached 'The Long Man' public house, Paul reduced his speed and prepared to take the next turning on the right. It was a cul-de-sac and our instructions were to drive to the far end. As we passed each of the detached chalet-style homes, up ahead we could see a house with its lights blazing and the front door wide open. I remembered one of the many phone calls earlier in the day alerting me to her eagerness to show me around her home.

In the doorway, a man's silhouette was beckoning us to proceed and park on the driveway. His signalling and arm-waving was something akin to bringing in a 747 jet and I suspect he'd been waiting all evening to perform that extremely important duty. As we climbed out of the car, we were instantly gripped by the freezing temperature; the girls immediately scuttled towards the open front door as the young man approached me, beaming from ear to ear. Dressed in a short-sleeved polo shirt, he seemed oblivious to the weather conditions.

'It's great to see you again, Karen,' he said sincerely, embracing me in a lengthy, heartfelt bear hug. The feeling was entirely mutual, I was so pleased to see him again. Our first encounter just one month earlier had been wonderful.

After eventually releasing me from his tight grip, I was delighted to be able to introduce him to Paul. Still not perturbed by the extreme conditions, he remained outside conversing with Paul, eager to discover the make and model of our hire-car before returning back into the house.

Once inside, his parents were waiting anxiously to greet each of us in turn with a kiss. It was with great pride and sheer delight that I proceeded to introduce each of my beautiful and talented daughters.

'Rosemary sixteen, Annie fourteen and Nancy eight.' As I spoke, I watched their reactions carefully, wondering if this encounter would stir something within them. Still standing in the hallway, the girls automatically removed their shoes and placed them neatly by the front door. Paul and I did the same. The woman seemed very puzzled by what was for us, a natural gesture.

'What's all this, what are you doing? Smelly feet, smelly feet,' she said, in a desperate attempt to amuse and appear familiar. With little else to say to these three very significant young girls, it only served to emphasise her anxiety.

The young man and his father ushered Paul and my daughters into the sitting room. The officious matriarch indicated that I should follow her into the kitchen. Unzipping my jacket, I perched on a small sofa while she remained standing and nervously busied herself making a pot of tea. She talked relentlessly in her strong Irish brogue, about the weather, our time at the airport, the flight and our car journey, leaving no time for me to get a word in edgeways. I watched her with secret amusement, removing the lid of the teapot, stirring furiously before replacing it and immediately repeating the same exercise several times over. I found myself fixated on this tense, nervous woman and although only our second meeting, here I was, observing her in her own home. Whilst she gabbled on, it gave me the opportunity to scrutinise her. Looking her up and down, I decided she was in good shape for someone in her late sixties. Considerably shorter than me and with a petite frame, she was smartly dressed in a plain straight skirt, which hung just below the knee and a round neck, short-sleeved jersey top under a delicate knitted jacket. I noted with a tinge of envy her high, black patent, strappy sandals and wondered how she could wear them with such ease and confidence; my inherited bunions had prevented me from ever enjoying such elegance.

The entire party from the sitting room soon appeared in the kitchen. The brief time together had proved decidedly uncomfortable for the elderly gentleman who could find no alternative but to seek help from his wife in entertaining these unfamiliar guests.

The kitchen table had been covered with a lace tablecloth and each place setting laid precisely with fine bone china. I was instructed to move from the sofa and join Paul and my daughters around the table. As she directed each of us to a specific seat, the young man and his father took to the sofa, whilst the woman remained stationed by the worktop, from where she probably felt better able to maintain a certain amount of control. I watched as she hurtled around the kitchen attending to everyone's needs, repeating the same questions, determined to prevent any awkward silences. She opened the oven door and removed a freshly baked apple pie, which she placed on the table together with a plate of carefully arranged chocolate biscuits. Her attempt to casually provide an impressive display of refreshments did nothing to disguise her obvious acute nervousness. Sadly, despite all her efforts, the gathering was tremendously awkward. Throughout, the two figures on the sofa had remained noticeably silent. The elderly man, sitting with his head bowed, was determined to avoid any eye contact, but the same could not be said for the young man sat beside him. Whilst I imagined he had been given specific instructions not to speak for the duration of our visit, it was impossible for him to contain his obvious excitement at our visit to his home. His surreptitious glances would break out into a beaming smile each time he managed to catch my eye.

It was 10.15 p.m. and conscious of the late hour, I was keen to bring this most bizarre and laboured gathering to a close. Whilst encouraging the girls to drink up, I gulped down my own cup of tea and hurriedly ate a slice of searing hot apple pie in record time, burning the roof of my mouth in the process. As we stood up ready to leave, we enthused at the array of late-night refreshments nonetheless.

'Do you want to use the bathroom?' she asked expectantly. Somehow I sensed this was her opportunity to instigate the threatened tour. Keen to make a hasty retreat, we all declined her offer, however, I couldn't help but notice her sudden look of disappointment. We followed the girls out into the hall to put on our shoes.

'We've got something for you,' she said abruptly, signalling to her husband to come forward. As he kissed them goodbye, he placed a 50€ note into each of their hands.

'Treat yourselves to something nice,' she insisted as she kissed them. Somewhat taken aback, the girls thanked them profusely, promising letters giving details of their purchases.

As we stood in the hallway ready to leave, Paul noticed the cut-string staircase and commented favourably. Immediately, the elderly gentleman came to life, talking freely and animatedly, delighted that his bespoke staircase had been noted and appreciated. Suddenly discovering common ground between them, he would have liked, perhaps, to have conversed with Paul at length, but it wasn't to be. I sensed something was standing in the way of any rapport or relationship. We said our goodbyes and I felt an immediate wave of relief that this ordeal had finally come to an end, but it was to be short-lived. To my utter surprise they announced their intention to join us the following day for afternoon tea – a prospect that filled me with sheer dread. How much more of this surreal situation could I take?

The front door was opened letting in a freezing blast of air. With a final goodbye we all scurried to the car and, as we drove away, we looked back to see the three waving figures silhouetted in the doorway.

'That was weird!' declared Annie.

'And why did he give us this?' asked a bewildered Rosemary, staring at the 50€ note she was still clutching in her hand. We continued on our journey south to Waterford, the true reason for our brief visit to the Emerald Isle, where we were guaranteed to find the warmest and most genuine of welcomes.

3. Karen Gay

On the 6th April 1962 at just fourteen days old, I was collected from St Margaret's nursing home in Hackney by Peter and Bernice Gay. They were a childless couple who named me, their much-wanted little girl, Karen Lesley Gay. However, for reasons known only to the adoption authority, this adoption hit some complications and was not officially sanctioned until some six months later, in November.

Our first home was a small rented flat situated behind Streatham bus garage and this is where we lived for the first two years of my life. However, my new parents were soon desperate to adopt a second child to complete their family, but their cramped one bedroom flat was considered too small and their only solution was to move to Morden, Surrey, to live with my paternal grandmother in her three-bedroom council house. Soon after our move, they returned to St Margaret's in East London to collect a baby son, whom they named Andrew Peter Gay.

I have fond memories of my time spent in Nanny's company, or Nanny Gay, as she was known. She became integral to our lives. An extremely kind, good-natured woman with a most generous spirit, she devoted a great deal of her time to Andrew and me. Nanny was a tiny woman with minute feet and a striking head of brilliant white hair who always dressed in a nylon button-fronted overall to project her clothing underneath, the two patch pockets on the front contained her cigarettes, a lighter and a handkerchief. Nanny had been a widow for some years and although our arrival must have caused tremendous disruption to her life, she appeared to enjoy her involvement in our upbringing and even agreed to an addition to the family, an Airedale puppy named Elsa.

My Dad was the youngest of four children and had been brought up in this modest end-of-terrace house with his parents, two brothers and a sister. The bathroom was downstairs, but lacked a hand-basin, so any washing or teeth-cleaning had to be done at the sink in the sparsely furnished little kitchen. My overriding memory of my time there was the severe cold.

The house had just one reception room, with a gas fire which provided the only source of heat in the entire property. Upstairs my parents slept in the box room, their bed touching three of the four walls and the modest wardrobe set against the fourth wall prevented the bedroom door from opening fully. Andrew and I shared the second bedroom, where a small Noddy rug alongside our bunk beds provided the only layer of warmth between us and the icy, linoleum floor.

Nanny had the largest bedroom, which spanned the full width of the house. She had arranged a small, work area at one end and at the other was her double bed, its thick, spongy eiderdown was always very inviting and made a marvellous trampoline for us children. And it was from this vantage point that I would sit and watch Nanny at her sewing machine, producing thousands of crêpe-paper party hats for a local shop. As I grew older, I was given the task of snipping the thread in between each hat to separate them and stack them neatly into boxes, ready for collection.

When Nanny wasn't toiling away in her bedroom, she and I enjoyed doing jigsaw puzzles together, spending many happy hours sitting at the gate-legged table under the window in the front room. Unfortunately, Nanny's chain smoking could be highly irritating, as I watched the length of her ash grow ever more precarious before eventually collapsing and landing amongst the puzzle pieces. Trying to remove the debris was always a most unpleasant job. One of Nanny's other great loves was her garden. Although the house was small, it was on a corner plot, giving us a sizable garden big enough for both a swing and a slide. The garden was beautifully kept and I have strong memories of my excitement on the days that Nanny chose to cut me a bunch of antirrhinums, roses and dahlias

17

to take into school for the teacher's desk.

Our standard of living was modest. Mum was a keen knitter and seamstress and while I was very young, she made most of my clothes, always worn with a matching ribbon in my hair. Mealtimes were regular and involved the whole family, Mum made simple home-cooked meals every day except Wednesday, as this was Nanny's day to provide us all with something equally wholesome. Our family holiday was only ever for one week a year and involved just the four of us, usually at a caravan park or, on a couple of occasions, at a holiday camp, but always on the south coast. Nanny would always accompany her daughter and family. For our birthdays, Mum organised a small party at home with a handful of friends, party games followed by a party tea. Although we had a family car, Dad used it to travel to work and it was many years before Mum learned to drive and therefore had to rely on public transport to ferry us children around much of the time.

Nanny liked to spend every Saturday visiting her daughter, my Aunty Frances, and occasionally she would take me with her. Guaranteed to be the most enjoyable of days, it always involved a serious shopping expedition. Aunty would decide upon the destination, often travelling far and wide on either bus or train and always taking in a very welcome lunch along the way. My cousin Barbara completed the band of happy shoppers, an only child seven years my senior, whose company I always much enjoyed.

The fact that both Andrew and I were adopted was never kept a secret. From a very early age my mother had made us both aware of our different circumstances, describing us as 'chosen'. Little more was ever said unless the need arose to explain to others why, as a family, we didn't look alike, or to remind our GP that there were no hereditary genes each time we had cause to visit him with an ailment. Despite Andrew and me sharing a unique situation, our relationship was fraught. Even from a very young age, there was something markedly different about him. An unwillingness to share his toys or play together was frustrating and he could be extremely demanding, my mother and grandmother constantly *bending to his every need. His awkward attitude towards me, his big sister, was seldom discouraged, which left me with feelings of immense rage and invariably resulted in me lashing out. My temper was born out of sheer frustration, for which I felt there was little understanding or empathy from those around me. From very early on, family life seemed to centre solely on Andrew's needs.*

For me, school was a pretty challenging time. Saddled with a surname like Gay was the first real difficulty I had to face amongst my peers. Initially my schoolmates thought it a frivolous, silly name guaranteed to provoke a titter each time it was announced in the classroom. Inevitably, as I grew older and the name was used to describe something with a very different meaning, my life became unbearable, as did my brother's. And this was not all I had to contend with. Covered in freckles, I had to endure relentless teasing and was made to feel extremely self-conscious. My hands too, which from a very young age looked quite odd, severely wrinkled and aged with extremely prominent knuckle joints, added to my embarrassment and my terrible habit of nail-biting left me with no alternative but to conceal my hands whenever possible. Inevitably there were times when I had no choice but to expose them and it was always to a barrage of cruel taunting. In fact, all my joints were unusually prominent, including – to me – very obvious bunions, making it difficult to find well-fitting shoes. My adoptive mother was always at pains to point out that she had no idea why my feet were so disfigured, as she had always ensured that both my brother and I had been provided with the very best footwear – Clarks. With no other family member sharing these unfortunate traits and features. it was impossible for them to show any true empathy. My protruding front teeth and the brace I had fitted at nine years old just added to the constant unwanted attention.

A far worse condition, though, was to have a lifelong effect. Around the age of five or six, following a severe bout of mumps, which I distinctly remember caused me difficulties with my balance, I discovered that I had absolutely no hearing in my right ear. I first became aware of this whilst lying in bed, when I noticed that if I lay on my left side I could block out all the noises around me and sleep soundly, but a deep-seated fear of hospitals dating back to my early childhood prevented me from sharing this alarming discovery with anyone for many years. This could be explained, certainly in part, by the fact that the whole family had never looked upon hospitals favourably. My paternal grandfather had died at the local hospital and each time any family member had cause to refer to this, it was only in a grave, rather scathing tone. Andrew also had two operations when very small, for removing both tonsils and adenoids and my memories of the large ward with its unpleasant smell and mysterious-looking equipment filled me with horror. All this reinforced my determination to avoid anything which involved needles and pain.

My deafness – or rather my reluctance to tell anyone about it – had far-reaching consequences: above all, my schooling was very much affected. As a well-behaved child, I was always directed to sit at the back of the class, but with over thirty children sitting between me and the teacher, I missed much of the lesson. We sat in pairs at twin desks and I would always make a beeline for the right-hand seat, so I could communicate easily with my neighbour. but, unfortunately, as soon as the teacher noticed I was left-handed, I was told to swap places. I failed abysmally at languages, unable to distinguish the phrases repeated over and over on an inferior reel-to-reel tape, which to me were just a blur of sounds. I was also no better at sport. My poor balance and the inability to determine the origin of any sound meant the PE staff despaired of me. Using my eyes as ears, I learned to lip-read, but with my gaze fixed on either children or teachers it would unsettle them and I was frequently accused of staring.

Looking back now, I am amazed at the lengths I went to in my effort to disguise this disability. Around the age of ten, the entire class was given a hearing test from a visiting medical team. There was no thought of privacy. Queuing at the open door, waiting their turn, my classmates watched curiously as each in turn donned a pair of headphones for the simple test. The prospect of my deafness being discovered and coping with the inevitable mocking that would follow terrified me. When my turn to be tested finally arrived, I slowly placed the headset over my ears as I watched the operator preparing to start the test.

'Turn around and answer with a 'yes' each time you hear a sound,' she instructed.

It was an awful moment. Facing the open door, I could see a mass of faces peering in at me. Many had already singled me out for mocking and bullying on previous occasions. I was overcome by a feeling of sheer terror at what was about to happen, both now and also later back in the classroom. Panic-stricken and still clutching the earphones, I turned to face the woman carrying out the test. Unbeknown to me she had already started to test the hearing in my right ear.

'Did you hear that?' she asked curiously.

'Um, I don't think this was on properly,' I said wiggling the headset, anxious about already drawing attention to myself.

'Ok, we'll start again,' she said kindly.

And to my surprise this time she didn't ask me to turn around. I watched her carefully each time she moved the dial and I simply acknowledged the unheard sound.

When she repeated the exercise on my left ear, it was with immense relief that I knew I had averted a near catastrophe.

Thanks to my concealment tactics, my parents remained oblivious to my deafness for nine years until eventually a serious attack of dizziness forced me to share my secret. I'd been experiencing debilitating dizzy attacks, which my Mum had thought were migraines, but I knew that something in the ears controlled balance and I was convinced it must be connected to my hearing loss. One day, whilst out shopping with a school friend, I had one of these terrible attacks and just couldn't manage the bus journey home. As I sat in an alleyway unable to move, my friend had no alternative but to go and telephone my parents and ask them to come and collect us both. Having taken my friend home, I finally told my parents my secret. They instantly dismissed my diagnosis, believing it to be nothing more than earwax and my Mum booked an appointment with

21

the GP for the following day. However, after a number of unpleasant tests with an ear, nose and throat specialist they confirmed what I already knew: I was profoundly deaf in my right ear and, furthermore, there was nothing to be done.

We had moved from Nanny's house to our new council house five miles away when I was eight years old and it was soon after this move that I began to notice significant changes to our family life. First and foremost, I was devastated to learn that my much-loved Saturday morning ballroom-dancing class would cease. Taught by a wonderful and very talented couple, who later became Latin American World Champions for five consecutive years, I had already achieved several awards. However, for my parents, the prospect of a regular journey across town each week to take me to the classes was out of the question.

Nonetheless, I soon made friends with Marian, the girl next-door-but-one. Together we joined the Girl Guides where we soon looked forward to all the activities and outings. Any camping holidays that occurred from time to time were an added bonus and becoming the Robin Patrol leader was a great achievement for me, and one that I truly embraced.

Since our move, it seemed to me that Dad's work commitments had increased and I saw very little of him. Monday to Friday he worked for the local council as a foreman managing a fleet of minibuses. His primary responsibility was to transport handicapped children to specialist schools, but even during the long school holidays his workload didn't appear to lessen. Every Saturday morning he maintained the council vehicles, then after he came home for a quick lunch, he dashed out again, this time to work for a large, mobile catering company. His return in the early hours of the following morning played havoc with our Sundays. He would wake late and then insist on a nap after lunch, leaving little time for our one and only family day together. He no longer came on the family holiday, preferring instead to look after Elsa our dog, and it was left to my Mum to take us, accompanied by either her sister and nephew, or a friend of hers from work.

Mum had a part-time job, also working for the council as a supervisory escort on the transport Dad managed. In addition to this, both my parents spent one night per week walking door-to-door, collecting coupons for a national football betting scheme. So family life was pretty non-existent and, despite all the hours they put in, lack of money was an ongoing problem. No doubt Dad's heavy smoking would have been a drain on the family's finances.

As I grew older, my teenage years were particularly lonely and unhappy ones. The appeal of pretty homemade dresses had long since diminished and, sadly, Mum no longer showed the same interest in my appearance as she once had and my limited wardrobe contained mostly mismatched, ill-fitting clothes. As if all this were not enough to contend with, I was not spared the inevitable acne and greasy hair. And to top it all, around this time for some unknown reason my front teeth took on a decidedly unhealthy shade of grey.

At fourteen my cousin Barbara asked me to be a bridesmaid at her wedding. Like most girls this was a much longed-for opportunity, having listened enviously to my school friends, who seemed to have an endless stream of relatives all requiring little girls for the role. I was torn though, not wanting to decline this once in a lifetime experience, but loathing myself as I did, I showed little enthusiasm for something I had wanted so badly. My poor cousin must have regretted ever having asked me. Aunty Frances was adamant we had to address the problem of my dingy teeth and bought some vile smokers' toothpaste, insisting I use it in the run-up to the wedding. Needless to say it had absolutely no effect. Mum booked my first ever wash, cut and blow-dry at the local hairdressers, but I had no idea about make-up. I watched with fascination as Barbara and her friend Debbie, the other bridesmaid, carefully applied the various colours to their faces. They appeared surprised that I had arrived without any make-up and hastily turned their attentions to me to enhance what I could only describe as my dour, unappealing face. Despite the attention administered to me, it did little to lift my spirits at a time when I felt immensely unattractive and self-conscious.

Despite the difficulties I faced, there were some brighter times.

23

Amongst my extended family, I have very fond memories of my Great-Uncle John who was married to my maternal grandmother's sister, Great Aunty Doris. A quiet man, he was raised in an orphanage and had never known his own family. Despite this unpromising start in life, he had learnt a trade and landed himself a successful job working as a carpenter, building stage sets and props for Thames Television Studios at Teddington Lock. Unlike the rest of our family, Aunty Doris and Uncle John were considered within the family to be rather 'well off'. They owned their own home and would purchase a brand-new car every couple of years. Each Christmas and birthday Andrew and I would receive a gift voucher for one guinea (twenty-one shillings as it was then, or £1.05 nowadays), which was always considered a far superior sum than a mere £1.00.

Uncle John's amazing job on studio sets meant he was on first name terms with many famous faces of that era and he was more than happy to collect signatures for my autograph book, the most prized one being Benny Hill's. I remember a very exciting trip to the television studio, where I was part of the audience during the filming of The Tommy Cooper Show, a wonderful experience.

During one particular visit to my aunt and uncle, I had expressed a longing for the latest fashionable toy – a pair of wooden stilts. Just days later, my parents woke me as usual before leaving for work and told me something had been delivered for me. Puzzled as to what could arrive before 7.15 in the morning, I ran downstairs to find a most beautiful pair of wooden stilts leaning against the kitchen cupboard. In just a couple of days my Uncle John had produced my greatest wish. They were very stylish and so beautifully made, painted white with coloured rings of shocking pink, electric blue and purple, with black foot supports. It was a truly unique gift and one that I treasured for many years.

Looking back, I think my Dad felt envious of Uncle John's generosity towards me. I can remember how he never particularly warmed to Uncle John and would make the occasional derogatory remark. Despite this, it didn't detract from the enjoyment I felt at the special attention he paid me. When I began to search for my first car, Uncle John wanted reassurance that I would purchase it from a main dealership, somewhere that would provide me with a guarantee. Sadly, I explained that my budget didn't run to that idea. To my utter surprise, after a moment's thought, he announced that he would lend me the money to buy a suitable car. A most generous offer but very short-lived, as the following day Aunty Doris telephoned Mum rather indignantly to dispel any thoughts of a loan. John hadn't been serious, she insisted categorically. I knew his offer had been totally genuine, but unfortunately nothing more was ever said on the matter. Sadly, Uncle John died months later. He was found at the wheel of his parked car at the television studios having suffered a heart attack.

As soon as I was able, I had found myself a Saturday job in a local florist shop. It was something that really interested me, but the conditions and the rate of pay were dreadful. At a time when Marks and Spencer were paying Saturday girls £9.00 per day, I earned a meagre £2.50. I lacked the confidence to apply for what seemed to me such an elevated position and so I resigned myself to a job where I felt exploited and chose instead to follow my parent's example and supplement my earnings as a football pools coupon collector.

In addition to the usual teenage angst, my home and school life was not easy. My parents left for work early, leaving my brother and me alone to get ourselves off to school. Although Andrew was in the house, I seldom saw him in the mornings. He was adamant about doing everything in his own time and was either late for school or didn't go at all. Left to my own devices, a proper breakfast went by the board and invariably consisted of a two-finger Kit Kat: not the most nourishing start to the day.

Unlike Andrew, I did attend school regularly, seldom missing a day, but it was a tough environment. Many of the pupils, like me, came from the large, new, housing estate nearby, and the standard of education on offer seemed to steadily deteriorate as I progressed through the system. In the early 70s, the newly built middle school was considered state of the art for its time: a single storey building with huge open-plan spaces, where classes were separated with just the very minimum of partitioning. The reality for me however was different, a totally impractical design concept, very disruptive and certainly not good for me with my hearing difficulties.

The high school I went on to in 1975 was even worse. Here the buildings were more traditional, with individual classrooms, but, bizarrely, all desk furniture was at a premium. For those who wanted to work, it was advisable to hurry to the lesson to guarantee a desk and chair. Many of the children were completely out of control and it wasn't unheard of to see a piece of furniture fly past the window before crashing onto the lawn. Lighting could also be a problem, it was considered a jolly prank by some to remove the starter switches from the fluorescent light fittings. Disruption was the order of the day. The uncontrollable behaviour of many pupils was shocking and, as teachers spent much of their time battling to maintain some kind of order, actual teaching time was severely reduced and inevitably resulted in a poor education for us all.

Sadly, my parents were accepting of the situation. Their own social status and poor education prevented them from understanding the effect of such an environment. My regular attendance and glowing school reports that described me as a polite, well-mannered child who tried hard was enough for them.

Yet, amongst the mayhem and chaos, I was to discover a kind, sympathetic and understanding teacher who took me under her wing. I became very fond of Mrs Heym, who taught needlework and prior to teaching, had acquired years of experience in the 'rag trade', something which intrigued me. Sitting together sewing in the classroom, it was easy to converse with her. I loved her needlework classes and took every opportunity to spend additional time in the large, bright and tranquil workroom, far away from the main part of this disruptive school. I soon became aware that it wasn't just her interesting career that connected me to her, I discovered that she had an adopted daughter named Jacqueline.

Suddenly, within the safe confines of Mrs Heym's classroom, I had found someone with which to discuss the subject of adoption. I'd often pondered on the bizarre idea that my birth mother might live somewhere close by and that, unknowingly, our paths may have frequently crossed. It was a romantic notion, which Mrs Heym was quick to dispel. By expressing my secret thought to her, she opened up and shared her own daughter's anxieties with me. In particular, Jacqueline worried about the colour of her eyes, which were brown, whilst her parents' were blue. Hearing how they were able to reassure their daughter that there were many natural families whose eye colour did not always match, made me envy Jacqueline and the way in which she felt able to address the many issues surrounding adoption with her mother. An opportunity that had been lacking in my own family.

It was unheard of for a pupil to be invited to a teacher's home, so the invitation to spend a Saturday with Mrs Heym came as a total surprise. She lived some distance from the school in affluent Epsom, Surrey. Her husband I soon discovered, worked as a customs officer at Gatwick airport.

One glorious Saturday morning, I waited outside the deserted school for her to collect me and my excitement knew no bounds as she bowled up in her Triumph Herald convertible. It was my first experience ever of driving in an open-top car and it was certainly a memorable journey. We spent some time browsing around the shopping centre and then collected her daughter Jacqueline from her grandparents, before returning to her chalet-style detached house. Feeling a little out of my depth, I didn't let Mrs Heym out of my sight. It had been impossible to interact with Jacqueline. She was several years younger than me and was more intent on showing-off; it was left to her father to curb her slightly unruly behaviour. So, instead, I chose to sit in the kitchen and watch intently as Mrs Heym made profiteroles for dinner later that day.

The meal seemed to me quite magnificent – steak and sauté potatoes with an assortment of vegetables, including red peppers – my first introduction to this outlandish vegetable. I took a small piece, only to find that it was raw and not only unpleasantly hot to the taste, but also difficult to chew and digest. I declined another piece and watched in amazement as Jacqueline ate it with relish. The profiteroles which followed for dessert were more to my taste, also a first and quite delicious.

Mrs Heym's exciting accounts of her time in the fashion industry had a profound influence on my future career choice and steered me towards my first job with a high street fashion chain. Her help with job applications and letter writing was invaluable. She had high hopes for me and was the one who suggested that I ask my employer for day release to study pattern cutting at the London College of Fashion. Much to my complete surprise, my future employer agreed. As it turned out, I was very unhappy at my place of work and left within a year to begin what became a successful career in the central buying office of British Home Stores. Although I completed my studies and gained a City and Guilds Certificate, I felt that in leaving the rag trade I had let Mrs Heym down and sadly I avoided any further contact with her.

I was seventeen when my parents separated under extremely difficult circumstances. Dad went to live with a lady who was not only a colleague at work, but also happened to live directly opposite us, a truly unthinkable situation. Living as we did in a cul-de-sac consisting of seventy terraced flats and houses, all arranged around a communal parking area, this enabled many to witness our very private pain and distress.

Dad handled the whole difficult situation with a great lack of sensitivity, leaving it to Mum to break the alarming news to both Andrew and me; he said nothing to us about his impending departure. His reluctance to make any attempt to explain his actions only served to make an already fraught situation worse. From that moment onwards, Andrew refused to have any association with Dad, electing to change his surname to that of my mother's maiden name and dropping his middle name of Peter. They never spoke again.

Much later, thinking about the timing of the separation, I realised it was just months after losing our much-loved Airedale terrier. Dad would never have been able to leave her behind.

The relationship between my brother and me was becoming increasingly fractious, our physical clashes were more regular and violent. Andrew's continual refusal to attend school resulted in him eventually being taken into care. Left to cope without Dad's support, Mum's attention was inevitably focused on Andrew more than ever. All this, added to her mounting financial worries, had a hugely detrimental effect on our relationship and any remaining family life. I continued to live at home and tried to help support Mum as much as possible until the age of twenty-three when I met and married David, a lawyer. The prospect of a home of my own in a more comfortable and stable environment was almost beyond my wildest dreams.

Surprisingly, on my wedding day when I finally relinquished the surname Gay, it was with an element of regret. After loathing a name that had caused so much embarrassment and anguish throughout my childhood, I had eventually learnt to live with, and even like, such a memorable name.

4. Motherhood

As I grew older, I was always struck by the surge of emotion that I experienced whenever I gave a conscious thought to Margaret Coleman, my birth mother. These overwhelming feelings, for a woman I'd never known, would often surface on my birthdays, when I was convinced that she too would be thinking of me. After all, how could she ever forget the sad circumstances surrounding my arrival into this world, already fatherless? What a most tragic story, as told to me many years earlier by my adoptive mother – that of a heavily pregnant woman losing her husband, after a freak accident while working on a building site. He fell to his death and left her prematurely widowed and she had made the heart-wrenching decision to give me, her first-born child, up for adoption.

I knew this harrowing tale to be true as, unbeknown to my adoptive parents, I had discovered my original birth certificate when very small. Rummaging around in the bottom of my parents' wardrobe, I had come across an old disused ammunition tin and after working out the complexities of the opening device, found inside all the important family papers. The two salmon-coloured documents relating to the birth of Andrew and me were easily recognisable nestled amongst numerous other papers. Just as my Mum had described, it clearly stated that my father, Patrick Coleman, was deceased.

The reality was that any thoughts and feelings I had towards my birth mother would remain secret. Neither Andrew nor I had ever been encouraged to talk openly about our adoption and so I never raised the subject with my parents. Bernice had been my Mum since I was fourteen days old and the idea of sharing my sudden unexplainable feelings with her now I was in my teens, seemed rather insensitive. Sadly, thinking back now all these years later, I wonder whether it might have strengthened our relationship had I talked more openly with her about my adoption.

Life has to go on though, and I managed it by suppressing any feelings for Margaret Coleman. However, standing in front of the mirror on my wedding day, shortly before leaving for the church, I deeply longed for her to have seen the daughter she never knew, about to be wed and most probably eventually to become a mother. Unfortunately, unlike the anniversary of my birth, Margaret had no idea that this was one of the most significant occasions of my life and her thoughts would not be with me.

It wasn't until many years later, however, that I faced the true heart-wrenching reality of adoption. It was 1990 and I was in the early stages of my first pregnancy. Delighted at the prospect of motherhood, I was overwhelmed by the idea of meeting for the first time, someone with a strong physical likeness to me, but my feelings of elation were soon to be quashed during my first lonely visit to the ante-natal clinic at the local hospital. In fact they were quickly reduced to ones of gross inadequacy. Faced with a formidable midwife, my inability to provide any medical history caused me extreme feelings of helplessness. I watched despairingly as page after page of the new medical record set up for me remained blank. It slowly dawned on me that my own unfortunate circumstances no longer solely affected me, but would also have an impact on the life of my very precious baby. The immense feeling of inadequacy combined with my life-long fear of hospitals was made worse by the absence of any comfort or support. I had a husband who could never be persuaded to take time out of work for anything other than a scheduled holiday and a mother who sadly had no experience of pregnancy or childbirth herself and would never have considered accompanying her daughter at such a time. Frightened, anxious and lonely, I found the whole experience highly traumatic, which resulted in me fainting.

The unsympathetic midwife had no understanding of what I was going through and, maintaining her brusque manner, made things even worse by seeming to take a delight in questioning my ability to undergo childbirth at all. Also, my fear of needles had not diminished and, alarmingly, I was informed that my blood group was O Rhesus Negative so that I would require additional blood tests throughout the pregnancy, a terrifying prospect. The prospect of the months ahead seemed quite daunting and the somewhat isolated life I had led before my marriage was still very evident, even now.

The far-reaching implications of adoption would surface two years later, during a second pregnancy. My ordeal and feelings of despair were no less painful, as I was reminded once again of my apparent shortcomings.

Life has many strange twists and turns though, and how was I to know at that time of terror and loneliness that it was to be the existence of my two very small daughters and the life changing effect they had on me, which finally convinced me of the desperate need to trace my own birth mother?

The overwhelming love and devotion I experienced towards my daughters had been immediate. A photograph of Rosemary, my eldest, cradled in my arms moments after her birth shows a contorted little face studying me intently. In the weeks that followed, I could not help but wonder how Margaret had been able to part with her own helpless child; it must have been torture for her.

Up until this point in my life, I had always defended the reasons for my adoption, but now, as a mother myself, Margaret's actions were incomprehensible. I needed to understand what led her to act as she did and how she had coped throughout her life. I wanted to hear her harrowing tale for myself. My heart went out to her and I longed for the opportunity to reassure her and relieve her life-long anguish.

There was also a deep sense of curiosity. More than thirty years had elapsed, but I was intrigued to know if I would feel a sense of connection between us, something that was sadly lacking with my adoptive mother.

Soon after the arrival of my second daughter, Annie, I noticed considerable media attention was being given to adoption and the tracing of birth relatives. I was absolutely riveted by the whole subject and the spate of articles in the press as well as the coverage on TV. When I followed other adoptees on their daunting and often painful journeys in search of their own birth mothers, I too longed to find myself in a similar situation.

I had also considered the prospect of half-siblings. The possibility of meeting a blood brother or sister was tantalising. And not forgetting my father's family, they too must have been aware of my existence, surely they would be interested to know what became of me?

Having made the monumental decision to begin the arduous search for my birth mother, it wasn't something I could dwell on indefinitely. I was thirty-one years old and I had no idea of Margaret's age or whether I would still find her alive, but this did not deter me.

I signed up with an adoption support agency and was sent an information pack giving me guidance on how best to search and notably, alerting me to the Adoption Contact Register. The Register provides an opportunity for an adopted person and a birth relative to register their wish to make contact with each other. Somewhat over-optimistically, I immediately placed my name on the Contact Register, expecting a positive result, but was mortified to discover there was no match. I discussed my disappointment with an adoption counsellor, who explained that in many cases the birth mother might be inhibited by guilt. Hearing this only made me more determined to find my mother and express sympathy towards her.

It turned out to be quite a complex process. First, as I was born before 1975, I was required to attend an interview with an approved adoption worker. Mothers who had given up their children had been reassured that there would be no further contact with their offspring and I needed to be made aware of this and the possible consequences and it was important to consider the prospect that I might meet with rejection once again. More importantly, the main purpose of the meeting was to authorise access to my adoption file. I met with a pleasant, middle-aged woman at the local town hall, but the session proved exceedingly frustrating. I felt under intense scrutiny as I battled to convince her of my need to trace my birth mother, as she continued to emphasise the possible implications. I resented having to justify my desire to know something that I considered a right and fundamental to my very existence.

Eventually, though, I did succeed in convincing her that my reasons were valid and was then able to embark upon my search. My adoption file was lodged with Wandsworth County Court and I applied for access, in the hope that it might provide me with significant information to assist me in tracing Margaret Coleman. To my disappointment, I then learned that my adoption file could not be found. This was a disastrous blow at such an early stage. I turned to my husband David for advice on how I might progress. Although he was fully aware of my decision to trace my birth mother, he was reluctant to assist or even encourage me in my search to find her. His reaction felt very unsympathetic.

'What could possibly be gained in finding her now? Why rake up the past? Why can't you just look forward? You've got me, Rosemary and Annie, why can't you leave it at that? And why embark on something that will inevitably end in tears?' he asked.

Beneath this very insensitive reaction, the message seemed clear: You've got enough shopping, cooking, ironing, cleaning, keeping house, looking after children and chauffeuring to keep you busy. What else does a wife and mother need?

David was unable to grasp the fact that this wasn't just about my heritage, but also that of our daughters. I could do nothing more without his help, as any further investigation would be costly and extremely time-consuming. I was devastated.

With my objective vetoed in its infancy, I continued for many years as a devoted mother and dutiful housekeeper. I even managed to contain my feelings of utter despair several years later when, in 1997, David was presented with a published copy of his father Tony's memoirs. It was a magnificent tome, complete with a comprehensive family tree for each of his parents spanning several hundred years. I watched pensively as the entire family congratulated Tony on his marvellous achievement. David devoured the publication and even allowed our daughters to take it into school during their studies on family history. As I observed David proudly placing the book on our bookshelf for posterity there was no reference to my situation or the effect it may have had on me. I felt worthless.

Once again, in 1999, during my third and final pregnancy, my overriding thoughts turned to Margaret. I had been drawn to yet another adoption story on television, which had a tremendous effect on me. Unbeknown to David, I noted the help line number at the end of the programme and called the following morning. Hearing a sympathetic female on the end of the line caused a rush of emotion, but after regaining some composure, I relayed a brief history of my personal circumstances to her, including my current pregnancy. Although she advised me to re-establish contact with the Adoption Support Agency, I chose not to. Just the opportunity to express my most pent-up feelings brought an immense relief. This one sympathetic ear enabled me to shelve and contain the inevitable a little longer, choosing instead to focus solely on my daughters and fully experience the overriding joy that a newborn baby brings.

5. A Thistle in the Flowerbed

January 1998

It was with great pride that I sent Rosemary, aged three, to a delightful prep school in Sevenoaks and two years later, Annie followed in her footsteps.

Their time at the school was idyllic and an experience that I could have only ever dreamed about during my own childhood. Dressed in their blue and white striped pinafores, matching floppy hats and unbeknown to many, matching striped bloomers, they learned in an environment in which every child is encouraged to reach their potential. This, in fact, did leave me at times feeling most envious. They would receive an excellent education and have the opportunity to pursue many additional activities. Good behaviour and social manners were instilled in them as a matter of course. They would also learn another notable life skill, the curtsey – invaluable!

How different my life might have been had I been given similar opportunities. And it was here, at the same school, that I went back to work after a seven-year break raising my family.

From the very outset I was slightly apprehensive about working in the same school which my two daughters attended. David had spotted the advert in the local paper. They required a Domestic Bursar, a part-time position working mornings, during term-time only. I chose to ignore his first attempt to draw my attention to the vacancy, but when the advert appeared for a second week running he was convinced this part-time job was made for me and remained adamant that I should apply. I could see through his ulterior motive. After a difficult period in our marriage, he saw this as a way to keep me occupied. So, after a slightly awkward interview with the Headmistress, the job was mine and it was with a little reluctance and apprehension that I returned to work in January 1998.

I shared an office with the bursar, David Trill, who had joined the school the previous term after a long career in banking. Married to Margaret and with two grown-up sons, he looked upon this post to take him through to retirement.

The first thing I noticed when entering the small office was its lack of natural light. The large sash window at one end was permanently sealed, covered in an opaque film and formed an internal wall of an extension built many years earlier. The fluorescent tube remained permanently on and a small Velux window above my desk provided the only ventilation. It was also evident that this was the school's dumping ground. The room was filled with disused computers, printers, files, boxes, various unwanted classroom exhibits, Christmas decorations and for some considerable time, a hot water cylinder, awaiting installation in the headmistress's home. Added to this was an eclectic array of tired office furniture. The bursar's office was not a particularly welcoming environment.

The office was located at a kind of internal crossroad, on the ground floor of the main Victorian building between two staircases, the back stairs and the much grander front staircase and surrounded by corridors and walkways. There were two heavy, solid doors directly opposite each other, both opening inward and each leading to one of the two stairways. At times it resembled something akin to a French farce with a constant stream of staff calling in with requests, queries and questions, entering through one door and exiting through the other. Often both doors would open simultaneously, leaving each visitor quite perplexed. Who was the first to vie for our attention?

My responsibilities, under David's watchful eye, were to manage the entire housekeeping for the school. This role covered a multitude of duties and whilst it made for a varied job with no two days the same, meeting the demands of the entire school would often leave me exasperated. Feelings of frustration and subservience soon came to the surface.

Although at first David appeared a somewhat reserved man, it wasn't long before we hit it off and any concerns that I may have had over sharing a room with another person soon evaporated. He lived some distance from the school and was unfamiliar with Sevenoaks and its surrounding area. Sevenoaks was a total mystery to him, but I was able to enlighten him. The high standard of living and people's consequent expectations continually surprised him. He teased me relentlessly over my expression 'going up to town', which for me meant a short journey to the High Street in Sevenoaks. His idea of town had always been London or as he liked to call it 'The Smoke,' a deliberate choice of dated expression ensuring a guaranteed reaction from me. As a parent at the school, I could help him put names (and cars) to faces and keep him up-to-date with school news beyond the confines of our office, something I soon realised he enjoyed greatly. With his preconceived and somewhat cynical view of Sevenoaks, we would frequently rib each other, he over my life in this 'Sevenoaks bubble', while I would refer to his tougher, harder life in the north. (The reality was he lived just fifteen miles from the school!)

He held the school's purse strings and in his tireless efforts to make continual savings would search out 'bargains, sale, value, and specials' as he thumbed through mountains of catalogues and surfed the Internet making various purchases for the school. I, on the other hand, would frequently remind him that here at this school, quality was always paramount, drawing his attention to the 'deluxe, premium and superior' ranges. The continual banter was always very tongue in cheek and I look back on my time with David as fun and enjoyable. Elsewhere in the school however, away from the haven under the stairs, my working life could be intolerable. It was David's ability to introduce humour to any difficult situation that would help lift my spirits during some of the more challenging moments.

The Headmistress could without doubt, be most taxing. A very overbearing woman, with little time for anyone other than herself, she had been appointed in 1990 following a glorious reign of some thirty years by the previous Head who, in turn was niece of the school's founder.

It didn't take me long to limit my time in her company – nothing positive for me ever came from it. Of course, that didn't prevent her from seeking me out. She could be heard throughout the building. The distinctive sound of her footsteps and her penetrating voice, resonating in the distant corridors, meant I would already be bracing myself for the invariably unreasonable demands that followed. The only moments of reprieve were each morning, during the regular tours for prospective parents. Aware of her close proximity as she circumnavigated the office, extolling the delights of the school, I was always safe with the knowledge that my very undesirable space never featured on their route.

As a new member of staff, I too had been subjected to one of her guided tours. On my first morning, after a comprehensive tour of the school, concentrating on matters relating directly to me, namely catering, toilets and cleaning, to my surprise it was pointed out that my breaks would take place in the school office or at my desk and not in the staff room. I soon became very aware of the protocol. The administration, catering and grounds staff were very much 'below stairs', making this clear divide a somewhat lonely existence. From my first day at the school, the teaching staff had been introduced to me as Mrs, Miss or Mr and so it felt impossible for me to refer to them as anything else. Not wanting to emphasise my subservient position, I soon learned an 'um' or an 'excuse me', before launching straight into conversation avoided the need to call them anything. Although the occasional social event was organised amongst the teaching staff and occasionally I was invited to join in, I was reluctant to socialise with people who, despite working with them, I really didn't know. Feeling very much the outsider, I had no intention of being temporarily 'elevated', only to then revert to my dutiful position. I also had a distinct fear that I might be called upon in my capacity as general dogsbody to perhaps fetch and carry. Aware of this uncomfortable relationship, it was sometimes difficult for me to remember that not only was I the domestic bursar, I was also a fee-paying parent.

An occasion at the annual Spring Festival, was a case in point. This delightful – if somewhat twee – event, with every girl wearing a chaplet of flowers on her head, brought together the entire school in a celebration of new life. A series of poems, songs and hymns were performed to an audience of parents. As a proud mum, I took my seat in the audience, carefully selecting a spot some distance from the front, tucked away expecting to remain unseen. I suddenly became aware of a familiar pair of eyes frantically scanning the seated audience. I slumped down into my seat, trying to avoid eye contact with the woman I knew was eager to track me down with no doubt another demand. In her failed and desperate attempt to flush me out:

'MRS BRAZEL, WE NEED MORE CHAIRS HERE AT THE FRONT,' bellowed the Head.

There was no hiding place now, as all eyes immediately turned to me. I straightened up and could see a great deal of arm waving. Her need was clearly urgent, the festival about to commence and a few teachers still unseated. As I approached the stack of chairs, I couldn't help but wonder why they themselves were unable to collect a chair from the same stack as I had done, before returning to my seat feeling somewhat humiliated.

The requests and demands in my job were wide and varied. Being the individual responsible for all catering matters, I found that providing suitable menus, in particular those which met with the staff's requirements, was a tall order. In fact, more time and effort was spent planning and organising their meals, than for those of the pupils. However, very early on in my employment, there was one most important fact relayed to me by the Headmistress that I could never forget.

'Ladies of a certain age cannot eat baked beans,' she declared during one of my regular Monday morning audiences, referring to the sausage, mash and baked bean lunch – one of the more popular meals amongst the pupils. In fact, it was decided that there were a great number of meals served to the pupils which were not entirely suitable for the staff and my brief was to provide a selection of assorted salads each day.

Every aspect of the school's catering was most important to the Head and her culinary demands were endless. She herself certainly enjoyed her food and had been known to attend both first and second lunch sittings on a number of occasions, but with the introduction of a salad option, new problems inevitably arose. As word spread, a sudden influx of additional customers appeared in the dining room and with space already at a premium, it wasn't long before I was brought in to solve yet another most frustrating dilemma. I was very seldom in the dining room during lunch service, but on this one occasion I had been spotted.

'MRS BRAZEL!' came the familiar cry. 'WE NEED ANOTHER TABLE AND MORE CHAIRS, THERE ARE STAFF HERE WITH THEIR LUNCH IN THEIR HANDS AND NOWHERE TO SIT.' She was correct. I could see staff with nowhere to sit. The existing space was already filled to capacity and short of moving walls and windows her request was a physical impossibility. As she looked at me, awaiting a miracle, I stood frozen to the spot. What did she really expect me to do? Eventually the unseated staff retreated to the staffroom to sit and consume their lunch. A proposal from me to consider drawing up a rota to alleviate the congestion was immediately rejected as the staff needed to be given priority and fed urgently, as they did get very hungry. This, I decided, probably explained the large quantities of cake and biscuits consumed in the staffroom on a regular basis. However, when considered logically, I struggled to find any correlation between their extremes of dietary needs. On the subject of cake, the occasional invitation for David and me to help ourselves to any 'leftover cake', was an unwelcome gesture. How could consuming anyone's leftovers be a welcome invitation?

A ray of light in my rather grim worklife appeared, however, when, to my utter delight, Rosemary was chosen to be Head Girl for her final year. In the tradition of the school, as her mother, I was the guest of honour at the annual swimming gala and invited to sit with the Headmistress and then to present the prizes. Any possible thought of allowing me to enjoy, however briefly, an afternoon in the limelight was out of the question.

In my capacity as domestic bursar, my priority was to ensure all the physical needs of the staff were met and I arrived laden with bottles of water, cups, programmes and the school camera. Everything went smoothly, races swum, prizes presented, everyone content. Only as the event came to a happy close, believing my duties to be complete and proudly clutching the posy presented to me by my own, beautiful daughter, I was suddenly stopped in my tracks.

'MRS BRAZEL!' That dreaded voice boomed above the chatter. As I turned, an assortment of unwanted items was thrust into my arms and having relieved herself of all clutter, the Headmistress swanned off, leaving me struggling with my additional load. Watched by stunned fellow parents, I was mortified. Whilst I had already recognised that this job was doing nothing for my confidence and self-esteem, sadly any thought of a change of employment was unimaginable. My successful career many years earlier at British Home Stores, was now just a distant memory. It was hard to even believe that the ambitious and responsible person, entrusted to make major corporate decisions, had once been me.

Despite being on the receiving end of such demands on virtually a daily basis, amazingly, David Trill still managed to keep my spirits up. With his presence, humour and support my situation was just bearable but without him it would have certainly been a very lonely existence. He turned out to be my mentor, friend and guardian angel. I valued his opinions, ideas and solutions to my ever-growing list of troubles, concerns and difficulties, which were threatening to overwhelm me – not only inside, but also outside the workplace.

David Trill seemed to me to be a fount of all knowledge – a kind of oracle – and yet he was modest enough to always be keen to learn and understand more. One of his great strengths was his gentle manner: never did I detect any sign of arrogance or superiority, and this quality made him very approachable. I found it refreshing to listen to and consider opinions other than those dictated to me by my husband.

Indeed, there was little that we didn't discuss, such was his wealth of knowledge. I would even ask for his diagnosis prior to a doctor's appointment for either one of my daughters or me, addressing him as Doctor Trill, before listing our current alarming symptoms. Most crucially of all, it was his financial knowhow that I was keen to explore, as I became ever more exasperated over the financial arrangements in my marriage.

I had tried to express my concerns to my husband David on numerous occasions, but each time I found his response and explanation to be tiresome and totally unsatisfactory.

Confident that any reaction from David Trill, good or bad, would remain between ourselves, I chose a time when we were unlikely to be disturbed.

'David,' I said, putting down my pen and turning towards him. I don't think he ever knew quite what to expect each time he heard me call his name, followed by a brief pause.

'Yes,' he said, bracing himself.

'Does your wife hand in all her debit card receipts and cheque book stubs for you to write up in a cash book?' I asked, referring to an infuriating system that I'd adhered to since the beginning of my marriage.

Knowing that his responses were always measured and considered, his reaction was a comfort and although not unexpected, I realised that much of what occurred within my marriage was unacceptable. Over the following weeks, whenever there was a quiet moment, we talked in more detail about my ever-increasing difficulties outside the workplace.

David had also made great efforts to get to know Rosemary and Annie and it wasn't long before they, too, felt comfortable in his company. If Mummy wasn't available, then Mr Trill would usually suffice. Whether urgent funds were needed for a cake or toy sale, or a bit of childminding at the end of the school day, (if I'd been held up in traffic during the afternoon) he was always happy to help out wherever possible.

Perhaps because David had no grandchildren of his own, he showed a keen interest in Nancy's development. From her birth in July 1999, she too benefited from his attention, and so was extremely familiar and comfortable with the school three years later when she joined the nursery. Her very early garbled reference to 'Mem Large's Restaurant' endeared her to the school's catering team throughout her entire time there and, in particular to the cook, Mrs Large herself.

David Trill and I did, in fact, make a good team, so it was not all gloom and doom. There were so many bizarre and ridiculous requests that we'd frequently be reduced to fits of laughter. There was the request for a machine to deal with the increasing amount of fox poo deposited on the school grounds each evening. The newly refurbished ladies toilet had also caused a stir. The aperture of the new toilet seat was considered too small and, as we pondered on how best to replace it with a more acceptable size, it conjured up a whole manner of amusing possibilities.

My job wasn't just limited to the school day. With a variety of evening functions to organise, life could be quite arduous. With a very limited team available to support me, these evening soirées were hugely demanding. Here the headmistress was very skilled at making everything appear absolutely effortless. She went to great lengths to get things 'right' in her own eyes, even stretching to the hire of candelabras on one occasion.

I can recall one particular event which resulted in a tremendous amount of additional work and organisation for both David and myself. In fact, such was its importance in her eyes, that the daily matter of the running of the school became almost secondary.

An important and lavish dinner was being arranged for Heads from other local prep schools. The Headmistress embarked on one final inspection of the school and, accompanied by her secretary, she toured the buildings and its grounds. David and I, along with the few support staff waited with bated breath for the hard-earned seal of approval. Having laid the tables with all the finery that I could muster, I had turned my attention to the last-minute details in the kitchen when disaster struck.

'MRS BRAZEL', came the piercing, familiar cry. My heart sank. Something was obviously very wrong. Although neither of us were within sight of each other, this didn't prevent her from trying to communicate with me as she approached the dining-room. At this late hour I dreaded to think what had not met with her approval, what unthinkable task would I have to turn my hand to now? As her footsteps drew nearer I waited to hear my fate and once again stood frozen to the spot.

'MRS BRAZEL', she repeated, catching sight of me. 'THERE'S A THISTLE IN THE FRONT FLOWERBED!'

The impending dinner had completely gone to her head and her concern over a single weed was a gross overreaction.

'I'll go and see to it,' came my ever-dutiful response, leaving her in the dining room with the open-mouthed kitchen staff. As I headed down the corridor to attend to the offending weed, I could hear a further drama developing as her attention had moved on to the disabled toilet. On occasions such as this, it provided facilities for Gentlemen, but being located in a quite large space, it also doubled up as permanent quarters for the Henry Hoover.

'MRS LARGE, CAN WE REMOVE HENRY FROM THE DISABLED TOILET, IN CASE THE MEN SPRAY ON IT.'

Only some time later, looking back, was it possible to see these events as amusing and laugh them off.

Many of her utterly absurd requests harked back to another era. She had failed to move with the times and also with the increasing number of Government requirements to comply with, it became more and more taxing to meet many of her demands. Repainting the large edging stones that lined the drive was one of them. Watching David on his hands and knees, assisting the caretaker as they undertook this most laborious task was reminiscent of a scene from Alice in Wonderland. Like the playing cards, armed with tins of paint they worked feverishly, no doubt with cries of 'off with their heads' ringing in their ears.

Away from these somewhat bizarre and strange goings-on which made life a little more entertaining, the job was essentially soul-destroying. I was torn between my need to regain my confidence and self-esteem (impossible if I remained in the school environment), and the convenience of the job, with a reasonable salary. In my private life I was desperately unhappy. Knowing that my marriage was about to end, how could I consider embarking on a new career when I needed some stability at what was going to be a very traumatic time? Despite the prospect of remaining at the school until my retirement being just too depressing to contemplate, I felt I had to persevere a little longer.

Finally, just before Christmas 2005, I ended my marriage, leaving the family home and moving with the girls, into rented accommodation. It was a most harrowing time. By then David Trill had become a key figure in my life, his utterly practical advice and guidance, which I so desperately needed, was invaluable and he was a true lifesaver. Always mindful of my three daughters, he made every effort to consider and include them in his thinking and our discussions. They have always returned his affection and consideration as he continued to be involved in many aspects of their lives. Looking back, I can see that it was inevitable that I would involve David in my second, and most determined, attempt to search for my birth mother. Directing me to various sources of information and helping lead me to my startling discoveries, his assistance proved to be invaluable.

Finally, after ten years at the school, the bursar's office was by then relocated to a new area with natural daylight and brand new furniture, but David had decided to retire and after one long term without him, I could see that things were never going to work with a new, very ambitious Bursar, who had little time for me. I didn't feel that I featured in her future plans and with nowhere else in the school to seek support and a friendly ear, I called it a day.

On my final day after almost eleven years, I was invited to the staff room for a presentation during morning break. I was not surprised to find that the two cakes purchased to mark the event had already been severely demolished. I declined a slice.

My time at the school was not a particularly happy one. Without David Trill to share the burden, life would have been intolerable. Convenient, yes, but a place where I felt continually undermined, put upon, forgotten and lonely. It was impossible for me to challenge the thinking and approach of others, the upstairs/downstairs mentality was antiquated and ingrained and not the best way to motivate employees. Whatever their position in an establishment, everyone has an important role to play.

6. The Doctor's Surgery

May 2006

'Have you thought about looking at your medical file?' suggested David Trill, one morning at school. 'Everyone is entitled to see their own file now and it just may have something in it,' he added.

Several months had passed since I'd embarked on the search for my birth mother, but so far to no avail. This was not only a search for her, but also an attempt to learn something of my own beginnings, so David's suggestion was an idea I intended to follow up.

Margaret Coleman had registered my birth on 2nd April 1962. I was then ten days old. My adoptive parents, Peter and Bernice Gay, collected me four days later on 6th April. So what had happened during those fourteen days? Did I spend any of that time with my birth mother or were we separated immediately? Would my medical records give any details of this time?

I couldn't wait a moment. That same afternoon, following David's suggestion, I immediately went to the surgery. Naïvely, I had expected to be able to report my findings to David later that day when I returned to collect Nancy from school. I joined the queue to speak to a receptionist.

'Can I help you?' she said eventually.

'Yes, I would like to see my medical records, please.'

There was a stony silence as the receptionists and staff looked up from their workstations to scrutinize the instigator of this very sensitive and irregular request. I felt most uncomfortable.

'Well you can't see it today,' said the very guarded receptionist. 'Firstly we need to inform your GP that you have made a request to see your file. Then you have to make an appointment with our practice manager and she will find a convenient time when we have a suitable room available. I've made a note of your request and I suggest you telephone and speak to her in a couple of days. In addition to this there will be a £10 administration fee,' she declared.

As the tiresome procedure was explained to me, it became clear I would not gain access to my file that day. Although the change in the law does indeed permit access, I sensed this was something to be discouraged.

Now fully aware of the system, I remained undeterred. An appointment was made and the following week I returned to the surgery full of anticipation. I followed a very efficient looking woman down the long corridor, where I was ushered into a vacant room. I had already noticed the sizeable and rather tatty, buff-coloured file tucked firmly under her arm. It was tantalising. She invited me to take a seat at an empty desk and placed the file down in front of me.

'Do you have everything you need?' she asked.

'Yes thank you.'

'I will leave you alone and when you have finished, just leave the file on the desk,' she explained.

Before leaving the room she walked across to the window and adjusted the blind, ensuring some privacy. The suspense was too much and with the practice manager still in the room, I couldn't resist turning over the front cover of the file to reveal the all-important first page, hoping to discover vital information relating to the start of my life.

Alas, there was no reference to my birth or my time in the nursing home and subsequent adoption. My medical record did not begin until May 1962, by which time I was already two months old. Within seconds I realised there was nothing to be gained from this file and before I was even left alone in the room, I shut the file and rose from my seat.

'Thank you,' I said, noticing her surprised expression. 'I've seen all I need.'

'What do you mean?' she asked.

'I only wanted to look at the first page and there's nothing there to help me.' She was obviously very curious and I gave her a brief explanation. Her business-like manner was suddenly replaced by one of genuine concern and empathy at the lack of information in my file.

'But I can't charge you £10 for that,' she said compassionately. 'And I do wish you all the luck in your search.'

I thanked her for her help and left the surgery, remembering as I did so that it had been a visit to my GP almost three years earlier that had had the most life changing effect.

7. The Praying Mantis

July 2003

Sitting in a state of bewilderment, waiting to be called, this was no typical doctor's appointment. I was totally unprepared for my consultation. I was unable to provide any symptoms for a condition that had brought my life to a debilitating standstill.

That morning, to my great relief, the surgery had allocated me a slot within the hour and it was in an almost cursory fashion that I rose from my desk and announced to David Trill my impending visit to the Doctor. Unlike other occasions, I refrained from my usual habit of relaying any ailments to him, for a much appreciated preliminary diagnosis.

I had chosen not to share my intention to visit my GP with anyone, least of all my husband David. Whilst he would acknowledge my current state of anxiety, it appeared impossible for him to truly grasp what I was going through. All he did was reassure me that it was just a difficult phase, which would soon pass. There seemed no alternative but for me to battle on in the total absence of any practical or emotional support.

My true inner life and feelings had to be kept masked by a pretence that all was well. Publicly, I strived relentlessly to present a very capable, contented front. I managed by focusing on everyone around me rather than myself but once within the confines of my own home, I was full of despair and unhappiness. My life had become intolerable. Finally, it was concern for my three daughters, which drove me to seek help. They were the most important people in my life and my effort to be the best mother to them was in jeopardy.

I hated myself. The prospect of each new day had become unbearable. Life had become ever more challenging, even the simplest of tasks were daunting. The grocery shopping was haphazard and the household chores neglected. I cried a lot of the time and totally lacked any resilience to deal with the day-to-day pressures of life. Totally lacking any self-esteem, any criticism was mortifying and I had allowed myself to be dominated by the unreasonable behaviour of many around me.

I was suffering deeply and without any outside support, I could see no end to these feelings of hopelessness. Perhaps the final straw had been the dreadful experience the previous weekend. The huge upset that it caused me finally drove me to seek help.

It was a Saturday morning in late June, Founders Day at Sevenoaks School where Rosemary had just completed her first very successful year of secondary education. To mark the occasion, all first year parents had been invited to a celebratory service at the local parish church followed by an awards ceremony and lunch to be held at the school.

The weather was glorious as David and I walked the short distance from our home to join Rosemary who had set off for the church a little earlier. We sat amongst the other parents and spotted many familiar faces that we had come to know during the last nine months. The uplifting service left me with a great sense of pride for my eldest daughter and all that she had achieved.

The congregation was then invited to take the brief stroll to the school campus. Still standing in the pew and slowly edging our way towards the aisle, David and I became separated. He had seized an opportunity to join the throng of departing parents heading towards the door. I had hesitated, not wanting to push in and so had to wait. One of the last to leave the church, I approached the south door alone and stepped out into the warm air, noticing the brilliant blue sky.

In high spirits, my thoughts were focused on my three daughters. How suited they were to their excellent schools and all the opportunities open to them. My own school days were a stark contrast – my opportunities and achievements had been non-existent. Supporting and encouraging each of them gave me immense joy and satisfaction. As I passed through the open doorway I was immediately aware of a man lurking in the entrance, watching me intently. A quick glance directly at him confirmed that I had no recollection of this middle-aged man. I felt uncomfortable and avoided any further eye contact, as I headed out along the path intending to catch up with David in the distance. My unease heightened as he came alongside me.

'Um, excuse me,' he said. He was now uncomfortably close and loomed over me like a praying mantis. I stopped and looked up at him. I didn't have a good feeling. Beyond what appeared to be a welcoming smile, I could clearly detect a grimace. He seemed to hesitate as he prepared to speak again.

'I hope you don't think me impertinent?'

There was a further pause. I glanced ahead in the hope that David might come back to find me but he was out of sight. Somehow I sensed that I needed to be rescued from this encounter.

'I was sitting in the row just behind you in the church and couldn't help noticing that you didn't sing any of the hymns during the service. Is there a reason for this?'

A wave of emotion swelled up inside me, this extremely rude man was certainly impertinent! Why should I explain to a total stranger that my severe hearing difficulties prevent me from singing in tune and never wanting to embarrass myself at events such as these, I've always chosen not to sing. I was mortified that not only had he monitored me throughout the service but also he was so incensed that he waited outside until practically everyone else had passed before finally accosting me. And now I felt very intimidated, as he waited patronisingly for an explanation.

I suspected he was ardent church, prepared to challenge anyone who didn't conform to his rigid beliefs. He showed a confidence and arrogance, which was determined to humiliate me. A sudden wry smile was apparent, as he prepared to pounce. Believing he had me cornered, he had every intention of highlighting my apparent disrespectful behaviour.

I look around again, desperate for the support of my husband. Completely incapable of retaliating by brushing him aside, I felt instead inferior and pathetic, and even defended and apologised for my actions as I explained my situation. I was desolate.

His smug expression, however, immediately vanished. Realising his excruciating gaffe, he showed a sudden transparent display of care and concern. Desperate to escape the company of this loathsome individual, I started to walk down the path but his disrespect knew no bounds however, as he remained beside me continuing to delve and question. To my shame, I felt unable to cut him dead and reluctantly responded. Why had I allowed myself to be crushed by this man? Instead of the rage and contempt needed to deal with this appalling situation, I remained vulnerable and distressed. Where was David when I desperately needed him?

Eventually, having shown what he believed to be a sufficient amount of sympathy and understanding towards my unseen disability, he quickened his pace to join his wife up ahead. Left alone I began to weep but unbeknown to me, someone else had witnessed the entire scene.

'How terribly rude!' she exclaimed. I looked up to see a mother of one of Rosemary's good friends.

'Do you know who he is?' she asked, implying that she already knew the answer. 'No,' I said, feeling very self-conscious that she'd observed my pitiful performance.

'He is the headmaster of an independent prep school, I heard him give a talk recently. It's disgraceful, how dare he speak to you in that way.'

I quickly brushed her concerns aside. I was too ashamed to discuss it any further. I scuttled ahead, avoiding the offender and by now absolutely desperate to locate David, still oblivious to my traumatic encounter. With tears rolling down my cheeks, I recounted the whole shocking episode to him.

'What an unpleasant man,' he said in a mildly comforting tone. 'Take no notice. People like him aren't worth bothering with. Now try not to think about it and let's get on and enjoy the rest of the day.'

I felt even more mortified at this underplayed response. Not only was he my husband and had a duty to defend me but he was also a very articulate man, who could certainly have challenged this loathsome man. Instead I had been treated patronisingly and without feeling, being virtually instructed to forget the incident, but this was impossible. For the rest of the day I kept a very low profile, battling to hold back the tears and longing for it to come to end.

Eventually my wish was granted. Back home and feeling terribly distressed, in need of comfort and solitude, I took to my bed. Throughout the weekend I chose to remain there whenever possible, holding tightly to the duvet as if a shield. I got up only to meet the demands of my family and return to my haven at the first opportunity. David was unable to lift my spirits.

Finally realising that I had to seek help, the following week, comforted by my GP, nothing would be the same again. He ushered me into his surgery and I sat in one of the two chairs adjacent to his large, sweeping corner desk. He sat in his hi-tech wheelie chair, complete with a large rubber cushion designed to encourage good posture (the finer details of which had been explained to me on a previous visit.) Over the years I had invariably sat in the seat furthest from his desk after placing one of my ailing daughters in the chair nearest to him, but now it was me in the hot seat.

Richard had been our GP since our arrival in Sevenoaks in 1994, an excellent doctor, with whom we had a good relationship. I'd always found him to be approachable and understanding. He turned towards me.

'What can I do for you?' he asked gently.

Suddenly finding myself the focus of attention was daunting. Richard sat patiently, waiting for me to gather my thoughts and divulge my symptoms, but there was no response. My head was bowed and my shoulders arched and raised, my knees were locked tightly together and both hands were in my lap. I glanced at him. He waited patiently. Still nothing. There were no aches, pains or a condition that could easily be translated into words. I felt unable to speak or even know where to start talking about the heart of my problems – if only I knew what they were. Suddenly the immense strain of the situation caused a surge of emotion and I was overwhelmed by a torrent of tears rolling down my face.

A large, white, crumpled blur suddenly appeared in my lap. Gratefully, I struggled to stem the tears and blow my nose simultaneously. I was flooded with feelings I'd harboured for many years, maybe an entire lifetime. Richard remained silent and manoeuvred his seat closer to mine encompassing my pitiful frame with his knees. The uncontrollable weeping came as a welcome release. I felt secure, but the prospect of leaving his safe haven was unimaginable.

Exhausted and emotionally drained, I needn't have worried about being incapable of words; I had communicated everything and Richard had made a very accurate diagnosis. I had severe depression and was experiencing some kind of breakdown.

To ascertain the situation, the gentle questioning that followed required only a simple nod of the head. After many comforting and reassuring words he instructed me to contact the local mental health centre immediately and prescribed some anti-depressants for some short-term relief.

'This can be sorted, you will feel better again.' he said encouragingly.

It was an idea too impossible to imagine, but I had a lot of faith in Richard and felt just a little better as I left the surgery and returned to work.

I embarked on some initial counselling and was advised to consider a more satisfactory long-term solution, somewhere safe and understanding where I could explore the life issues which had brought me to the state I was now in.

At this very desperately sad and lonely time, I was keen to accept any help available. It was for me to select a name from the list of registered therapists handed to me and to make direct contact.

8. Maggie

September 2003

Maggie met my initial, very simple criteria: close to home and female. I had spent hours trawling through the extensive list of registered psychotherapists in the southeast and eliminated them one by one. Three children and a part-time job meant I had limited time for myself and only a woman would have some real understanding and empathy for a busy working mother's timetable.

With my husband's agreement to fund the sessions, I called to arrange an appointment. Desperately unhappy, I needed to talk to someone urgently.

Maggie lived just fifteen minutes drive out of Sevenoaks in a small semi-rural village. Her home was a pretty, detached single-storey cottage, smothered in a Virginia creeper which turned a most spectacular, glowing crimson each autumn. The weekly sessions took place in an annexe to the side of the property and it was approached by a magical meander through beautiful trees, shrubs, plants and ornaments. The concealed entrance was protected by a prolific clematis and variegated ivy, a combination that provided a welcome shield whilst waiting for Maggie to operate the door entry system from within.

I stepped into a small, sparsely furnished waiting area with a solitary wicker chair and always a vase of fresh flowers. The seat of the wicker chair was such that it was impossible to perch on the edge. Instead it had a way of drawing me down into it, almost forcing me into a relaxed position whilst I waited for Maggie's arrival.

Maggie could always be heard approaching the adjacent room by another entrance from where she would open the waiting room door and invite me in. It was a cosy, compact room, furnished with a couch, two chairs and an entire wall lined with books, all on psychology.

Maggie sat in an elaborate, padded rocking chair between the head of the couch and the book-lined wall. The couch was positioned against a window and dominated the room. It looked most inviting, covered in a throw and with plenty of plump pillows and a fleece blanket folded at one end, all in deep warm tones.

However, despite its appeal, I chose instead to sit on the other chair opposite Maggie, my first thought being that in this unfamiliar situation I needed the reassurance of being able to lip read if necessary. It was many months before I felt confident enough to rely solely on the sound of Maggie's voice to conduct our sessions, but having done so, I soon found the experience very agreeable. Lying down beside the bay window was quite tranquil. The sight of the swaying treetops and the frequent vapour trails of aircraft high in the sky was something to focus on during some of the more reflective moments. The room was always warm, even on a mild day the central heating was evident and provided a comfortable, relaxed and safe environment that I would continue to visit for many years.

Maggie herself was most compelling. Somehow she created an atmosphere of curious enchantment. An attractive woman, probably in her early fifties, with a petite, delicate frame, olive complexion and a mass of dark reddish shoulder length hair. I envied her extensive wardrobe and dress sense. Her clothes were of good quality, often displaying a sense of fun, almost elfin-like, with interesting tights or leggings teamed with some unusual footwear.

Initially I relished the sessions, Maggie conveyed a sense of calm and empathy and the luxury of having someone devoted solely to me was a new experience. Burdened and troubled by many difficult issues during my life, I was intent on providing her with a detailed picture. I bombarded her with information, concealing nothing. Maggie's ability to retain practically everything I told her was astounding and a great comfort.

Over a period of time we identified the many painful events I had experienced throughout my life, slowly and carefully addressing each of them in turn, in an attempt to help me understand the effect they were having on me today, but I was overwhelmed. Absolutely every aspect of my life had been affected by my past experiences.

The sessions became ever more challenging, as I struggled to accept that I did indeed have the power to change my way of thinking and thus turn my life around. I increased my visits to twice a week and despite the traumas each visit made me face, I was determined to do my utmost never to miss this most precious time. Childcare was arranged whenever necessary, and occasionally I drove in severe weather conditions. I even went to the extent of choosing to match my holidays with Maggie's whenever possible. Inevitably though, the more sessions I had, the greater my dependency on her. I felt a strong connection and her reaction towards me on two occasions in particular, affected me greatly.

The first concerned my adopted brother Andrew. Although I had already made Maggie aware of Andrew's difficult behaviour as a child, which eventually resulting in living in a care home, she decided to enquire further. As this episode had occurred whilst I was in my teens, my knowledge was patchy, however, I described as much as I could remember.

'He wasn't living anywhere local,' I explained. 'It was in Guildford, one hour's drive from where we were living at that time.'

'Do you remember the name of the place?' she asked curiously.

'Oh yes. It wasn't actually in Guildford, but close by, in Godalming, it was a place called Peper Harrow.'

'Peper Harrow,' she repeated. The name was obviously familiar to her.

'Yes.'

'I know of it,' she said.

I could see real concern in her face. I didn't immediately understand the implication, I was just surprised that she'd heard of it, but, as a very experienced therapist, she knew a great deal about Peper Harrow. In the early seventies it had been a centre where pioneering work with disturbed adolescents had been carried out.

'Karen, this was no ordinary care home. Any young person sent there would have been extremely troubled. I can certainly understand that living in that family environment would have been exceedingly difficult. In fact, it must have been impossible for you.'

Finally, in my forties, somebody realised and sympathised with just how tough my life had been. Growing up with Andrew had been intolerable at times and I don't think anyone else, until now, had ever truly understood. Throughout that session, I sat and wept and then went home and cried uncontrollably, out of sheer relief. Her surprising insight into Peper Harrow convinced me that my sessions with Maggie were meant to be.

The second occasion was in April 2004. I drove to Maggie's house as usual, having just returned from a family holiday in Mexico two days earlier. My four-year-old daughter Nancy had been very unwell during the previous two nights. Her breathing

62

was laboured and each night I had lain beside her as she slept, monitoring her every breath whilst David slept soundly in our bed. I'd had little sleep and was exhausted. Operating Maggie's intercom I was alarmed to hear her voice asking me to return in five minutes or so. I checked my watch, clearly oblivious to everything including the time and found I was indeed too early and had encroached on her previous appointment. Eventually, sitting in front of Maggie, it was obvious to her how exhausted I really was and completely unable to make any rational decisions as to what was best for my family and me.

'You need to go home and rest, either in bed or on the sofa. You're totally drained. You shouldn't have lain there each evening alone with Nancy. In fact if her breathing was laboured you should have telephoned the emergency doctor. You must get her looked at. Also, I would recommend that you stay at home tomorrow and certainly don't even think about going to work.'

Her concern and advice was much appreciated. Unable to think clearly for myself, I returned home and followed her instructions. Nancy's health was immediately addressed and she was diagnosed with asthma. I was so very grateful to Maggie that day. In the absence of any other caring person in my life, she alone had been able to help and guide in a way a mother might at the sight of her daughter in such obvious distress.

I knew the time ahead would be even more challenging. All was clearly not well in my marriage. When asked if I had a happy marriage, initially I was keen to reassure her. I truly believed it, but as I explored and analysed the intricacies of the relationship between David and myself, I realised it was far from happy, balanced or healthy. I struggled to face issues that had become apparent. The reality of ending my marriage was something I didn't even dare contemplate, as I worried endlessly over the effect this would have on my three daughters. Frightened and daunted at the prospect of facing the practicalities of what might be looming, some days were terrifyingly bleak, but throughout this time, Maggie's help and support continued to be immeasurable.

As a psychotherapist, Maggie has ensured that our relationship has remained a professional one. I still know little about her. Nevertheless, the number of unexpected coincidences between us has surprised me. Not only her in-depth knowledge of Peper Harrow, but also she has revealed a detailed knowledge of both my place of birth, Hackney in East London, and the location of my adoptive late mother's ashes, a hundred miles away. However, whilst I noted each of these strange coincidences, Maggie chose not to elaborate on them. It hadn't gone unnoticed that, although only ever referred to as Maggie, her name is an abbreviation of Margaret, the same name as my birth mother. Maggie's unequivocal support during every stage of my traumatic and heartbreaking search for Margaret Coleman has been crucial.

Looking back to the start of my therapy, I had a mountain to climb. Maggie's ability to challenge my thinking and decisions has at times left me angry and perplexed. The simple notion that I have choices in life, whilst difficult for me to comprehend, has been key to the emotional and physical changes I have since brought about. When faced with daily life-decisions, I am learning to consider my own thoughts and feelings and not just of those around me. I make a conscious effort to try not to succumb to the relentless needs of others, unless it is my choice to do so. Physically much has already changed in my life. Today I am in a new, happy and contented relationship. I feel loved and considered, and I can be myself. I have left a job behind that did nothing for my self-esteem and I am now free to embark on something new. This new-found confidence has strengthened my relationship with my daughters. I'm no longer the 'stressy' mum they once knew and I have embarked on the most extraordinary search to discover my own identity.

This entire life-changing journey and the many traumas on the way would have been unthinkable without Maggie's support. She has given me the strength to turn my life around. I now have the confidence to take risks in the hope that my life can be more fulfilling.

Despite the many difficulties that surround me, I have learnt there is only one person I am capable of changing – me.

It's hard to imagine my life without Maggie. I have grown very fond of her and I sense a great warmth and affection between us. Amongst the difficult times there has been a lot of unexpected fun and laughter, as I relay to her yet another strange happening in my ever-taxing world. On many occasions I have arrived armed with photos or a laptop. Sitting together, observing her as she eagerly studies and retains the images of each important individual in my life, has always been heart-warming. For me, as well as being my therapist, she has acted out the role of a much-needed mother, sister, aunt and best friend.

9. Up Before the Judge

February 2006

To my complete surprise, I'd received notification that this time, my Adoption File had been found and I was advised to book an appointment at the court. My first attempt to locate my file thirteen years earlier had proved fruitless and had resulted in a compliments slip sent from the Chief Clerk with a scribbled message simply reading: 'Not Wandsworth's Case Number.'

I knew at the time this reply was incorrect because I had the Adoption Order in my possession, which clearly stated it had been issued by Wandsworth County Court in 1962. In my opinion it had been a poor response to something so sensitive. With no further assistance offered nor any explanation given, I assumed that it had been lost or destroyed. However, many years later, I'd decided to apply one more time. This time, unlike the last failed attempt, I was now utterly focused on my search for Margaret Coleman and with the complete support of my new partner Paul and my three daughters, I would not be deterred.

As Paul and I travelled together to Wandsworth County Court on Wednesday 15th February for what had been described to me as an informal meeting with a Circuit Judge, I had high expectations. The prospect of viewing a file untouched for almost forty-four years was fascinating. I was curious as to its content. Surely something in that file would provide me with a clue to help me discover more about Margaret Coleman and ultimately lead me to her.

However, my excitement soon subsided as we entered the Court. Sitting in the waiting area clutching the letter confirming my appointment, I found my surroundings very intimidating and not, in my opinion, the right environment for someone about to undergo something so sensitive. Fortunately, the Court had advised me to bring a family member or close friend. Looking up, I noticed the list of cases scheduled for that day. My name appeared at the very top:

10.00 a.m.   Karen Brazel   Private Appointment

I even resented appearing publicly on a list in such an establishment. The sheer nature and procedure of a court seemed to provide an intimidating environment. The necessary counselling back in 1994 for access to my full birth records, had taken place at Bromley Town Hall under far less stressful conditions. This was an extremely sensitive time for me personally. I was about to uncover details of another life, my brief existence as a Coleman.

A Clerk of the Court arrived and announced my name. I stood up.

'Is it OK to bring my partner?' I asked, expecting a reassuring nod, but it was not forthcoming.

'Err, I don't know, I'll have to check, follow me please.' He looked perplexed and uncomfortable. Clearly he was not prepared for the nature of my visit or my request. I should have been more assertive and pointed out the content of my letter to him, stating that I may be accompanied by a relative or close friend. I didn't need to gain the approval of the judge, intimidated by this overwhelming environment, I was apprehensive and unnerved by the entire process and I reluctantly followed him, glancing at Paul as I left.

I followed the clerk at some considerable distance. First, we passed through a large doorway into an empty courtroom, then crossing to the other side, I was taken behind the Bench and out through the doorway used by the judge. The journey continued through a labyrinth of corridors until eventually we arrived at his private chambers. Not expecting to cover such a distance, it occurred to me that even with the approval of the judge, it would take some considerable time for Paul to join me.

As expected, the judge was in total agreement that I should have someone else present and so the clerk was immediately despatched to collect Paul.

I looked at the elderly and distinguished man sitting behind a very large oak desk. Speaking slowly and clearly, he invited me to sit down. The room was dark and imposing, and I felt very uncomfortable. I caught sight of his wig on a stand beside him, reminding me of the gravity of the occasion.

These initial impressions were replaced by a sudden overwhelming feeling of excitement, as I spotted the open file in front of him. The judge began to explain one or two details, but I really didn't want him to say anything of any significance until Paul's arrival, as I feared my inability to retain any information. As I sat facing this austere looking gentleman, I felt nervous and anxious. He explained that he had been called upon at short notice to conduct this meeting, as the original judge was suddenly unavailable. He also added that he had a particular interest in adoption cases, as he'd been heavily involved in the process spanning over many years.

As expected, he enquired as to my reasons for wanting access to my file and how much information I had already uncovered. I talked briefly about my desire to know more about the circumstances of my adoption and, if possible, to try and trace my birth mother. I also disclosed the small amount of information that I had found so far, including my uncertainty concerning

Patrick Coleman.

'This file is extremely sparse, it contains very little information,' he began to explain, just as Paul and the clerk entered the room. I breathed a sign of relief as Paul sat down beside me, with the clerk next to him. After a quick introduction the judge continued.

'As I have just explained, I've looked through this file thoroughly and it doesn't contain a great deal of information and I really don't think that there is anything in here that could be of any help to you in tracing your birth mother.' There was a brief pause. 'But it is also for me to assess whether releasing the little information I have is best for all concerned. I do have to consider all the parties involved in your adoption, you understand. However, in this particular case, because of the lack of information in the file, the decision does not arise.' He said, slowly turning the pages.

Listening to his measured words, my heart sank as it dawned on me that I wasn't going to have direct and unlimited access to this file. Quite wrongly, I had imagined that like my medical file, I would be free to browse the documents at my leisure. Instead, the file would remain at arm's length on the other side of an oversized desk, making even upside down reading out of the question. The notebook and camera carefully prepared and waiting in the bottom of my handbag were redundant.

'As I said, I have been heavily involved in adoption cases over the years and, compared to others, this file is very thin. However, I have read what little there is and I will disclose to you two important facts.' There was another pause, which seemed endless.

'The first is that Patrick Coleman was not deceased at the time of your birth, as stated on your birth certificate.'

There was no great reaction from either Paul or me. It confirmed the words of Jim Donovan, which initially I had refused to believe.

'The second, is that Patrick Coleman was not your natural father.' he paused again, waiting for me to digest his statement.

With the information we had uncovered to date, this came as no great surprise. I turned to Paul and could see that he too, was unfazed by the disclosure. Patrick Coleman had already become something of an enigma and this had already been considered as one of many theories. Nonetheless, confirmation that I was illegitimate, despite the information on my birth certificate, was particularly poignant.

'Would I be able to have copies of those documents?' I asked, hopefully.

He thought for a moment.

'I don't see why not. I can give you copies of what I have, although it's not much,' he said, as he began to remove the reports from the file. 'Are your adoptive parents still alive?' he asked.

'Only my father.' I said.

'In which case, I will refrain from giving you a copy of the report on your adoptive parents. I'm sure you understand and of course it doesn't have any bearing on the whereabouts of your birth mother.'

I agreed, I could see the lengthy report in question and whilst it would have been an interesting document to read in its own right, I was prepared to accept the opinion of the judge. My main concern for today was to discover something about Margaret Coleman.

The judge handed three documents to the clerk and instructed him to take a copy of each. Although I was delighted to be taking away something to examine, I was still disappointed that there appeared to be so little in the file.

Throughout the course of the meeting, I had studied the elderly gentleman sitting across the desk intently. During the short time we had spent together, he had appeared to mellow, realising my appeal was genuine. Waiting in silence for the clerk to return, I seized on what might be my final opportunity.

'Is there a date of birth for Margaret Coleman?' I asked.

'I don't think so,' he said, turning the pages and shaking his head.

'Or a National Health Number?' I enquired hopefully.

'No, I'm afraid there isn't,' he replied, turning the pages of the file yet again, to reassure us both that he hadn't missed anything. 'As I said, there is very little information in here,' he reiterated. He turned to the beginning of the file once more and began to slowly turn the pages for a final time.

'I've seen many adoption files over the years and I must say this one has a surprising number of blank pages,' he commented. 'But you must also bear in mind that it is you who would have been the primary concern of the authorities. Your birth mother's details would have been of very little interest to them. However, despite this, I would still have expected to see a little more in here,' he said, shaking his head. 'Also, I notice there appears to be no amendment to your birth records, correcting the details of your birth father. I'm surprised that wasn't done.'

The file had been exhausted. No amount of further questioning would reveal anything more.

'I am very sorry that I cannot be of more help to you.'

The clerk had meanwhile returned and handed the photocopies to the judge, who in turn passed them to me. We stood up to leave the room.

'I do wish you luck in your continued search,' he said. 'The clerk will escort you back to the main entrance.'

The brief meeting, lasting only twenty minutes or so, was over. If the journey to the chambers had been circuitous, then it had not prepared us for our escorted departure. With the Courts now sitting, our alternative route took us back through a seemingly endless corridor system, up a flight of stairs, through an entire open plan office filled with clerical staff surprised by our sudden presence, down a further flight of stairs, before finally arriving in the waiting area. After an apology from the clerk for the diversionary route, we left the building.

Driving home, we talked of my disappointment and the mystery surrounding my birth father. If Patrick was indeed not my father, then why did his name appear on my birth certificate, dead or alive? There was no legal requirement to provide a father's name.

The morning's events had been exhausting and I was feeling totally drained. To sit before a judge in a county court is quite an undertaking. Surely suitable agencies could be given access to these files, allowing this important information to be relayed in a more comfortable and a less intimidating environment.

Once home and with so little new information to go on, all that remained was for us to study the documents given to us earlier that day. Although I was already convinced that nothing we had learnt that morning was going to lead us any closer to Margaret Coleman, my hopes of at least discovering her date of birth had been dashed.

The first document we examined was hand written and, despite being neither on headed paper nor dated, it appeared to come from the Social Services. They were clearly suspicious about the information that had been given to them by Margaret, and were concerned at the lack of a death certificate. Unfortunately, however, they came to the wrong conclusion as to her marital status.

This read:

Mrs Coleman was not aware that Mrs Davey of 156 Wimbledon Park Rd. had helped to arrange the placement. She told me that

Mrs Coleman was not aware that Mrs Davey
of 156 Wimbledon Park Rd. had helped to arrange
the placement. She told me that her husband
died in Ireland in Aug of last year & that she
had destroyed the death cert certificate. I think
it is quite likely that she is unmarried rather than
a widow but she assured me that her husband's
parents as well as her own & agreed it was best for
the baby to be adopted.

(Miss) J. Moncrieff

her husband ha died in Ireland in Aug of last year & that she had
destroyed the death cerfi certificate. I think it is quite likely that
she is unmarried rather than a widow but she assured me that
her husband's parents as well as her own I agreed it was best for
the baby to be adopted.

(Miss) J. Moncrieff

The second document was dated 18th May 1962, when I was
exactly eight weeks old. It appeared to be the result of a formal
interview with a Mrs Winifred Davy, a member of the adoption
board who acted as an intermediary. Reading this I learned that I
was collected from the nursing home on 6th April. There is little
additional information, other than another reference to Patrick's
alleged death in August 1961 and also to my blood group, O
Negative, the implications of which I wouldn't discover until I
was expecting my first child.

Finally, the third document was the most surprising of all. A
declaration made by Margaret, sworn and signed in the presence
of a judge at Ilford County Court, stating that her husband Patrick
Coleman was alive but was not my birth father. According to the
document, I was illegitimate and she had no knowledge of my
true father's whereabouts. However, above all, the information
that disturbed me the most was the reference to Karen Lesley

ADOPTION ACT, 1958

Interview with

Name *Winifred DAVEY (Mrs)*

Address *156 Wimbledon Park Road SW.18*

who is described on an application for an Adoption Order in respect of
Baby Coleman born *23. 3. 62* as a person
who appears to have taken part in the arrangements.

1. What part did you take in the arrangements aforesaid?	Acted as 3rd Party
2. Are you related to the infant, its parents or the persons with whom the infant is placed?	No
3. With whom was the infant placed?	Mr Mrs Gay 5 Ellora Rd SW.16
4. On what date	6. 4. 62
5. Who are the natural parents of the infant (to your knowledge)?	Mother Address Mrs Margaret Coleman 13. Herbert Rd. Ilford Father Address Deceased during Aug. 1962
6. (a) If you ever had charge of the infant yourself please give dates (b) Details of any payment received for caring for the child for this period	From To No None
7. If the infant was not in your custody prior to placement with the applicants from whose custody was it transferred?	Name Mrs Eldridge Address St Margarets Nursery 262 Victoria Park Rd E9
8. If you have knowledge of protective inoculation given to the infant, please give details and dates	Treatment Date not yet. started
9. Who has the medical record of the infant?	None in existence Normal Birth. V.D. Negative
10. Do you wish to be present at the hearing of the application?	No
11. Have you made or offered to make, or received or agreed to receive any payment or other reward for or in consideration of adoption, or for making arrangements for adoption, or for transferring the care and possession of an infant for adoption or for the grant of any consent required in connection with adoption? If so, what is its nature?	No

The answers to the above questions were recorded by me at an interview
with the person concerned on *18/5/62*

Signed *Maurice Brown*

Description *Child Care officer (S.D.)*

Acting as agent for the Children's Off

74

This is to state that the Birth Certificate
relating to KAREN LESLEY COLEMAN born the
23rd March 1962 at St Margaret's Nursing
Home, 263, Victoria Park Road, Hackney E.9.
and signed by me, is incorrectly filled in.
My husband is not deceased and the baby
Karen Lesley Coleman is illegitimate. I
regret that I have no knowledge of the
present whereabouts of the true father and
cannot get in touch with him.

Signed... M... Coleman...:
Date ....25.th Oct '62.:

Sworn at the ... in the County of ...

To the Judge,
Wandsworth County Court,
Garret Lane,
London. S.W.18.

FILED 26 OCT 1962

This is to state that the Birth Certificate relating
to KAREN LESLEY COLEMAN born the 23rd March 1962 at
St Margaret's Nursing Home, 263 Victoria Park Road,
Hackney E. 9. and signed by me, is incorrectly
filled in. My husband is not deceased and the baby
Karen Lesley Coleman is illegitimate. I regret that
I have no knowledge of the present whereabouts of
the true father and cannot get in touch with him
Signed .....M.   Coleman
Date   25th October '62

75

Coleman. At no time did I ever possess this name. When Margaret Coleman gave me up for adoption it was simply under the name of COLEMAN, (Female). I became Karen Lesley after Bernice and Peter Gay collected me from St Margaret's nursing home.

I vehemently objected to Margaret Coleman having knowledge of my given names after her decision to abandon me.

However, despite confirmation of Patrick Coleman's existence in March 1962 and a court document stating that he was not my biological father, Paul remained unconvinced. The conflicting information puzzled him and he was adamant that we were lacking all the facts.

'I still believe that Patrick Coleman could be your biological father,' Paul insisted.

He was referring to the adoption procedure and the ease with which a child could be adopted with only one parental signature. For a married couple to give a baby up for adoption it was likely to have raised many questions. However, I remained unconvinced. We had uncovered a catalogue of lies and were left wondering: what was Margaret Coleman really trying to conceal?

10. Mum and Dad

My parents, Bernice and Peter Gay, were a working-class couple from South London, who coincidently shared the same occupation as Margaret and Patrick Coleman at the time of my adoption. They were bus conductors.

Unable to have children of their own, they embarked on what turned out to be a lengthy and difficult adoption process. Having endured a relentless ordeal of paperwork, assessments and interviews over several years, on 6th April 1962, they finally arrived at St Margaret's Nursing Home in Hackney, East London, to be handed their 2-week old baby daughter.

For Bernice and Peter, the initial period as new parents was fraught with uncertainty and anguish. Informed by the authorities that the Adoption Order could not be granted, they were advised to avoid drawing attention to my sudden appearance until the relevant documents could be finalised. Without any explanation for this unexpected delay, it only served to convey one heartbreaking message to my parents: I could be returned to my birth mother at any time.

Bernice reacted to this unbearable stress by making me utterly dependent on her. Cradling me constantly throughout the day, I would immediately show my discontent the moment I was parted from her. Her thinking was that, should an official suddenly arrive to take me away, they would be faced with a distressed and unhappy infant and have no alternative but to revoke the decision to return me to my birth mother. Thankfully for my parents, that day never materialised.

It was November before they finally heard that the Adoption Order had been granted and a further two months passed before they received notice of a copy of the entry in the Adopted Children Register. At long last I was now officially Karen Lesley Gay. After almost ten agonising months they could begin family life, free from any outside interference.

My mother spoke fondly of our time in the small one-bedroom flat behind Streatham bus garage. The mountain of photos of my early life recorded a contented, chubby faced infant with a head of fine, wavy, fair hair. Wearing pretty, smocked dresses and surrounded by soft toys, life appeared idyllic, as I spent much time either in the garden or in my elegant Silver Cross pram on regular outings with my mother to Streatham Common. It was soon after my second birthday that we moved to live with my paternal grandmother.

My parents were very kind, easy-going people, if a little dated in their outlook. Only when I went to school did I realise that they were significantly older than the parents of my peers, but I was certainly a daddy's girl. Dad was a man with a cheery disposition, who never shouted, lost his temper or used bad language. I naturally gravitated towards him, as a great deal of Mum's time, with nanny's assistance, seemed to be taken up with Andrew, my new brother, whom they adopted in August 1964.

Andrew's idiosyncrasies had a grave effect on the family, who were ill-equipped to deal with him. Their meek and unassuming dispositions prevented them from seeking the appropriate help they needed. Dad was inclined to shy away from situations he felt unable to understand or manage, thereby avoiding any confrontation. This left Andrew to Mum's somewhat misguided approach, as she continued to justify and defend his strange and often unacceptable behaviour. It would be many years before Andrew's complex mental disorder was finally diagnosed. With little or no support from Dad, it was my Mum who single-handedly devoted ever more time to Andrew, placing my parents' relationship under a great strain and eventual divorce.

Mum had given both Andrew and me several months' notice of Dad's intended departure. That six-month period was tremendously difficult and the tension in the house was intolerable. When Dad did eventually pack up his belongings and relocate to live with Eileen his new partner in the house immediately opposite ours, I was devastated. I suppose I never quite believed that he would actually carry out his intention.

Mum understandably made her feelings very clear to both Andrew and me, which made the possibility of any future communication with Dad very difficult. Our relationship was severely affected. Although I saw him frequently at a distance, the only contact between us was by telephone or an occasional visit to a pub a short distance away. Visiting him in his new home was not an option and any contact with Eileen was out of the question whilst I was still living at home with Mum.

Rather than helping defuse the fraught domestic situation, Dad's departure only served to exacerbate the existing problems within the family. Mum was left with an even greater financial burden and had no alternative but to seek full-time employment. She had neither skills nor qualifications to offer, and finally landed a job as a receptionist with a security company, often working twelve-hour shifts.

My relationship with my mother was not easy. Somehow the true mother/daughter bond had never been established, despite our early months together. Her continual focus on my brother had had a very detrimental effect. We spent no quality time together and, as was common at that time, sharing any of my feelings and concerns with her was never encouraged. Unable to voice any anxieties or emotions in a safe family environment, my adult life was flawed and troubled. Feelings of rage, sadness and frustration festered inside me for decades as a result.

I believe my mother had good intentions, but plagued as she was by her own personal troubles, her life had not been easy. Evacuated as a child during the Second World War, she was sent, together with a younger brother, to Weston-Super-Mare. Separated from her mother, I believe her time there was not an entirely happy one and after she died, I discovered a record of her memories from that time, where she referred to an unpleasant incident that she had never forgotten, although she didn't elaborate.

Married to a man who proved unable to father her much wanted family, she remained committed and loyal, only for him eventually to leave her. Living on a housing estate with her estranged husband co-habiting with another woman, literally across the street, must have been a daily torture. However, the prospect of a move and a fresh start was impossible, as we were tied to our council property. Despite my parents' lengthy, childless marriage they never considered buying their own home. Having both been raised in council properties themselves, my father in particular had a firm mindset about property ownership. He felt that it was never a good idea to be solely responsible for a property. He saw it as a financial burden taken only by the very wealthy or the foolhardy. So Mum, unable to make any independent decision without his support, had no option but to resign herself to the status quo.

My own thinking couldn't have been more different. Six years after my parents' separation I was engaged to David and delighted at the prospect of owning our own home.

Although I was keen to share this most exciting news with Dad, our infrequent contact inevitably meant he had little knowledge of my life. I had a good job, new friends and a fiancé whom he had never met. Nevertheless, I talked excitedly to him about my wedding plans, but as I did so, I detected some reticence. Firstly, he expressed a reluctance to wear the top hat and tails that I had naturally assumed would be part of my wedding plans. Secondly, he was most anxious about the proposed seating plan, insisting that not only should Eileen be present at my wedding, but that she should sit beside him at the top table. The prospect was unthinkable. My parents had not communicated since their separation and there was, understandably, much bitterness on my mother's part. Whilst I reluctantly accepted Eileen's presence at the ceremony, I tried in vain to tactfully suggest she could sit elsewhere. My main priority had to be for my mother, it was her day too.

Faced with apparently insurmountable family problems, all my enthusiasm for my big day waned. Trying to cope alone with this most traumatic situation, I had no one to turn to for help and advice. Revealing my dilemma to Mum was not an option and it seemed inappropriate to involve David and his family. They were all terribly joyous at the prospect of our forthcoming nuptials and had little experience of estranged families and how best to handle them. They had also, very generously, offered to fund the entire event and so I was in a way beholden to them. Sharing my anxieties would have been embarrassing and was likely to dampen their spirits.

However, determined not to jeopardise the most important day of my life, I felt compelled to make a drastic decision. Turning things endlessly around in my mind, I saw that the only way out was to ask someone else to give me away at my wedding. I asked a work colleague I respected and got on well with, who was delighted to oblige. Once the decision was made I also realised that it was for the best all round. Ultimately, it may have been the lesser evil for Dad, a reserved man, who may have lacked the confidence under the very strained circumstances to carry out his duties as father of the bride. As my wedding day drew closer and feeling somewhat ill at ease with my decision, I suggested that both he and Eileen might like to attend simply as guests. He declined.

But my Dad wasn't the only difficulty I had to contend with. To my chagrin and puzzlement, Mum lacked the enthusiasm I would have hoped for over my plans to marry and seemed almost indifferent. She needed persuading to look at wedding dresses, and most upsetting of all, was her reluctance to view the property David and I had purchased together. I'm sure she felt out of her comfort zone amongst David and his family and despite their every effort to embrace her, she was always reticent. Much of her attitude stemmed from an intense jealousy on Andrew's behalf. Sadly, she resented what I had achieved and believed that Andrew should be entitled to the same hard-won opportunities and had no qualms in expressing this to me. This was most hurtful from my own mother and a totally unreasonable stance, which would continue to surface throughout her life.

Soon after my marriage, and away from the family home and prying eyes of the neighbourhood, I was able to re-establish a relationship with

Dad and also get to know Eileen a little. As our relationship improved and developed, I could see that Dad was a happier and more contented individual.

Once my first daughter Rosemary was born, I was determined to create an environment for her that would not be weighed down by events from the past. My children would have a good relationship with all of their grandparents. Dad and Eileen embraced their role as loving grandparents and my daughters certainly looked forward to regular visits from Nan and Granddad. It was also pleasing to see my own relationship with them flourish after so many difficult years.

I chose not to challenge Dad over his handling of the separation. Reflecting many years later, I had a greater understanding of the entire situation. When I finally separated from my husband it was to Dad and Eileen's home that I first introduced my new partner, Paul.

When my Dad died in May 2008, my daughters were dreadfully upset. They had each established a special relationship with their granddad and for them he had been such fun.

Sadly, my ongoing relationship with my Mum was beset with difficulties. Unfortunately for Mum, soon after Rosemary's arrival, at sixty-one years of age she was diagnosed with a form of Ataxia, an incurable muscle-wasting illness. She was forced to retire and two years later, around the time of Annie's birth, was confined to a wheelchair. Sadly, with her speech severely affected and little control of her limbs, she was unable to enjoy her grandchildren fully, but it didn't deter me from ensuring that she had regular contact with them. As soon as Rosemary and Annie could communicate with each other, they soon devised a tailor-made name for Mum which greatly amused her: 'Number One Nanny in the Buggy'. The buggy referred to her wheelchair and the number one distinguished her from Mum's own mother, my grandmother, who was fondly known as 'Number Two Nanny'. In sad contrast to her own daughter, she was very sprightly and a great help to me and my young family in the early years. Counting David's parents, known as Ma and Pa, my daughters had accumulated a significant number of grandparents.

Eventually, Mum was transferred to a warden-assisted flat with care facilities and although I would take the girls to see her on a weekly basis, every visit left me exasperated. Andrew now had a quite overpowering influence over her which I found maddening, but, for reasons I could never fully understand, she seemed completely beholden to him. He lived alone close to Mum, in a one-bedroom council flat and had complete control of her life, including access to her finances, influence over her diet and even her thinking. She was completely manipulated by him. He and I had ceased communicating with each other some years earlier, our disputes always centred on the same topic: Mum's welfare. His strange outlook and peculiar habits prevented us from ever seeing eye-to-eye.

Although I continued to dutifully visit Mum regularly, it wasn't without difficulty. After a thirty-mile drive that involved the notorious M25, I would arrive laden with a week's grocery shopping for her, (although living so close by, Andrew could never be relied upon to shop for her) a packed lunch for us all, toys and games to occupy Rosemary and Annie and after Nancy's birth all the additional items required for a young baby. On arrival I would have to wait patiently outside in all weathers while Mum slowly made her way to operate the entry phone system. This would positively infuriate me, as I knew she had allocated keys to both her sister and a couple of friends. I, however, was not so fortunate. Andrew had, in fact, forbidden her to give me a key. If he happened to be visiting, it gave him time to flee, either out of the window or using a service entrance, thus avoiding any contact with me. All efforts to voice my absolute frustration concerning this ridiculous behaviour fell on deaf ears. Mum continued to defend and support him, as she had done his entire life.

Whilst visiting, as well as looking after my daughters, I would vacuum, clean the kitchen work surfaces and wash the floor. I would also feed Mum a tasty treat, satisfied that for a short time Andrew had no influence on what she ate. Sadly, despite my efforts to please Mum, there was little gratitude. I was exasperated by her actions on numerous occasions; one in particular was extremely hurtful. As Christmas approached I had spent a day with her writing out her Christmas cards and organising any monetary gifts. As one of the few still able to understand her progressively worsening, slurred speech I was able to follow her instructions. I wrote a card to her great nephew, a young child around Nancy's age, whom although she had never met, still liked to remember. She asked me to take £15 from her purse and place it inside the envelope. Next were the cards for each of her three granddaughters – my own daughters.

'Can you put £10 in each one?' she said.

With total disbelief and feeling immensely hurt, I quietly carried out her instructions. Regrettably, I understood her actions completely. Once again her jealous streak was evident. Unlike her great nephew, her granddaughters' privileged upbringing had not escaped her.

I tolerated a great deal from Mum and was always sympathetic to her condition, but I hardly felt like her daughter much of the time.

When she died in March 2002, her will stated that £500 be given to me to purchase a new sewing machine, whilst the entire contents of her flat and the remainder of her money which came, after funeral costs, to approx £4000 were to go to Andrew.

A note on the bottom of her homemade will read: 'Karen, I hope you understand.'

11. A New Beginning

New Year's Day, 2006

My three daughters were with their father, at the family home. I was alone in a rented house, after recently ending my marriage of twenty years. The past six weeks in these unfamiliar surroundings had been dreadful. Any personal belongings that I had acquired during my life were minimal and did little to improve the conditions in this sparsely furnished property. Desperate to hide away from the rest of the world, it had not been easy in central Sevenoaks with three daughters each attending different local schools and one of those, my place of employment. Whilst the shame and guilt of my actions continued to weigh heavily, the prospect of returning to work and a much-needed routine had some appeal. I longed for this isolation to end. The festive period has an unfortunate habit of magnifying feelings of loneliness and despair. I felt condemned. David appeared the innocent victim and took the opportunity to inform his family and many of our friends that not only had I left, but that there was somebody else in my life. Without understanding my circumstances, I had been immediately shunned by them. Their reaction only emphasised my feelings of shame and lack of self-worth. I felt powerless to insist that my daughters spend more time with me; instead they remained cocooned by David and his family. Sadly, I had no such luxury to match this. My Dad and stepmother lived in a modest property fifty miles away, making it impractical for myself and the girls to spend time there. To add to my misery, I had developed flu-like symptoms. Wallowing in self-pity, I'd advised Paul to stay away.

New Year's Eve had been intolerable. Noisy celebrations nearby made it impossible for me to sleep and so I climbed out of bed and peeped through the curtains. Looking out onto the very small garden I could see a large gathering just the other side of the back fence, where, with much jollity they waited with excited anticipation to welcome in the New Year. Amongst the crowd, I could make out familiar faces from my new neighbourhood. Feeling forgotten, uncared for and unloved, I slipped back into bed waiting for the fireworks to end before finally going to sleep.

Today was the first day of a new year and a new life and I was determined to lift myself out of this debilitating situation. I wanted a happier life, one that enabled me to regain my self-confidence and a feeling of independence. I no longer had to comply with the endless emotional and financial constraints imposed on me by my husband. The thought that I now had the ability to make my own life changing decisions, whilst quite daunting, was also very liberating.

Determined to turn my life around, I took little time in deciding my first course of action. At last I had the opportunity to embark on a quest that had eluded me for so many years, the search for my birth mother. This time I knew I would have the support of those closest to me. Paul had stressed many times, the importance of searching for her. My daughters, too, had expressed a healthy interest in their unknown heritage on numerous occasions.

Technology had improved considerably over the last thirteen years and much of my search could now be carried out on the internet. Before leaving the family home I had retrieved the old obsolete computer and, despite its laborious pace, it could still serve a purpose. I used it to re-register with the adoption support agency I had originally used many years earlier and eagerly awaited an updated information pack, with instructions on how best to conduct my search.

My momentous decision had lifted my spirits. I thought of Paul and wished he was here with me – I was terribly lonely. Still feeling feverish, I wrapped myself in a blanket and sat on the floor clutching two of the documents that my mother had handed to me shortly after my marriage. I unfolded my birth certificate and laid it out beside me, tucked inside the document was a small flimsy piece of paper that I had never paid much attention to before.

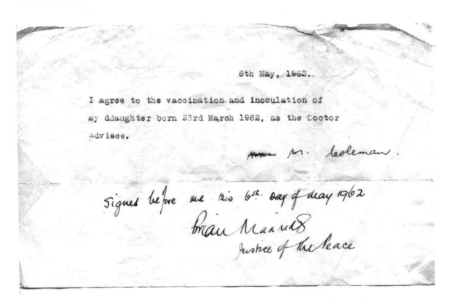

6th May, 1962.

I agree to the vaccination and inoculation of my ddaughter born 23rd March 1962, as the Doctor advises.

M. Coleman.

Signed before me this 6th. Day of May 1962

Brian Manuel
Justice of the Peace

The family name was Coleman, the name under which I had been registered but, rather poignantly, I had not been given a Christian name. The allotted space had been left blank. I found myself wondering whether Margaret had ever thought of a name for her daughter? Casting my mind back to my own pregnancies and the experience of carrying that energetic bundle, as it grew ever larger, it was inconceivable not to have made a strong connection with my own baby before its long awaited arrival.

COLEMAN, (Female)

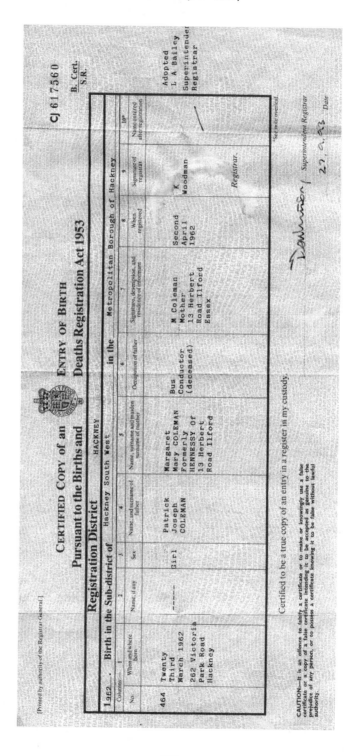

[Printed by authority of the Registrar General.]

CJ 617560

B. Cert.
S.R.

CERTIFIED COPY of an ENTRY OF BIRTH
Pursuant to the Births and Deaths Registration Act 1953

Registration District HACKNEY

1962 . Birth in the Sub-district of Hackney South West in the Metropolitan Borough of Hackney

No	When and where born	Name, if any	Sex	Name, and surname of father	Name, surname and maiden surname of mother	Occupation of father	Signature, description, and residence of informant	When registered	Signature of registrar	Name entered after registration
464	Twenty Third March 1962 262 Victoria Park Road Hackney	------	Girl	Patrick Joseph COLEMAN	Margaret Mary COLEMAN Formerly HENNESSY Of 13 Herbert Road Ilford	Bus Conductor (deceased)	M Coleman Mother 13 Herbert Road Ilford Essex	Second April 1962	K Woodman Registrar.	

Certified to be a true copy of an entry in a register in my custody.

Adopted
L A Bailey
Superintendent
Registrar

Second overleaf

Dominter Superintendent Registrar

27.9.83 Date

CAUTION—It is an offence to falsify a certificate or to make or knowingly use a false certificate or a copy of a false certificate intending it to be accepted as genuine to the prejudice of any person, or to possess a certificate knowing it to be false without lawful authority.

Something else puzzled me. My adoptive mother had been insistent that St Margaret's Nursing Home had been a private establishment and 'the father' as she liked to refer to him, when sharing the story with a select few, had funded it. How could this be possible if he were dead? I assumed that she must have been referring to Margaret's father, my maternal grandfather.

'Margaret Coleman, where are you?' I said aloud, still hopeful of finding her alive and well. I had no idea of her age, but envisaged a woman remarried and with a family, my half siblings. I assumed it unlikely I would find any other offspring from Margaret and Patrick Coleman. If she had given birth to any children prior to me, then I would have expected to remain within the existing family.

I studied the Christian names of my parents again: Margaret Mary and Patrick Joseph. Margaret and Patrick or, notably, Mary and Joseph. There was a wealth of names between them and yet, not one for me. Patrick Coleman's occupation was recorded as a bus conductor (deceased). This too was puzzling, as once again my adopted mother had always insisted that his death had occurred whilst working on a building site. Maybe he was in the habit of moonlighting.

There were two addresses on my birth certificate: one was my place of birth, St Margaret's Nursing Home Hackney, the other was the address of my birth mother at that time, Herbert Road Ilford. It also gave her maiden name as Hennessy.

I scrutinised the small, delicate piece of paper dated 6th May 1962. It was a single typed sentence giving permission for me to undergo my course of vaccinations, signed by Mrs M. Coleman and witnessed by a Justice of the Peace.

Engrossed in my thoughts, I was startled to hear a key in the lock. I turned to see Paul standing in the doorway. Overcome with joy at his unexpected arrival, my ailments and feelings of loneliness were immediately dispelled. As I shared with Paul my plans to trace Margaret, I knew that this time around with his understanding and support, I had the best possible chance.

I contemplated the months ahead. Would I be successful? If so, how long would it take? Where would my search take me? And what would I discover at the end of it? Suddenly the new year didn't seem quite as bleak. I had a focus and a mission.

The recent changes to our family circumstances gave me time each weekend to undertake the search and while the girls were with David, Paul and I could devote the endless time required.

With the start of the new school term, I decided to share my plans to trace my birth mother with David Trill. David's calm and rational approach to everything was just what I needed. Already fully aware of my marital circumstances, he had been supportive and understanding and happy to offer advice on a variety of issues as they arose. Discussing my latest intention with him could only be positive and I was delighted when he expressed a true interest in my mission. Suggesting, guiding and assisting wherever possible, his input would be invaluable. He studied my birth certificate and the additional document.

'Of course, you know it's likely to be an Irish Roman Catholic family don't you?' he said eventually, after scrutinizing all the information.

'Is it?' I asked surprisingly, as I peered over his shoulder wondering how he'd come to that conclusion.

'With names like these, I'm pretty certain.' David's theory seemed obvious, I felt foolish, why hadn't it occurred to me? His observations suddenly triggered several distant memories for me, none of which I had dwelt upon at the time, but which now bore some significance.

Firstly as a young child during my fits of rage, I had a vague recollection of my mother muttering something about Irish blood, as if to justify my outbursts and secondly, many years later at the age of seventeen I recalled a strange encounter.

Part of my journey to work each day involved a bus ride from Victoria mainline station to Kings Cross. It was early in the morning and travelling alone I felt somewhat vulnerable. I found comfort in the shape of an elderly lady who, each morning, would acknowledge me with a warm friendly smile as she too waited in the bus queue. With the regular greeting established, one particular morning, as we boarded the bus she sat in the seat beside me.

'Good morning,' she said, smiling at me, very keen to engage me in conversation. 'Do you mind me asking, where you're from?'

I noticed a very strong accent, probably Irish.

'Mitcham,' I told her cheerfully. I was more than happy to converse with her. She seemed kind and genuine.

'Ah, but where were you born?' she asked inquisitively. Clearly I hadn't given her the reply she had been expecting.

'Oh, um … Hackney,' I said, remembering my place of birth.

'You know you're certainly Irish?' she said confidently.

'Oh no,' I said politely, not wanting to disappoint or offend. She looked puzzled.

'I live in Mitcham, Surrey and I was born in Hackney.' I repeated clearly.

'Well, I don't care what you say, you have Irish blood running through you without a doubt. With eyes like that and all those freckles, let me tell you, you're definitely Irish,' she said adamantly. Soon after this I changed jobs and began working at BHS, which meant a different journey. I never saw the elderly lady again.

Furthermore, I knew that my adoptive parents had chosen not to have me Christened, believing that religion was a decision for me to take alone, as I grew older. Perhaps for my parents, to be handed a baby from a Roman Catholic family, caused them unease. With little or no faith of their own, the question of my origins and how best to deal with them, were to be avoided.

David Trill turned his attention to the small piece of paper with Margaret Coleman's signature on it.

'She's crossed through the Mrs,' he pointed out. 'I wonder why she would have done that?' he asked curiously.

'Mm, I don't know,' I said, acknowledging his observation as I folded the documents and returned them to the envelope. He'd given me a lot to think about.

Meanwhile the search pack arrived from the adoption support agency, but once again I was disappointed to discover a negative response from the contact register. Sadly it would seem that Margaret still had no desire to make contact with me.

Nevertheless, this time I'd made a successful application to the court for access to my adoption file and thankfully it had been located and an appointment was arranged for me to visit the Court. Whilst I waited patiently for this date to arrive, I turned my efforts to exploring the birth, deaths and marriage register for England and Wales. Now that this information was online, searching was easier than ever before, but I was not at all prepared for the surprises it revealed.

In order to first familiarise myself with the index, I decided to search for Patrick Coleman's death entry. Much to my surprise, I was unable to locate it. Being sure of my facts regarding the limited period within which the death occurred, this left me at a total loss. The only assumption I could make was that perhaps my moonlighting theory had taken place in Ireland rather than the UK. Unfortunately, as Irish records were not available online, my search for Patrick Coleman had to be aborted. However, tracing the death record for my father was not essential in my search for Margaret, but still keen to acquaint myself with the national register, I searched for the birth records of each of my daughters and to my great relief – success.

Birth records are listed in yearly quarters under the father's surname, and each individual entry is recorded in alphabetical order, using the given Christian name of the child. It also states

Name	Mother's Maiden Surname	District	Vol.	Page
COLEMAN, Gillian A.	TILL	Ilford	5 a	503
-- Gillian M.	McRECROFT	E.Glamorgan	8 b	489
-- Glenn	MOORE	Nuneaton	9 c	1830
-- Glenn A.	HOWES	Plymouth	7 a	766
-- Graham H.M.	MIFFETT	Wandsworth	5 d	1143
-- Greta L.	CARTER	Bristol	7 b	467
-- Guy	COLEMAN	Kettering	3 b	862
-- Ian	TAYLOR	Middlesbro'	1 b	1094
-- Ian D.	BALL	Liverpool N.	10 d	445a
-- Ian P.	BROWN	Marylebone	5 d	556
-- Jacqueline	MEADE	Bournemouth	6 b	360
-- Jacqueline A.	GREEN	Bromley	5 b	182
-- James P.	SCROOP	Leicester	3 a	1077
-- Jane E.	CONWIG	Pontypool	8 c	427
-- Jay	HERMAN	Hitchin	4 b	390
-- Jennifer M.	COUMBaR	Bristol	7 b	93
-- John E.J.	ANDREWS	Bolton	10 b	847
-- John L.	SOMAN	Bradford	2 b	364
-- John M.	WOOLLEY	Meriden	9 c	1624
-- John W.	TARLING	Banbury	6 b	1453
-- Joseph N.	CASsELLS	Middleton	10 e	824
-- Julie A.	ABBOTT	Oxford	6 b	1581
-- Julie A.	TILSON	Northampton	3 b	920
-- Julie V.	SAUNDERS	Tonbridge	5 b	1482
-- June	SKELTON	Surrey N.	5 g	539
-- Karen H.	BRAZIER	Smethwick	9 b	649
-- Karen L.	LUNN	Lower Agbrigg	2 c	781
-- Katrina M.	KEOGH	Middlesbro'	1 b	1291
-- Keith A.	EDWARDS	Winchester	6 b	1356
-- Keith J.	SPARROW	W.Hartlepool	1 a	1657
-- Kevin	CURRAN	Liverpool N.	10 d	663
-- Kevin	GREENALL	Doncaster	2 b	629
-- Kevin J.	WILTON	Yeovil	7 c	501
-- Kevin R.	WITTMAN	Edmonton	5 c	486
-- Lee R.	COPELAND	Hammersmith	5 c	1072
-- Lee R.	HENRY	Birmingham	9 c	181
-- Lesley	DRAYTON	Croydon	5 g	77
-- Linda B.	KETTLE	Barton	10 b	412
-- Linda J.	OLLIVER	Worthing	5 h	636
-- Lindsay S.	TURNER	Surrey S.W.	5 g	1466
-- Lorraine	CLEARY	Oxford	6 b	1625
-- Lynne	IRELAND	Nthmbld.C.	1 b	385
-- Marianne L.	MINCHIN	Maidstone	5 b	1102
-- Marie L.	COLGMAN	Hackney	5 c	981
-- Mark	CURRAN	Liverpool N.	10 d	662
-- Mark A.	GILL	Leeds	2 c	729
-- Martin P.	SILCOCKS	Bristol	7 b	141
-- Martin V.	TOWNSEND	Reading	6 a	131
-- Melanie D.	GARDNER	Coventry	9 c	1398
-- Michael E.	GOODE	Southwark	5 d	713
-- Michael G.	PUDDEPHATT	Watford	4 b	692
-- Michael J.	DUBOIS	Blackpool	10 b	697
-- Michael J.	BARHAM	Leicester	3 a	937
-- Michael J.	BLAKE	Bristol	7 b	292
-- Michael P.	RYAN	Fulham	5 c	543
-- Michelle	MURPHY	Bermondsey	5 c	65
-- Michelle B.	WOLVERSON	Rother V.	2 d	1012
-- Nicholas	MITCHELL	Wrexham	8 a	462
-- Nicholas A.G.	KINGHAM	Wycombe	6 a	1018
-- Nicholas J.	PAINTER	Ipswich	4 b	1435
-- Nicholas J.	SARGINSON	Rugby	9 b	1869
-- Nicola J.	AIKEN	Weymouth	7 c	1160
-- Nicole	NURMEY	Bermondsey	5 c	65
-- Owen	KELLY	Greenwich	5 c	681
-- Pamela	WILLIAMS	Worth Valley	2 c	37
-- Paul D.	STREET	Southampton	6 b	1093
-- Paul D.	WILLS	Southampton	6 b	1118
-- Peter	LAYBOURN	Gateshead	1 a	1216
-- Peter	MILLWARD	Liverpool N.	10 d	185
-- Peter A.	ELFORD	Gipping	4 b	1402
-- Peter J.	WILLIAMS	Middlesbro'	1 b	1136
COLEMAN, Philippa J.	OATES	Westmorland	3.1 b	860
-- Rebecca J.	HAYNS	Amersham	6 a	528
-- Richard C.	LOWE	Norwich	4 b	1150
-- Richard N.G.	HOWE	Harrow	5 f	612
-- Robert J.	HEMSLEY	Paddington	5 d	270
-- Rochelle M.	LAMBERT	Edmonton	5 c	379
-- Roger	HALL	Penrith	1 a	223
-- Ross	MANN	Cheltenham	7 b	534
-- Roy B.	BARRERO	Chelsea	5 c	322
-- Roy L.	WEBSTER	Manchester	10 e	298
-- Royston D.	CARTER	Bristol	7 b	467
-- Sarah R.	BARNES	Trowbridge	7 c	909
-- Saverio P.L.	DORIA	Chatham	5 b	614
-- Sharon	KERRIGAN	Hackney	5 c	880
-- Sharon Y.	GOULDEN	Basingstoke	6 b	238
-- Sian E.	FAULKNER	Surrey S.W.	5 g	1362
-- Sonia H.	HALL	Stamford	3 b	221
-- Steven R.	WRIGHT	Dartford	5 b	777
-- Stuart T.	KING	Uckfield	5 h	204
-- Susan	CULLAN	Islington	5 c	1670
-- Susan	ROBINSON	Northampton	3 b	966
-- Suzanne H.	COLLEY	Warwick	9 c	2259
-- Terence A.	BYERS	Coventry	9 c	1291
-- Terence A.	NORTHMORE	Plympton	7 a	869
-- Thomas J.	DELAFUENTE	Surrey N.E.	5 g	679
-- Timothy J.	JONES	Pontypool	8 c	333
-- Timothy M.	TURRELL	Yarmouth	4 b	954
-- Tony A.	BUTLER	Wednesbury	9 b	1359
-- Trevor	OLIVER	Barton	10 b	355
-- Trevor K.E.	COLLINS	Cardiff	8 b	346
-- Valerie	HARDING	Basford	3 c	56
-- Vanessa J.	GRANT	Hammersmith	5 c	1244
-- Vincent	WILKINSON	Whittlesey	4 a	702
-- Walter G.	MOUTINHO	Bootle	10 b	931
-- Wendy	STOKES	Poole	7 c	987
-- William F.	WARD	Sheffield	2 d	120
-- (Female)	HENNESSY	Hackney	5 c	830
COLEMERE, Michael	GRIFFITHS	Shrewsbury	9 a	320
COLE-MORGAN, Tina J.	ROWLAND	Northampton	3 b	949
COLENSO, Jane M.	PARISH	Kingswood	8 b	839
COLENUTT, Martin	MILLS	Dartford	5 b	700
COLsRIDGE, Keith	BASHFORD	Croydon	5 g	mens
COLES, Adam F.	SCRIVENER	Eton	6 a	907
-- Alan J.	BAINTON	Bristol	7 b	36
-- Amanda	COLES	Southend	4 a	1503
-- Andrew L.	FRASER	Uxbridge	5 f	294
-- Andrew M.	LEE	Worthing	5 h	621
-- Angela R.	DURSTON	Bridgwater	7 c	132
-- Annette A.	OLAY	Hitchin	4 b	408
-- Barry J.	MOORE	Tonbridge	5 b	1546
-- Bridget M.	GAUNT	Luton	4 a	362
-- Christina A.	CANDLIN	Alton	6 b	162
-- Christopher S.	BERGSTROM	Romford	5 a	614
-- Claire S.	FOURACRE	Cardiff	8 b	344
-- Colin J.	PRICE	Bucklow	10 a	165
-- David	DEALEY	Braintree	4 a	765
-- David A.	WILLIAMS	Hereford	9 a	42
-- David A.	VAGGERS	Bristol	7 b	446
-- David A.	WOOD	Barnsley	2 b	40
-- David A.	QUELCH	Alton	6 b	159
-- David J.	POWELL	Barton	10 b	454
-- Deana M.	CARPENTER	Totnes	7 a	947
-- Della M.	INGLES	Worcester	9 d	359A
-- Denise J.	BUTLER	Aylesbury	6 a	705
-- Elaine	KILSBY	Whittlesey	4 a	705
-- Elaine R.	SMITH	N.Cotswold	7 b	890
-- Elizabeth	OWEN	Caerleon	8 c	181
-- Elizabeth M.	COLES	Birmingham	9 c	385
-- Elizabeth M.	CAMPBELL	Stourbridge	9 d	285
-- Gareth D.	COLLING	Newport	8 c	248
-- Geoffrey B.	BAS	Banbury	6 b	1440
'Coleman Robert J.	Herman	Hitchin	4B	390A
2. — , Steven	Lawley	Noddres field	2B	1167

Full page from the Register of Birth Entries

the place of birth and the mother's maiden name.

This exercise was invaluable as it helped develop my thought process. Realising that Christian names were essential for the records, I was intrigued to know how, without a Christian name, my own entry would be displayed. Although my birth certificate gives no Christian name, it occurred to me that I might discover the name Margaret Coleman had intended for me. There just had to be a name.

COLEMAN, Philippa J.	OATES	Westmorland	S.1	b	860
— Rebecca d.	HAYNS	Amersham	6	a	528
— Richard C.	LOWE	Norwich	4	b	1150
— Richard N.G.	HOWE	Harrow	5	f	612
— Robert J.	HEMSLEY	Paddington	5	d	270
— Rochelle M.	LAMBERT	Edmonton	5	e	379
— Roger	HALL	Penrith	1	a	223
— Ross	MANN	Cheltenham	7	b	534
— Roy K.	BARRERO	Chelsea	5	c	322
— Roy L.	WEBSTER	Manchester	10	e	298
— Royston D.	CARTER	Bristol	7	b	467
— Sarah E.	BARNES	Trowbridge	7	c	909
— Saverio F.L.	DORIA	Chatham	5	b	614
— Sharon	KERRIGAN	Hackney	5	c	880
— Sharon Y.	GOULDEN	Basingstoke	6	b	238
— Sian E.	FAULKNER	Surrey S.W.	5	g	1362
— Sonia H.	HALL	Stamford	3	b	221
— Steven R.	WRIGHT	Dartford	5	b	777
— Stuart T.	KING	Cuckfield	5	h	204
— Susan	CULLEN	Islington	5	c	1670
— Susan	ROBINSON	Northampton	3	b	966
— Suzanne H.	COLLEY	Warwick	9	c	2259
— Terence A.	BYERS	Coventry	9	c	1291
— Terence A.	NORTHMORE	Plympton	7	a	889
— Thomas J.	DELAFUENTE	Surrey N.E.	5	g	679
— Timothy J.	JONES	Pontypool	8	c	333
— Timothy M.	TURRELL	Yarmouth	4	b	956
— Tony A.	BUTLER	Wednesbury	9	b	1309
— Trevor	OLIVER	Barton	10	b	355
— Trevor M.E.	COLLINS	Cardiff	8	b	346
— Valerie	HARDING	Basford	3	c	56
— Vanessa J.	GRANT	Hammersmith	5	c	1244
— Vincent	WILKINSON	Whittlesey	4	a	702
— Walter G.	MOUTINHO	Bootle	10	b	931
— Wendy	STOKES	Poole	7	c	987
— William F.	WARD	Sheffield	2	d	120
— (Female)	HENNESSY	Hackney	5	c	830
COLEMERE, Michael	GRIFFITHS	Shrewsbury	9	a	320
COLE-MORGAN, Tina J.	ROWLAND	Northampton	3	b	949
COLENSO, Jane M.	PARISH	Kingswood	7	b	839

Detail of page, showing my entry, fourth from bottom

I began searching under the Coleman name for the second quarter of 1962, looking for a Hennessy match. The alphabetical listing of Christian names spanned several columns and starting at the top, I meticulously read each entry until finally reaching the very last one. It was a different entry to the others and simply read: (Female). The mother's maiden name – Hennessy, and the area of registration – Hackney, confirmed this to be my entry.

My discovery was devastating. This permanent record of my birth appeared less valid and the reality of seeing my inferior entry just reinforced those ever-frequent feelings of worthlessness. It seemed incomprehensible that a married Roman Catholic woman could not provide me with a name. I have met with a number of adopted people and although their birth names were subsequently changed, each of them was given a name by their birth mothers.

Paul had suggested trying to locate a record of Margaret and Patrick Coleman's marriage, hopeful that their wedding had been here in the UK. Choosing the second quarter of 1961 as his starting point, he trawled back through each quarter until reaching the mid-fifties, but without success. Fast coming to the conclusion that their marriage had taken place in Ireland, he decided to make one last attempt, this time moving forward and looking at the third quarter of 1961.

'Karen I've got it!' came an excited voice from the study. I hurried to join him, eager to see something relating to my parents. We were both struck by a wave of emotion as we witnessed evidence of their brief life together. They were indeed married in either July, August or September of 1961 but we would need to order the marriage certificate to obtain a precise date. Did this make me a honeymoon baby or more likely, had I been conceived out of wedlock?

We couldn't wait to follow up these new clues and so, the following Saturday, Paul and I headed to Ilford. Our first stop was 13 Herbert Road, the address of Margaret Coleman at the time of my birth. It was quite easy to find and as we sat in the car in silence, I studied the mid-terraced Victorian house with mixed feelings. How many times would Margaret have walked the length of this modest suburban road, clearly pregnant? And then was hit by personal tragedy and obliged to give up her newborn baby? Did she keep her sorrow to herself or had the neighbourhood perhaps shared in her tragedy?

We discovered that the local library held the electoral rolls for the area, which would tell us how long both Margaret and Patrick lived at the Herbert Road address. We searched the records covering several years before and after my birth, but strangely neither name appeared. To my mind, the trip had been fruitless but Paul had picked up on some more interesting clues and was not so downhearted. He had noticed that not only Herbert Road but the whole surrounding area was populated by a large Irish community. Interestingly, the occupants of 13 Herbert Road in the early 60s had also remained there until the late 1980s. He made a note of their names, James and Mary Donovan.

Before returning home we drove to the place where I was born in Victoria Park Road, Hackney, but there was no longer any trace of a nursing home. Instead there stood a seventies housing block.

Later that evening, Paul drew my attention to a 192.com entry. It could be a long shot, but he had picked up on a James Donovan living alone, just a few streets from Herbert Road.

'What do you think of this?' he asked, pointing to the screen. 'It could be the same James Donovan.'

'Is there a phone number?'

'No, he's ex-directory.'

'That's a nuisance, we'll have to write to him.'

'No, we'll go and visit,' announced Paul. 'We'll go tomorrow, strike while the iron's hot,' he insisted.

Back in East London the following morning, this time at the newly-discovered address of James Donovan, we were again sitting in the car studying the house intently. It was a well-maintained bungalow with cream render and brown painted window frames. The small area to the front of the property had been entirely crazy paved to provide off-road parking for a metallic mustard coloured, Ford Focus.

'We could be in luck here,' said Paul confidently, pointing to a large green shamrock mounted on the wall beside the front door.

Little could we know at that moment that we were about to

have an extraordinary encounter. Nor could we have guessed that soon after, our visit to the court for access to my adoption file would actually verify the information given to us by Jim Donovan that day.

The arrival of Margaret and Patrick's marriage certificate in the post a few days later confirmed our suspicions. The marriage took place on 26th August 1961. Margaret would have been approximately ten weeks pregnant. If Patrick Coleman was indeed not my father, did he give Margaret an ultimatum? Was he even aware of the pregnancy at the time of the wedding and if so, how did they begin married life with Margaret carrying another man's child? Then again, why was Patrick's name on my birth certificate? So many unanswered questions!

The marriage certificate did, however, validate Margaret's occupation as given to us by Jim Donovan. She was a bus conductor. I recall how adamant Jim had been about having no memory of her pregnancy, or any length of time absent from work. How did she continue to work as a bus conductor whilst heavily pregnant? The marriage took place at St Dominic's Roman Catholic Church, Harold Hill, which also confirmed David Trill's suspicions that they were indeed Roman Catholics.

A visit to the church was next on our list. We met with the incumbent priest who happily located the entry in the marriage register and provided us with a copy. He did however, notice that it had been a visiting priest by the name of Michael Dunleavy, who had performed the service. Unfortunately, on checking his current register of Catholic priests, he was not listed. He also checked the baptism register in the hope of finding an entry for me, but not surprisingly there were none.

Although the marriage certificate also gave an address for Margaret at the time of her wedding, our search on the electoral roll for the Hennessy name drew a blank. A family named Whytock appeared to be living at the given address, not a name we had come across before.

I was determined to follow up any other possible avenues, which might help us find more answers to our questions. At the time of her wedding, Margaret was twenty-two years of age, but my tentative search for her birth record was to no avail and so I assumed her place of birth was Ireland. I also considered the likelihood of her remarrying, but searching for a further marriage certificate with little to go on was costly and time consuming. This line of enquiry was soon halted.

All my efforts over the past months had made one thing very clear: that this search was by no means straightforward. Sadly, I now had a greater understanding of the trauma, which my adoptive mum had described regarding the delay in issuing the Adoption Order. I now realised that the delay was never due to Margaret's inability to make the right decision over my adoption, as my parents had been led to believe, but instead due to Margaret's catalogue of lies. She clearly had no thought for my parents' suffering as a consequence, nor their terrifying fears and worries. The small, delicate piece of paper kept safely with my birth certificate all those years came to mind. Without the relevant paperwork, my parents had been unable to authorise my vaccination programme, and after four weeks of parenting, they still required the intervention of a woman they feared had the ability to turn their world upside down at any time. Margaret Coleman had still been very prominent in my parents' lives. Sadly it was only after my mother died in 2002 that I was, at last, able to uncover the truth behind those agonising months of 1962. Without a complete understanding of Margaret Coleman's actions, I could only feel anger towards her for the pain and unnecessary suffering she unwittingly inflicted on my parents.

As the months past, I had established a good relationship with the counsellors from the adoption support line and at each stage had reported my findings to them. Early on they had advised me of a facility available to adopted people searching for their birth relatives. It was a helpline number with the National Health Register, set up specifically to inform the adoptee if the person they were searching for was alive or dead. Finding out this information prior to a highly emotive undertaking helped to avoid what might prove to be a devastating outcome. My own enquiry had proved inconclusive as Margaret's record was not a current one. The most likely explanation they could give was that she had moved to another country. Assuming she had returned to live in Ireland, my search had now drawn a blank.

I tried in vain to unearth further information. My place of birth, St Margaret's, was a private nursing home and whilst the authorities were aware of its existence in the 1960s, surprisingly, there were no records. I wrote to the London Transport pension and archive departments, Margaret and Patrick's employer back in the 60s, but to no avail. Next, Paul and I spent an unsuccessful day at the Romford Library using the microfiche, in the hope of discovering a wedding photograph of Margaret, again without success. We even followed a fruitless lead from Jim Donovan, who was convinced that an aunt of Paddy's still lived in the East London area. He sent us to a council flat to talk to an elderly couple. The wife was most welcoming and, eager to assist me in my search, ushered us into the flat to introduce us to her husband. He was a small man, something akin to a leprechaun, who sat listening to traditional Irish music on an old radio with poor reception. After explaining the reason for our visit we waited expectantly while he contemplated our next move. He was adamant that we should visit O'Grady's Irish Bar in Seven Kings, Ilford, where a man by the name of Murray would be able to assist us further. Surprisingly, he and his wife expressed great concern as to how we might make the two-mile journey across town. Reassuring them that we not only had our own car, but that we had travelled that morning all the way from

Sevenoaks in Kent, left them in awe. As I looked around their dark, dated, highly cluttered room, they could have lived there for the past hundred years, oblivious to the pace of life around them. Unfortunately, our subsequent visit to O'Grady's proved to be unproductive.

Finally, desperate by now for more clues, I resorted to cold calling. David Trill had introduced me to the White Pages, the Irish telephone directory and finding out from Jim Donovan that Margaret had originated from Kilkenny, I worked my way through a number of Hennessys asking if they knew of her. Although I found a number of very kind and sympathetic individuals, that too was a wasted effort.

The girls also had become disheartened by our inability to trace Margaret. Annie in particular lived in the romantic hope that the search would take us far and wide. North-east London and possibly Ireland did not fall into this category. She continued to seek assurance from me that when Margaret was finally tracked down, school would immediately be abandoned and we could set off on our travels. Although I didn't say as much, I myself secretly hoped this situation would not arise.

It was nine months after our first meeting with Jim Donovan and by now early autumn when, out of the blue, he provided me with the photograph of Margaret Coleman. The following day David Trill scanned the rather blurred old black and white snap in the hope of providing a clearer image of this young woman who was pictured holding the hand of Jim's daughter, Eileen. It was after analysing the computer screen for some time that he made a most remarkable statement.

'I'm not sure that Margaret is your mother.'

'Really?' I exclaimed, turning to look at the photo again.

'That doesn't look like a woman who gave birth just six months earlier,' he declared. I disagreed, thinking back to how I had regained my figure soon after childbirth.

However, he remained sceptical.

'In those days women didn't spend time in the gym and their diets were very different to nowadays.'

It was hard to accept David's theory, but on reflection, I slowly came round to thinking that perhaps it wasn't quite as unbelievable as I first thought. If I accepted Margaret was not my mother, then suddenly I had the answers to many of my questions. Maybe it wasn't such an outrageous idea. If she really was the good, kind, helpful young woman that Jim Donovan had described, then had she carried out this deception to help and protect someone else, a sister perhaps? Not only had the lack of information in my adoption file surprised the judge, but also Jim Donovan was adamant that she was not pregnant whilst living as a lodger in his home. Margaret had spent many hours with his wife Mary, helping with her own young daughter: it would have been almost impossible to hide the pregnancy from her. Finally the funding of the private nursing home also remained a mystery. Had the family in Ireland been desperate to avoid shame in their community and provided the financial support? The question that still troubled me the most was, if Patrick Coleman was not indeed my father, then why name him on my birth certificate and why was he declared deceased?

I clearly had to widen my enquiries and I made contact with a research agency in Ireland, who managed to trace the birth certificates of both Margaret Hennessy and, to my delight, a younger sister – Catherine. However, disappointingly, the documents were illegible and I had to wait further whilst they tried to obtain clearer ones.

With my search on hold, Paul and I now focused on our impending house move. After one year in the rented property we were about to purchase our first home together.

12. Angels and Baubles

June 1980

Despite my unsatisfactory schooling and minimal qualifications, at eighteen years of age, I unwittingly stumbled upon a job that would eventually become an extremely successful career. My greatest achievement to date had been my appointment as patrol leader in the Girl Guides but, here in the fast-moving world of retail, I found something that I soon excelled at and could realise my true potential. It is with great fondness that I look back on this time and see it as one of the most fulfilling phases of my life.

My first job had lasted less than a year. After leaving school at seventeen, half way through my sixth form studies, with a desire to work in the fashion industry, I joined the pattern-making department of a ladies' fashion chain. Unfortunately, faced with a manager intent on making rather unpleasant approaches towards me, it was imperative that I found alternative employment. Naïve, frightened and in a fit of haste, I spotted an advert in one of the free London magazines seeking retail distributors. With little confidence and no real understanding of the job's requirements, I attended an interview at BHS in their central buying offices. Much to my surprise and great relief, I was offered the job as a trainee distributor in their fashion accessories department. This job not only paid well, but also provided an environment where I immediately felt at ease. Assigned to the distribution of gloves, umbrellas and belts, I settled in immediately.

The large open plan office was home to a number of buying teams, each responsible for several product ranges. Each team consisted of a buyer, whose role it was to source and select products, a merchandiser, who managed the considerable budget, as well as several distributors.

Under the watchful eye of the merchandiser, the distributors would monitor sales and issue instructions for stock replenishment nationwide, throughout the entire BHS chain. I was delighted to discover that the many distributors were predominately young people, much the same age as me, and I soon became involved in an active and enjoyable social scene. Nightclubs, parties, sleepovers and weekend breaks were all experiences that I thoroughly relished. The perks too eased some of the financial difficulties within my family. A staff discount card was a much-welcomed benefit, as were the many in-house departmental sales that gave the staff the opportunity to purchase products at very reduced prices.

Although the atmosphere could at times be fraught and pressurised, it was an exciting place to be. The feeling of unity within the workplace was a new experience for me, which I found very gratifying and the kindly actions of the buyers did much to create a cordial and cohesive environment. Just like thoughtful aunts and uncles, they would return from their buying trips around the world with small gifts for us junior members of staff.

I soon discovered that I had a real aptitude for this particular kind of work. The more I learned about the retail industry, the more compelling it became and no two days were the same. I found this fast moving business enthralling and analysing customers' buying habits quite fascinating. Sales of umbrellas really did increase when it rained and the position of all merchandise within the store was paramount. I worked hard and after a series of promotions, I soon reached the position of senior distributor.

Around this time BHS had decided to expand significantly the company's range of gift products, with a particular focus on Christmas merchandise. One of the existing buyers in the fashion accessories department, Alan Kramer, had already established a successful range of motorists' and mens' gifts and had recently also introduced a limited range of Christmas cards and wrap. Following an internal reshuffle, he was moved, together with his Christmas ranges, to the toys and toiletries department elsewhere in the building, but to my utter dismay, I learnt that I had been selected to join him. The news filled me with dread. I was terrified, and not least because, of all the buyers, Alan was undoubtedly the most formidable. A Jewish man, around the same age as my own father, he had a reputation for not only his wealth of experience, but also his demanding approach, short temper and intolerance towards others. A longstanding, loyal employee, he was one of the few to hold the position of senior buyer, however, it was also true that he didn't hesitate to use his elevated position, intent on differentiating himself from the abundance of mere buyers throughout the company.

The prospect of working with him was incredibly daunting. Until then, I had given him a wide berth, choosing to speak to him only when addressed and always answering as politely and as competently as possible. One thing I quickly learned was his insistence on being addressed as Mr Kramer. He was adamant it should be pronounced in a particular way. Kramer was to rhyme with farmer, as if spelt with an additional 'r' after the 'a'. He constantly corrected any poor unsuspecting individual, bellowing KRARMER at them after their failed attempt to address him. I always felt particularly sorry for any prospective supplier, eager to make a good first impression, but alas invariably destined to fail.

So, after three years in the fashion accessories department, I said my farewells and headed off with Mr Kramer to develop the new Christmas Department. The situation became even more alarming with the news that our section would not be allocated the usual merchandiser. Instead, it was deemed that I, as a very experienced distributor, with the help of a senior departmental manager overseeing my efforts, could assume that role in the short term.

At just twenty-one, without an immediate supervisor and someone to shield me from the rigours of a very demanding buyer, I had no alternative but to rise to the challenge. Our little team was soon joined by an additional buyer and several distributors brought in from elsewhere in the company and we quickly settled into our new surroundings.

David Hancock had been a buyer in housewares and was drafted in to develop specific sections within the new Christmas Department. He was a totally different character to Mr Kramer, younger and very amusing, with the ability to inject a great deal of fun to the proceedings. He caused much hilarity by renaming what for him were his more ambiguous lines. Thus fairies became angels and the round glass objects that adorned Christmas trees were spheres.

We all worked extremely well together and, as the department successfully evolved, we were joined by yet more staff. Working in a somewhat surreal environment, surrounded by a forest of artificial Christmas trees, created a scene similar to Santa's Grotto, it was a unique working experience. Totally absorbed in the whole festive process, I flourished. As the products developed and the ranges increased, so did my encyclopaedic knowledge of all things Christmas, making me an invaluable member of the buying team and earning me the title of Queen Bee or QB for short.

My thorough understanding of the department also ensured that I avoided the wrath of Mr Kramer and, as he came to depend on me, our relationship went from strength to strength. I discovered more about him and gained some insight into his life outside BHS. A keen golfer and a freemason, but in an unhappy marriage, work had become his life. This explained in part, his devotion to the business, and the reason why he could often be found in the office working at his desk most weekends. It was commonplace for me to receive a call at home on a Saturday, as Mr Kramer always found it quicker to call me for an instant answer to a product query rather than trawl through mounds of paperwork. Somehow I could always answer his questions and it was wonderful to feel indispensable. Affectionately referred to by him as luvvy, dolly, or sweetie, the fear of working with him subsided and together we became an excellent team.

With the difficulties I was facing at home with my own father, it was Alan Kramer that I approached to give me away at my wedding. Our relationship had come a long way over the five years we had worked together. I had watched this intimidating man mellow and become someone whose company I not only enjoyed, but who had become a significant part of my life. For this Jewish man with two sons of his own, the prospect of walking down an aisle of an Anglican church had been inconceivable. However, he was genuinely moved by my request and accepted my invitation with gusto and much to the amusement of our work colleagues, he even insisted that we regularly practice the all-important walk up the aisle as the big day approached.

On 19th October 1985, I left my home on the Mitcham council estate with Alan Kramer at my side. As I stepped into the white Rolls Royce waiting to take us to the church, I glanced across the road at the home of my father. Was he standing behind those thick, net curtains imagining what might have been?

Once settled deep into the seat of the car, I had little time to reflect on those significant individuals not present on this most important occasion. Alan Kramer believed he had something far more pressing to deal with. It was mid-October and during my two days away from the office some of the Christmas stock had begun to arrive in the stores. One of those lines was the best selling motorists' trace-a-route. A vinyl covered road atlas, complete with a black felt tip pen and a wipe clean see-through plastic sheet that enabled you to trace out your route prior to your journey. The year was 1985 and much was changing on the road network around London.

'Now luvvy, we've got a problem,' said Alan before we'd even pulled away. Somehow I knew it would be work related.

'The first batch of trace-a-routes has just been delivered to stores without the most recent sections of the M25 printed in them. What should we do?' he asked desperately.

He was eager to know what action he should implement first thing Monday morning. For me, talking through the appropriate course of action whilst en route to my wedding was an experience I shall never forget. With a near catastrophe averted, Alan settled back to enjoy the *remainder of the journey, but something had not escaped him. Although for Alan, my area of London south of the river was completely unfamiliar, several hours earlier he had driven in convoy with my cousin to the church to leave his own car waiting there for collection after the service. Suddenly and completely unexpectedly, he sat forward in the seat, poised to address our chauffeur.*

'This isn't the way to the church,' he declared, as if to query the competence of the driver. The chauffeur paused before responding slowly and eloquently.

'Sir, when you travel in a Rolls Royce, you certainly don't take the back roads.'

I chuckled as Alan slid back into his seat somewhat deflated.

For the remainder of the day, Alan carried out all his official duties faultlessly and at the wedding reception provided an excellent and most entertaining speech. So chuffed was he with his entire performance throughout the day, he was intent on taking a keepsake of the day with him. However his insistence on 'doing a deal' with the wedding photographer later that evening in an attempt to purchase the proofs, got him nowhere.

News of my wedding together with a photo of Alan with the happy bride, made it to the dizzy heights of the BHS in-house magazine.

I returned to work two weeks later under the new guise of Karen Brazel. Fortunately for me, a merchandiser never materialized and instead, I was invited to join the management training programme and embark on a rigorous scheme, eventually resulting in being promoted to the highly rewarding role of merchandiser. With an attractive salary, a company car, private medical insurance and non-contributory pension and share option schemes, I was immensely proud of my achievements.

My job was demanding and varied, and my knowledge of Christmas goods was second to none. Regular communications and negotiations with stores and suppliers took me all over the country and with my travel came some wonderful opportunities. Notably, invitations to dine in fine restaurants, attend product launches and the chance to attend some of the most renowned sporting events. One particularly memorable time for me was a trip in an airship over central London.

However, along with the excitement there were constant pressures and deadlines to adhere to. The toughest of these occurred once a year, when we presented our entire Christmas range for the coming season to the board of directors, which included Sir Terence Conran, Chairman of The Storehouse Group. The prospect of this encounter was always guaranteed to raise all our stress levels and provoke much anxiety within the department.

Poised to answer the abundance of questions fired at us by the Board of Directors, the buying team had to retain copious amounts of information relating to each and every product. Any attempt to fumble through reams of paper to provide an answer was highly frowned upon. Consequently these were extremely tense meetings, not helped by the fact that in the past, our department had not always fared well. Sir Terence, an international style icon in his own right, often struggled with the concept of traditional Christmas merchandise and low value novelty gifts. In a fit of displeasure it had been known for him to throw an offending item across the room.

I worked very hard indeed at this job, which I loved, and never failed to rise to the challenge, always shouldering the accompanying responsibilities. Within the constraints of the company I had an extraordinary freedom to make major decisions and was prepared to face up to their impact, whether good or bad. I had grown with the job and developed the confidence to justify and explain my reasoning as and when needed and provide a coherent and sound argument for something that I strongly believed in. I had indeed come a long way from my childhood council estate background. Meanwhile in bleak contrast, in my personal life, things looked very different. Within the confines of my own home all these skills, and the fact that I was now earning a generous salary, counted for nothing. My husband imposed a draconian system of checks and balances, which I had to comply with to the last letter.

Regrettably, my working partnerships came to an end as colleagues moved on. David Hancock was the first to leave. I had so enjoyed my time working with him, there was never a dull moment. I'd also discovered that, like me, he was adopted and this certainly created a special bond between us. He had chosen to take a very different career path. After leaving BHS to join theological college he was eventually ordained as an Anglican priest at a ceremony in Canterbury Cathedral, which I felt very privileged to attend. I was delighted that he was later to baptize each of my daughters.

Alan was the next to leave, reluctantly faced with retirement. BHS had been his life. His intention to utilize his wealth of experience and work as a retail consultant for existing suppliers, never really materialised. Sadly away from the retail giant any interest in him soon dwindled. His unhappy marriage did finally come to an end, giving him the chance to embark upon a new and happy relationship with Edna. I remained in regular contact with Alan as he continued to be very much involved in my life, often referring to me as the daughter he never had. I included both him and Edna in any family events and they regularly travelled to Kent, to visit us all. That tough exterior had long since disappeared and for me he had become a warm, charming, individual. Immediately after the birth of both Rosemary and Annie he rushed to my side, armed with some beautiful, carefully chosen baby gifts.

After ten years in the buying offices, with increased pressures to work even longer hours and enforced store visits at weekends, I decided to respond to a blanket request for voluntary redundancies. All applications were accepted, although mine was conditional. Unlike most other employees, the company was keen for me to see out the current season and I was asked to remain in employment for a further six months, until the end of the calendar year. When I finally left BHS on Friday 14th December 1990 after ten-and-a-half years, I was pregnant with my first child and much to my surprise even qualified for maternity pay until May of the following year. Laden with an array of baby gifts, it was with a good feeling that I eventually ceased employment. Delighted at the prospect of full-time motherhood and family life, I embarked on the role with sheer pleasure. It would be many years before I had a true sense of the unexpected void left in my life.

Whilst tremendously rewarding, motherhood was very lonely. I missed the camaraderie and the daily buzz of the working environment. Without the network of support and the continued financial constraints imposed upon me by David, it was a difficult and challenging time. Unaware that my confidence and self-esteem had slowly dwindled, my life was far from happy.

Sadly, in May 1998 Alan was diagnosed with cancer of the liver. The prognosis was not good and his time was limited. He quickly got his affairs in order, which included a hasty marriage to Edna. Their plans for a more lavish event had to be immediately cancelled. I travelled to his home in Stanmore, North London, to visit him for what would be the last time. It was sad and distressing to see the man that had been such an important part of my life looking so weak and frail. He died just two weeks later.

As I stood in the synagogue for his funeral service, reflecting on our remarkable time together, I listened as the Rabbi addressed him (incorrectly) as Alan Kramer, (without the extra 'r'). I resisted my overwhelming urge to bellow KRARMER, on Alan's behalf.

13. Friends and Loneliness

Friends and loneliness: two seemingly incompatible words which, on reflection, go some way towards describing a large element of my life. Surrounded as I was in the early years of motherhood by what I believed to be a number of exceedingly loyal friends and an active social circle, when I look back now at this period of my life, I see myself as a very isolated and deeply unhappy individual. It took the trauma of separation and divorce for me to fully understand and appreciate the true meaning of the word friend.

It was November 2005 and sitting alone in the recently rented house, just days after walking out of my marriage, I was desolate. The time I could spend with my daughters was now limited and even with Christmas fast approaching, it failed to lift my spirits. I had no intention of penning a single card this year. This was undoubtedly the most traumatic time in my life. With the exception of my father and stepmother Eileen, who lived over an hour's drive away and supported me as best they could, what little remaining family I had was distant, both physically and emotionally. Never before had I needed friends as much as I did now. Racked with shame and guilt at my actions, I lacked the confidence or the inclination to broadcast my whereabouts. Instead I had chosen to hide away and leave it to David to explain our sudden change of circumstances and pass on my new contact details to anyone who asked for them.

Many of my friendships were longstanding. As well as those that had been initiated during our marriage, my own friends had become David's and his, likewise. As I waited anxiously for their comfort and support and the chance to finally speak out about why I'd acted as I did, it was with a sense of foreboding that once again in my life, I faced the prospect of rejection.

I had valued the many friendships that I had developed over the years and enjoyed their involvement in my life and that of my family. This was in marked contrast to my childhood. For reasons which I never understood, friendships had never really been encouraged by my parents. Apart from birthday parties when my brother and I were very young, the idea of inviting other children in to play was a no-no. All my interaction with my peers was confined to school or out on the street on the council estate where we lived. Curiously, friends also did not really feature in either the lives of my parents or my grandparents. For them, other than a visit from a relative, any other social contact was always confined to a chance meeting with a neighbour in the street. It was practically unheard of ever to invite anyone else into the home. My father certainly never had a single friend throughout his entire life and although my mother befriended a couple of work colleagues: Anne and Doris, who would not only become her good friends but also permanent surrogate aunties to me and Andrew, they too seldom came to visit.

I soon learned that on the rare occasion I did return home with an unexpected school friend it was always very awkward. Brushing my manners aside as we approached my front door, I would forge ahead leaving any friend trailing behind. This was intended to give me valuable seconds to forewarn my mother that I was not alone and thereby giving her time for that despairing look, which could be translated into:

'Oh Karen how could you spring this on me?' followed by a deep sigh. I would cringe, as I turned around in the hope that any friend had not hotfooted it after me and witnessed my mother's reaction.

Whether it was due to lack of time or money, I never knew, but our home was neither particularly inviting nor presentable and looking after the home was not high on my mother's list of priorities, or so it seemed to me at the time. Although she claimed to be a slave to it, I seldom saw any evidence. No doubt with little consideration from Andrew and me, she looked upon it as a thankless task, exacerbated by my father's tendency to hoard all manner of clutter.

Andrew, with his strange behaviour, only added to my anxiety when it came to friends. He lived on a diet of faddish concoctions, which he would prepare at irregular times of the day or night and then eat directly from the saucepan whilst watching the television, leaving the empty vessel, lid and utensils strewn across the lounge floor. This, together with an invariably unpleasant, lingering odour was hardly a welcoming sight for the uninitiated.

Despite all these hurdles, I did have one extremely good companion, Marian. She was the same age and lived 'next-door-but-one'. We moved onto the new housing estate within a day of each other in October 1970 and became firm friends. We spent a great deal of time in each other's company, playing together out in the street throughout our entire childhood. As well as attending the Girl Guides together, we also went to the same primary, middle and high schools and for much of the time found ourselves in the same class. She had two brothers, one much younger and the other, a twin brother named Barry, who relentlessly tried to strike up a good friendship with my brother Andrew, without success. I was particularly envious of Marian's immaculate house. Her parents took great pride in their home, complete with its fitted carpets. Unlike my own mother, I noticed how Marian's mum would get stuck into housework with gusto.

Once married though, with a lovely home of my own and away from all the traumas associated with a council estate, I was free to invite friends. My cooking skills were certainly lacking initially, but with the help of several reliable cookbooks, I coped admirably. I also discovered that these occasions were often reciprocated and that too was a new, pleasurable, experience.

As my family grew over the years, so did my friendships. Immediately after Rosemary's birth, through the National Childbirth Trust, I was put in touch with a group of women all in the same situation as me and this turned out to be an absolute lifeline. Having a baby was a tremendously exciting time, but I was soon to discover that it could also be an immensely lonely one. One day was just like another and attending solely to the needs of my new arrival, whilst achieving little else in my day, could be very disheartening.

What a great relief to regularly meet with and share these frustrations with a like-minded group of women, and to discover I was by no means alone. This close group of ten friends grew from strength to strength and as most of us embarked on our second pregnancy, we were all in a position to offer each other help and support. Every effort was made to attend those regular weekly Thursday afternoon gatherings. It didn't matter if you felt and looked dog-tired or your baby was irritable with evidence of its last feed down its front. The important thing was to sit together and talk, somewhere where nobody minded or judged, as you described your wretched week, only to find somebody claiming theirs was worse. As our children grew, the Thursday afternoons changed to regular evenings out at local restaurants or a supper in one of our homes.

So strong was this group of young mothers that eventually the fathers formed their own gang and enjoyed regular monthly curry nights together.

In 1998, at my suggestion, all the families (including pets) embarked on a marvellous weekend away together in the New Forest, more than forty people in total. So successful was this get-away weekend, it was to become an annual event.

I was more than happy to organise these events and social gatherings, many of them in my own home. Our house in Sevenoaks had plenty of space to entertain and whether it was a dinner party, Sunday lunch, children's gatherings or a major celebration, I rose to the occasion. I now considered myself a capable hostess and for a long time I gained a tremendous amount of pleasure from the success of these events.

Frequently surrounded by family and friends, I wanted my daughters to have a happy, memorable childhood that would remain with them throughout their lives.

Behind my seemingly confident, exuberant and capable exterior, I was sliding into a deep depression. So many other aspects of my life had become intolerable. A busy working wife and mother, I strived relentlessly to achieve the very best for all those around me without ever having time, space, support or even the finances to take time out for myself. Any concerns I may have voiced to my husband David, were always immediately brushed aside. His response was to rationalise my feelings by reminding me of my tremendous abilities and encouraging me to continue in the same vein.

Ever since the beginning of our marriage, I had allowed myself to become indoctrinated by David and any thought of perhaps voicing my concerns to others close to me was inconceivable. A victim of my own success, how could I begin to convince anyone that what I'd strived so hard to portray had been my absolute downfall? Changing people's perceptions is never an easy task.

David and I had already encountered difficulties in our relationship several years earlier. Somehow he lacked the ability to look upon our relationship as a partnership and despite seeking help, nothing had really been resolved. His overbearing ways were suffocating and my life was intolerable. Our marriage was destined to failure.

My move into this temporary home close by had occurred quietly and discreetly. It was notably different to the euphoria that I'd experienced on other house moves during my married life. I had somehow managed to furnish the property sparsely with budget furniture using the limited funds I had accumulated in recent times, together with a few unwanted items from the loft at the family home. Unfortunately, with the financial restrictions imposed on me during my marriage, I possessed very few personal belongings. The house with its bleak, minimalistic interior lacking any adornments, seemed cell-like, serving as a punishment for my recent most appalling actions.

The marriage had ended at my instigation and yet there was no feeling of euphoria or relief on my part. Instead, I just remained hidden away. It was the only place where I could be guaranteed complete sanctuary, contemplating financial worries, concerns for my daughters and even for my own sanity. Any trips into town or the local supermarket invariably led to uncomfortable confrontations with acquaintances, who were obviously unsure how to react to me.

In the days and weeks that followed, there were certainly some unexpected good moments, as well as some very alarming discoveries. For, as it turned out, many of those friends in whom I had happily invested time and energy over the years, had chosen to show their allegiance to David. As the apparent instigator of our separation, I'd been unfairly judged. No doubt news that Paul, my new partner, was waiting in the wings only fuelled their support for my estranged husband. I was deeply affected by their actions, I genuinely believed they would be supportive and understanding. How could they be so judgemental without talking to me first?

There were a remarkably small number of very special

individuals prepared to comfort and stand by me. When they heard what I had been going through, they offered me the reassurance that I wasn't the bad person that I'd convinced myself I was. Feeling absolutely wretched, in the depths of despair and unable to provide anything more than a cup of tea and a pool of tears, I was in dire need of their frequent attention and discovering true friendships for the first time.

Marian, though, was the first friend I felt I could confide in over my decision to leave David. Very shocked and surprised, she refrained from giving her own opinion and has continued to support me throughout.

This was not only a difficult time for me, but also for my daughters. I welcomed those special friends who were able to find a way to continue a relationship with both David and myself. It proved to be a tremendous help during that transitional period when, under the difficult circumstances, their ability to maintain normality for the sake of my daughters, was much appreciated.

Although my entire family continued to communicate with David, sadly his family (with the exception of an extremely understanding elderly cousin), felt unable to continue any kind of relationship with me. The same can be said of many of our friends who chose to stand by David, thereby completely disregarding me. I truly believed that these friendships were strong enough to withstand life's traumas, but sadly, I was wrong.

Regrettably, my daughters' relationships with these individuals have been detrimentally affected too, including their contact with David's parents – their grandparents. Even as the mother of their granddaughters, all my sincere attempts to retain some sort of relationship with the couple whom I had completely embraced throughout my marriage and made so central to my life, were in vain. We would never be reconciled.

The long-established group of mothers, who had remained in regular contact for fifteen years, also showed a very surprising hand. Just three weeks after my separation, I received news of an early Christmas get-together. News of my sudden change of circumstances had reached the group and someone had telephoned to suggest that I might like to join them all, keen to encourage me out of the prison-like house that I had resigned myself to. The idea was most appealing, where else could I go and be guaranteed to receive sympathy and understanding?

This was my first social outing as an estranged woman and perhaps the only one I could have possibly contemplated at that time, but never could I have envisaged the outcome. To my utter despair the entire evening went by without mention of my current situation. In fact, I was not even spoken to directly. I found it very difficult to initiate a 'normal' conversation myself. Eventually I could stand it no longer and I stood up to say my goodbyes. 'Good luck for my time ahead' was the best a couple of them could muster. Completely distraught, I suppressed my emotions until safely home. I had put my faith in them and they too had chosen to reject me.

There was also another group of seemingly caring individuals, whom I had yet to endure. Many I had only considered acquaintances, but all the same I was delighted by their concern. After hearing the news of my predicament, I received several invitations for lunch, a chance for a good natter and a sympathetic ear, they had said comfortingly. In reality, their only motive was to delve and discover the most intimate details of my marriage break-up and, once satisfied, I never heard from them again.

The people who did come forward and offer me real support, help and understanding were not always the ones I would have expected. Likewise, some of the people I believed would be there have chosen to remain absent from my life, whilst still staying in regular communication with David.

During this most traumatic time in my life I have learned that with true friends, I can be myself. We can share and listen

The exceedingly engaging Jim Donovan.

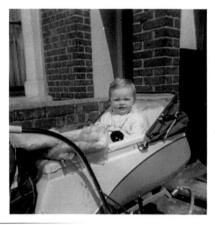

Mummy was very proud of our Silver Cross Pram.

This is me, Karen Lesley Gay, aged 4 months, July 1962.

Mummy, Daddy and me,
1963.

On the stairs at Nanny
Gay's house with my cousin
Barbara. Seven years my
senior, I always looked
forward to her visits.

My younger brother Andrew,
our Airedale terrier Elsa and
me.

My first school photo, aged 5, 1967.

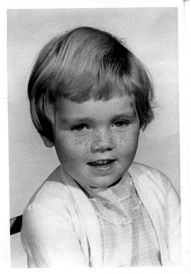

Andrew and me with our matching red scooters, 1970.

Aged 7 and my freckles are becoming prominent, c. 1969.

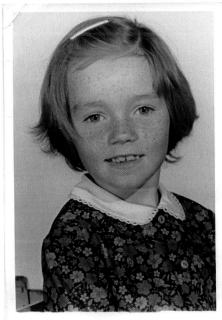

*My kind and gentle
Nanny Gay.*

*Another school photo,
aged 11.*

*Tuesday evenings meant
Girl Guides,
c. 1974.*

*My teens were a bleak time,
c. 1977*

My late teens, c. 1981

The wedding of my cousin Barbara. She had two bridesmaids, her best friend Debbie and me, an extremely self-conscious fourteen-year-old, 1976

With Alan Kramer on my wedding day, October 1985.

*Dad looking dapper,
enjoying a cruise.*

*Rosemary, my eldest
daughter, peering at
me intently soon after
her birth, March 1991.*

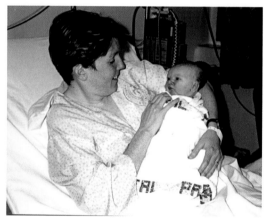

*Mum with my daughter,
Annie, 1993.*

to each other's problems and dilemmas and offer comfort and support to each other. I have learned how vital a true friend is and will always feel truly indebted to each of these very special individuals who loyally supported me during the most harrowing time of my life.

Victoria has proved to be one such special friend. As the mother of four children of similar ages to my own, our paths had crossed many years earlier at numerous after school activities. Several years later she was to be employed as a teaching assistant at the girls' prep school where I worked and although, unlike me, she was 'above stairs', her brief furtive visits to my office under the stairs were always welcome. She has remained a tower of strength since the early days of my separation and throughout the many significant events that followed.

One particular occasion sticks prominently in my mind. Immediately after the first Christmas in my rented house, during that bleak period between Christmas and New Year, she insisted on looking after my three daughters whilst I disappeared for a scheduled hair appointment. I returned with my coiffed hair to hear excited squeals and stories of raucous antics in an unexpected snowfall. After insisting that we all stay for a late lunch, Victoria proceeded to lay the table with a wonderful array of Christmas leftovers. As we all sat down to enjoy a hotchpotch of festive fare, I was moved by both her display of generosity and her genuine thoughtfulness towards my family and myself, at what would otherwise have been an exceedingly lonely time. Her gesture touched me to the heart and, as she continues to be a very loyal, valued and much appreciated close friend, I know I can call on her at a moment's notice.

14. 'Darling, We've Hit the Jackpot!'

November 2006

Over the preceding months, I had become very frustrated with the adoption support agency and in particular, their accredited researchers in Dublin. The long-awaited copies of both Margaret's birth certificate and that of her sister Catherine simply never materialised. They were impossible to contact by telephone as nobody ever answered and any communication from them via email was sporadic. Dissatisfied with their service, Paul and I had set aside the February half-term of the following year to travel to Dublin to retrieve and follow up the relevant information for ourselves.

Although Paul was always hugely supportive and his enthusiasm never flagged, living on my own and facing the initial difficulties and inevitable consequences of my marriage breakdown, I experienced many emotional peaks and troughs that year. My search was a welcome distraction in many ways, but that too presented its own low, as well as the occasional high. My hopes would rise as we followed yet another lead or waited anxiously for the delivery of another document, only to find myself, despite all possible effort, no closer to completing the puzzle. Whilst I remained unconvinced that Margaret Coleman was indeed my birth mother, as it was her name on my birth certificate, only she could explain the truth behind my adoption and I needed to find her.

Our imminent house move had provided a much-needed distraction from an almost year long, fruitless search. However, after just one week in our new home and still surrounded by unpacked boxes, I received an unexpected email from the researchers in Dublin. They posed a question that was very far reaching.

'If Patrick Coleman was not dead, had I looked to see if he and Margaret had had any further children together?'

With so much conflicting information surrounding my adoption, the idea just hadn't occurred to either Paul or me, but suddenly it seemed highly feasible. After all, Jim Donovan had been adamant that they were still together and living under his roof at a time when I would have been six months old.

Since our visit to the court, Paul had been of the opinion that I could still be Patrick's daughter and the reason for my adoption was related to me being conceived out of wedlock, something most unacceptable in the Catholic community – certainly at that time. But why and how did Margaret Coleman convince the Social Services that her husband was dead, when he was very much alive and they were still living together? To us it was still a total mystery.

We wasted no time with the possibility of siblings now firmly planted in my mind; we ignored all the remaining unpacking and sat down that evening at the computer to check through page after page of birth entries, beginning with the first quarter of 1963, one year after I was born. The process was slow and tedious. For each quarter of each year we scrutinised the Coleman listings, looking for the mother's maiden name of Hennessy, for a match with my own birth record.

We reached the third quarter of 1965 and suddenly Paul and

I found ourselves transfixed to the screen. The entry read: John F. with the mother's maiden name Hennessy and the place of birth was Barking in Essex, surely this was no coincidence. I put my head in my hands, as the implications of this birth entry became a reality. This was probably a blood relative. On paper we shared the same two parents; this made us full siblings. It was the most amazing feeling and I was overcome with excitement and emotion. After making a note of the birth reference we continued the search. We reached 1969, four years since the birth of John, and in the third quarter we found a Michael J., place of birth, Redbridge in Essex. We ploughed on, the second quarter of 1971, nine years after my own birth, to find an Oliver T., his place of birth was also Barking.

Margaret would have been over thirty years old in 1971 and somehow I was convinced there would be no further matches, so I decided to end our search. It was past midnight and I was utterly exhausted. It was impossible to sleep, as I lay there that evening turning our discovery over in my mind, together with the many possible consequences – it was almost unimaginable.

Although I remained uncertain as to my own parentage, on paper these three individuals appeared to be my full blood brothers. After forty something years, to discover that I'm not alone (I do have blood relations after all) was just a total revelation and one which felt almost incomprehensible. Did these three men know of my existence?

The thought of there being a complete family unit, living out their lives day-to-day so close by, which had been purposely hidden from me, was difficult to grasp.

Throughout my life I had believed my father to be dead. How could I have ever imagined this outcome? This had changed everything. Now I was no longer searching for just my birth mother.

The following day I ordered all three birth certificates of my supposed blood brothers. It was hard to contain my excitement and curiosity as I waited impatiently during the week that followed for the absolute confirmation I needed.

At last, the sight of three white A4 envelopes waiting for me on the doormat was awesome. Feverishly ripping open each one, I sat dumbstruck as each of these birth certificates confirmed what I'd already suspected: Margaret Mary and Patrick Joseph were their parents. On paper certainly they were my brothers. Somewhere, there were three men who probably looked like me and maybe had no notion of their sister's existence.

After telephoning Paul to share the news with him, I sat down and reflected on this new-found revelation and the prospect of three real brothers. Andrew had never felt like a true brother to me, not just because of his own adoption but because his odd and disturbing behaviour prevented us having any kind of relationship. There was no contact between us, which in essence had made me an only child.

I was determined to do my utmost to locate them; they too may have families of their own. I thought more carefully about their ages. When I married in 1985, Michael and Oliver were fifteen and thirteen respectively, the current ages of both Rosemary and Annie. Margaret would have been forty-four, the same age as I am now: it was a strange concept. I knew that Margaret had left this country in the early 70s, and her sons would have returned to Ireland with her. I was overwhelmed by a strong sense of sadness and loss for the three brothers I had never known. I thought about my aborted attempt to locate my birth mother in 1993. If only I had remained steadfast in my desire to trace her then, I would have been aware of, and maybe even have established, a relationship with these three brothers.

Once again, I called the services of the National Health Register helpline for adopted people, I wanted reassurance that the three men in question were still alive and more importantly, I hoped to find one or more residing in this country. After explaining my position, the assistant remembered me from my previous enquiry, expressing surprise at my latest discovery – this was certainly something she had never encountered before.

'I would like you to check whether perhaps any of them are now living here in the UK?' I asked hopefully.

'OK, lets have the first one,'

'John Francis Coleman, born 20th August 1965.' I waited anxiously as she searched her computer.

'Yes, I have that name and there is a current file on him.'

'Really, oh my goodness,' I replied almost in disbelief. My thoughts were racing. If he were living here in the UK, he would be much easier to find. If I could locate John, then I would find Margaret. Would this find be the key? The end of my search was now in sight.

'The next one?' said the voice on the end of the line. In my excitement I'd almost forgotten about the two remaining brothers, I fumbled around for their birth certificates.

'Michael Joseph Coleman, born 15th August 1969.'

'Yes, there's a current record for him also.'

Two out of three, my heart was racing.

'And the last one?'

'Oliver Thomas Coleman, born 11th April 1971.'

'No I have no current record for this name. If your mother returned to Ireland in the seventies he would have been very young and she would have taken him with her and perhaps he remained there. The first two have a gap in their records, suggesting that, although they also left in the early seventies, they have since returned to the UK.'

The helpline was only permitted to provide me with limited information relating to these two most coveted individuals. Although I knew that they were forbidden to give enquirers any contact details, I was determined not to let this opportunity pass.

'Is there anything else you can tell me?' I asked tentatively. She hesitated.

'I can tell you that there is only one John Francis Coleman with that date of birth and the same for Michael Joseph,' she said assisting me a little further. I was now desperately trying to think how I could tease any further information.

'Um, John Coleman, are you able to give me any indication of where in the UK he might be? I know he was born in Essex,' I added, hoping to engage further with her.

There was a brief pause as she considered my desperate request. My circumstances were certainly unheard of, I needed all the help I could muster.

'All I can say is that he is in the south, in the most obvious place.'

'Err, yes...' I said vaguely.

'In the London area is all I can tell you, they both are. That really is all the information I can give.'

'Thank you so much,' I said, wishing I could express the true depth of my gratitude, but words failed me.

Feeling that my arduous search was about to end, I wanted to dance round the house and shout for joy at this discovery, but it was late Friday afternoon and I needed to wait until Monday when I would call a contact with access to a national database. Only then would I have the contact information on both John and Michael, my brothers!

Monday morning, 9.05 a.m., and I was already armed with the all-important addresses. I searched 192.com to check the current electoral roll and clicked onto Google Earth, for an aerial image of each property.

Michael's information turned out to be inaccurate. The address I had was a flat above a parade of shops, but his name did not feature as a current occupant. I turned my attention to John and found his particulars seemed far more reliable. He shared a house with a Helen and Lisa Murphy, but unfortunately any plans to attempt a discreet drive-by were thwarted. The semi-detached property was in a small crescent and positioned at the furthest point of a tight loop; with a narrow roadway, it would be impossible to either cruise by or sit outside and observe without causing suspicion. Despite this slight setback to my plan, I decided to approach John. I gave careful thought to my next move. At this stage I was reluctant to reveal my identity to any of my brothers, I felt it was important to make contact with Margaret first and to give her the opportunity to disclose my existence to them. Using the information I had gained from Jim Donovan, I composed a carefully worded enquiry.

4th December 2006

Dear Mr Coleman
  Please accept my apologies for contacting you in this way. I am writing to all the John Colemans in the London area in the hope that I will find some information.
  I am trying to locate the Donovan family. They lived in Herbert Road, Ilford in the early 60's.
  There was a Margaret and Patrick Coleman living with the Donovans at this time and if they are your parents, I would very much like to contact them to see if they could be of any help.
I have enclosed a stamped addressed envelope if you have any information that could help me.

I look forward to hearing from you in due course.

Yours sincerely

Karen

Although the information was not entirely accurate, I was convinced that if John contacted his mother, there would be enough clues for her to be sure of the enquirer's identity.

I had of course only written to one John Coleman and it

was on David Trill's advice that I retained some anonymity and change my surname and home address to that of the school's. I also provided a mobile phone number belonging to Paul.

Delighted with my plan, I posted the letter immediately and waited eagerly for a response. From that point on, Paul regularly checked any missed calls and David Trill religiously scoured the post first thing each morning for that all-important envelope.

A week passed and I was starting to feel a little despondent. It was mid-December and almost the end of term. In two days the school would close until the New Year and there would be no access to the postal delivery. However, on the day of the school Christmas party, when pupils were not required to arrive at school until mid-morning, Nancy and I were still at home when the phone rang at 8.45 a.m. Paul had left for work sometime earlier and it was his number I noticed on the caller display as I answered it.

'Hello,' I said casually.

'Darling, we've hit the jackpot!' he announced jubilantly.

'What do you mean?' I asked, bemused.

'I've had the call, the call from John Coleman!' his excitement was palpable. Momentarily stunned, I could barely comprehend what Paul was saying. Somehow, I had expected a letter, not a 'phone call. After just a moment's hesitation, I bombarded him with questions.

'What did he say, what did he sound like, do you think he's suspicious? I can't believe it. It's so hard to think straight. Tell me everything,' I insisted, finally giving Paul a chance to respond.

'He sounded fine and he's given me his work phone number for you to call him, he's there all morning,' he explained.

'Oh no, what now? What do I say? How am I going to manage that?' I asked, anxiously.

'Listen, you'll be OK. He sounded very nice, although I nearly put my foot in it. When I answered the phone he asked to speak to you using your temporary pseudonym and so without thinking, I said is that John Coleman? He then expressed immediate surprise that I should know that, so I mumbled something about us looking forward to this call and how important it was to you and I think he believed me.'

'So he's not suspicious?'

'No, I don't think so.'

Paul read out the phone number for me to jot down.

'What else did he say?'

'Nothing really.' He's got a slight Irish accent and he speaks well. Go on, ring him and let me know as soon as you've done it.'

'I don't think I can do it, I can't think straight. I'm so nervous.'

'You'll be alright, I'll talk to you later, good luck.'

We ended the call and I sat motionless. I was so desperate to make the call and yet I was completely overcome. I was about to talk to someone for the very first time in my life who was almost certainly a blood relative.

I tried to organise my thoughts and re-read my letter yet again. In order to conceal my real identity it was important that this call sounded no more than a chance general enquiry, but under the circumstances, I questioned my ability to remain composed. I pushed the buttons on the handset, shaking as I did so. It took several failed attempts before I finally heard the terrifying ringing tone.

The male voice which answered spoke too rapidly for me to make out the name of the business.

'Hello, I'd like to speak to John Coleman please.'

'Yes hello, John Coleman speaking.'

I was dumbstruck. Somehow I hadn't expected to get straight through to him.

'Um, yes, my name's Karen,' I said, failing miserably to sound composed and relaxed. 'You've just been speaking to a friend of mine and he's passed your telephone number to me.' After this briefest of introduction, I felt totally drained.

'Yes, I must say it was strange to call the phone number on your letterhead and to find a man who appeared to be expecting my call,' he said guardedly. I was quick to dispel any suspicions and just as Paul had done, I stressed the importance of my search.

'That's OK,' he said reassuringly. 'But perhaps you can understand my point of view, in these current times you need to be extremely careful when it comes to possible identity fraud. I just wanted to be sure there was nothing untoward.'

'Oh, no.' I said, desperate to allay any concerns. It was imperative that I gain his confidence. As I listened to him, I tried to form a picture in my mind but it was impossible. Although he was likely to resemble me in some way, his unfamiliar accent prevented me from visualising him.

'I received your letter last week and wondered if you could tell me a little bit more?' he asked. I hadn't expected this, I'd told him everything I wanted him to know and I had no intention of revealing anything more at this stage. All I could do was to repeat the contents of the letter.

'Yes, I am trying to find the Donovan family, I've been doing a lot of research and I'm struggling. What I do know is that they were living in Herbert Road, Ilford in the early sixties and I think that a Margaret and Patrick Coleman may have been living there around that time.' I waited desperately for him to respond.

'Well, my parents are Margaret and Patrick Coleman.'

Knowing that he was under the impression I had sent out numerous letters, I expressed surprise. This was a defining moment, the first verbal confirmation of Margaret being alive. I was overwhelmed with an immense feeling of relief, mixed with excitement. I also discovered that she had remained with Patrick. I had to be careful though, not to betray any of these feelings to him.

'I have spoken to my mother, but unfortunately neither she nor my father have any recollection of this name.'

This was puzzling and very odd. Their response, claiming to have no recollection of Jim Donovan simply didn't add up. The information in the letter to John left them in no doubt as to who was trying to make contact with them after forty-four years.

'And they have no information at all?'

'No sorry, I have to tell you that my Mum is pretty sharp and on the ball. She has a very good memory and if she could help you I know she would.'

That last remark just confirmed my suspicions. They had rejected any opportunity to communicate directly with me. It needed all my strength to contain the sense of anger welling up inside me. Sensing disappointment, John asked if perhaps I had any additional information that might jog their memory. My thoughts were in turmoil. I was desperate to keep the conversation flowing while battling with my quivering voice and spinning head. Here I was, not only talking to a possible relative, but I'd also just discovered news of Margaret and Patrick's existence and in the same breath their denial of the events of 1962. The conversation was surreal.

Frustrated and completely overcome, for a brief moment I contemplated screaming down the telephone. 'I THINK I MIGHT BE YOUR SISTER!' but somehow, with almost superhuman control, I managed to resist the urge. I needed thinking time. I asked if I could call John back after I had gathered further information.

'Yes, by all means, you can catch me here most days. Feel free to call me back if you need more help. I'm quite happy to ring my parents again if necessary.'

'Thank you very much.'

'That's OK, bye Karen.'

The call had lasted less than five minutes, but seemed like much longer. Somehow it wasn't at all what I had anticipated. The rollercoaster of emotions I had struggled to conceal during the conversation now turned into red-hot fury. From the tone of the call, I sensed that John Coleman had not the slightest inkling of a possible sister. I couldn't understand Margaret and Patrick's actions. By choosing to deny all knowledge of events in 1962, and thereby my existence, they ran the risk of me revealing my true identity to John. I replayed the conversation over and over in my head before relaying it to Paul.

Nancy and I left for school and as David Trill and I sat together pumping up hundreds of balloons for the imminent Christmas party, I enlisted his invaluable help in preparing for a follow up call to John.

Later that day, with just a few embellishments, I prepared to make the call, this time determined to catch the name of John's work place. David had traced the phone number to the Watford area, but unfortunately yet again the speed of his voice prevented it.

'Hello, John, it's Karen again.'

'Hi Karen, how can I help?' In order to establish a relationship with him, I took the opportunity firstly to reveal my real name, explaining that like him I too had concern over my own security. He accepted my explanation and I continued.

'I've had a bit of a think and I do have a little more information.'

'OK, fire away,' he said cheerily. I spoke slowly, in a somewhat vague manner as I pretended to recall details from the long and distant past.

'The Donovan father's name was James or Jim, he was a bricklayer and his wife's name was Mary. They had five or six children and I think the eldest daughter's name was Eileen.'

'OK, I've made a note of all of that, I will telephone again,

131

I can't promise anything, Mum had no recollection before but you never know, it just might trigger something.' Unlike John, I knew this information would not make the slightest difference in jogging Margaret and Patrick's memory but if nothing else, it would relay to them that I remained steadfast and would not be dismissed easily.

'Are they in Ireland?' I asked.

'Yes, that's right.' He replied, confirming my suspicions.

I had just one final question.

'If I had their telephone number, I could always call them myself, it saves bothering you?' I suggested tentatively.

'By all means, if you want to try yourself that would be fine but you'll probably be wasting your time.' To my absolute surprise he read out their telephone number, complete with international code and I carefully wrote it down.

'Um Karen,' he said, suddenly realising his actions. 'Could I ask you to refrain from calling my parents until after I've had another conversation with them? I will speak to my mother this evening and get back to you tomorrow.'

I reassured him that I would wait and we ended the call. I stared at the digits on the scrap of paper in front of me. Unbelievable, I now had Margaret Coleman's phone number! This was the woman whose name I'd been aware of my entire life and whom I'd tried so desperately to find for the past year. Now she was within my reach. I had the information I needed to pick up the telephone, dial the number and hear her voice.

David Trill wasted no time in reminding me of the Irish white pages, which enabled me to find their home address; I now had everything I needed.

'I've done something unbelievably stupid today.' John announced to Helen as he returned home.

'What's that love?

'You know that letter from Karen in Sevenoaks, well I spoke to her

132

today.'

'Yes, and?'

'I've given her Mum and Dad's phone number and I don't even know the woman.' 'Don't worry about it. I'm sure it will be OK,' said Helen reassuringly.

'You're probably right, but I still can't understand what made me do it.'

Two days had passed since our conversation and life was quite unbearable, as I waited anxiously for John's call. It was Thursday and the last day of term, I went home resigned to calling John myself, but before doing so, I rang the adoption support agency. I had been communicating with them throughout my search, sharing with them my inexplicable findings and seeking advice and help at every stage. It was important for me to keep them informed, as ultimately they would act as the intermediary for any initial contact with Margaret. After listening to the very latest developments and stressing to me the importance of not revealing my identity, I made the call to John.

'Hello John, it's Karen, I'm sorry to chase you but I wanted to know if you'd spoken to your parents yet?'

'Karen, sorry, I meant to call you but I've been a bit busy these last couple of days. Yes, I did speak to my mother again and she still has no recollection of the Donovan family. In fact, although she said they used to live in Ilford, it wasn't Herbert Road.'

'Oh, really,' I said with fake surprise, hiding my absolute rage at her audacity to deny me.

'I know you've got their phone number, but there really is no point in you speaking to them. It would be a complete waste of time. I'm sorry, but your search appears to have come to a dead end.'

'It does seem that way,' I replied. My voice relaying something far removed from my thoughts and feelings.

'One last thing,' he asked. 'I wondered, would you mind telling me the exact nature of your search?' Had something been said that had made him think more deeply, was he suspicious? I thought very carefully about my reply to his question. At that moment I was so furious I was tempted to tell him everything, but remembering the advice from the adoption agency I resisted.

'I'm looking for someone and it's very important that I find them. I thought that Margaret Coleman would be the only person that could help me.' I chose my words carefully and spoke very slowly. If possible, I wanted to provoke some deep thought in John.

'I'm afraid that's not the case,' he said, regret in his voice. 'I'm sorry I can't be any more help to you, but I do wish you luck in your continued search.' he added.

I thanked him and ended the call, quite distraught. John would think no more of this encounter, but he had left me feeling terribly upset. The knowledge that we would undoubtedly speak again and that we would inevitably meet, was crippling. I was convinced that Margaret was determined to ignore and fend off my persistent attempts to contact her. How long did she intend for this ridiculous scenario to continue? I was both angry and distressed that she had chosen to dismiss me in this humiliating way. I couldn't understand why she would run the risk of me revealing everything to John.

I called the counsellors again, repeating the conversation, sobbing as I did so. They were very sympathetic and understanding as I described my feelings of utter despair. I was in urgent need of their help, but as they explained their course of action, I realised that it was completely unacceptable to me.

The adoption agency has to consider all the individuals involved, not just my birth mother. Although I knew that there was never any intermediary service available during the month of December or the week running up to Mothering Sunday, as these were highly sensitive times, I felt, maybe unjustly, my circumstances should receive special consideration. The agency explained that this was not to be, nothing would happen until after the New Year. In the meantime they would send out a four-paged application form for me to complete. This request for an intermediary would then be submitted to the manager for assessment and consideration. If my application was approved, an initial letter would be sent from an intermediary to Margaret Coleman, advising her that someone would like to make contact. She would be given one month in which to reply; if she did not respond, they would send a similar follow up letter. In the event of this too being ignored, then a third and final letter would be despatched, explaining to Margaret Coleman that she would not hear from the intermediary again. It would also point out that it is the person seeking to make contact that has provided the intermediary with the contact details.

Hearing about the process of letter-sending only served to infuriate me. I had kept the adoption support agency abreast of my search at every stage and the counsellors were very familiar with my abnormal circumstances. What was it exactly which needed further consideration? My careful handling of the situation had got me nowhere and my patience had worn thin.

I also expressed my concern over the time frame. If, as I suspected, Margaret chose to ignore each of these letters, I calculated that I would have to wait (bearing Mothers Day in mind), until late April before I could contact her directly. And what of my three possible brothers? Margaret may have chosen to abandon me, but I wanted the opportunity to tell them that I existed. I was reminded again of the risk of upsetting her and her family's Christmas. However, all I could think about was my Christmas. Life had become intolerable. Who was thinking about my daughters and me? I wasn't exactly predisposed to consider Margaret's feelings. Her incessant lies at the time of my birth and more recently, did nothing to endear her to me, whatever her circumstances. I had given her every opportunity to approach me discreetly, but she had chosen to ignore my efforts. Margaret had forty-four years to prepare for my sudden appearance, whereas I could never have been prepared for my discovery. How unreasonable that I should be expected to shelve any idea of contacting Margaret; the agency seemed to place the feelings of the birth mother before those of the adopted child. I was the innocent party and yet I felt penalised. I began to regret involving the agency at all: I felt let down by them. I had wasted a great deal of time, effort and expense telephoning the counsellors regularly throughout the year only to meet with a totally unacceptable response. I would take responsibility for my next move.

John picked up the letter that had occupied the kitchen table for just over a week. With the matter now closed he headed towards the bin but as he did so he glanced at my request one last time. After a moment's thought and unsure of any reason for his actions, he folded the letter and headed towards his study to tuck it away for safekeeping.

15. My Pride and Joy

On the 14th March 1991, just nine days before my 29th birthday, for the first time in my life I came face to face with a true blood relative, an event which, up until that moment had been almost unimaginable. The growing anticipation throughout my pregnancy and the sense of wonderment at the prospect of our meeting reached their peak, as at long last I cradled my daughter Rosemary in my arms. Never before had I looked into the eyes of another human being with whom I had a genetic connection. Totally overcome by the realisation that together we shared the same heredity, whatever it may be, my lifelong pain of isolation and lack of any sense of real belonging had at long last ceased.

My feelings of love and devotion towards Rosemary were overwhelming, and no less so for the subsequent arrival of both Annie in January 1993 and Nancy six years later. In truth, strangely enough I had never expected to bear a daughter. Long before David and I were even married, I had visited a fortune-teller at a local fun event. It was a tame, light-hearted consultation, during which she predicted that I would eventually marry the man I was currently with and I would bear him two sons. This seemed most plausible, as David was one of two boys and so too was his father. It never occurred to me to even consider what my own genetic family history might be.

Years later, in the early stages of my first pregnancy, I had already given credence to the prospect of a son and so too had David's family. My impending departure from BHS would mean the loss of a much welcomed discount card for The Storehouse Group, which fortunately included the babyware retailer Mothercare. As I intended to make full use of its benefits, buying as much clothing and equipment as possible before my impending departure, I decided to get confirmation of the sex of my baby at the twenty-week scan. Such was our surprise to discover that our first offspring would be a daughter that we refrained from sharing this news with anyone else until her birth and thereby surprised family and friends too. Concealing all things pink for the duration of the pregnancy had been quite a challenge.

In less than two years I was a very proud mum with two beautiful daughters. However, it was to be my own experience of motherhood that would arouse such immense feelings towards my own birth mother, Margaret Coleman. As I nurtured and cared for my daughters' every need, I couldn't help wonder how a woman could carry a child for nine months and finally, after bearing that child, hand over such a vulnerable and dependant progeny forever? As my thoughts towards her intensified, so had the idea of trying to locate her. Sadly though, in 1993, after my initial attempts to find her were jettisoned, there was no alternative but to suppress my extremely deep feelings and emotions. This could have been the end of the story if it were not for the fact that years later my own daughters raised the subject of my adoption. Suddenly I realised that not only was I affected but they were too.

Driving home one day after a visit to my disabled mother, their grandmother, one of them burst out.

'Are you going to get ill like One Nanny?'

'I hope not,' I replied, keen to reassure them.

'How do you know that?' they both asked.

'Well, I wasn't born from One Nanny.' I reminded them, implying that any hereditary disorders in the family could not be passed on to me. They knew that I'd been adopted, as we had spoken about it several times, but on this occasion they wanted to really understand its implicit meaning.

'What do you mean? If you weren't born from One Nanny who were you born from?' they asked, determined to try and understand Mummy's strange circumstances once and for all.

'A different lady,' I said. 'I know her name but I don't know who she is. She gave me away to be adopted when I was just a few days old.' They were puzzled by this.

'Why didn't she want you?' they asked sympathetically. The idea that a mummy could want to be separated from her child was inconceivable to them.

'I don't really know,' I said. Even as I explained the tragic events surrounding my adoption, I struggled to find an answer that would suffice.

'But that's so sad,' said Annie. 'Don't you want to find her and see what she's like?'

'Maybe one day,' I said, thinking back to my aborted attempt soon after Annie's birth.

'I do think about it sometimes, but it wouldn't be easy, it could take a long time and even then I might not find her,' I explained.

'I think you should try,' they all agreed. 'I wonder where she is now?'

'I just don't know. She could be anywhere.'

Discussing my adoption with my own daughters was a new and very welcome experience and unexpectedly thought provoking. They were as curious as I was to discover something of our shared but unknown family history.

As the bond between my daughters and myself grew ever stronger, it also highlighted for me once again the deficiencies in my own relationship with my adoptive mother. As a child, not only was there no encouragement to talk about my adoption, but also, I'd never really felt able to broach any other childhood concerns or worries with her. Conscious of these inadequacies in my own upbringing, I have always been determined to ensure that my own mother/daughter relationships were very different.

There were many reasons for ending my marriage in 2005, not least because of the effect my unhappy life was having on my daughters. After hitting a rocky patch in 1996, I had at that time been resolute in providing a stable environment for my family. The girls should never *experience, as I had done as a child, the horrors of a broken marriage. As the years passed, their frequent use of the word 'stressy' to describe me had not gone unnoticed. Feeling myself sinking into an ever-deeper depression, it was impossible for me to be the diligent mother I so wanted to be. I was forced to face and consider what appeared to be unthinkable possibilities, but how could I inflict such trauma on them? I continued to battle with an internal conflict until I finally had to face what I knew was inevitable.*

Breaking the news to our three daughters of our planned separation was the most difficult experience I have ever had to encounter in my life. Their world suddenly fell apart and, as I feared, they were naturally very distraught. By then Rosemary was fourteen, Annie twelve and Nancy only six. They listened to David and I with disbelief, as they sobbed uncontrollably. There was nothing I could do to ease their pain or take away their hurt, it was a truly distressing experience. It seemed to me that I had caused the most unimaginable upset to the very people that were most dear to me.

'I'm only six, I'm too young for this to happen to me!' cried Nancy. Her words penetrated my heart like a sharp arrow and only compounded my already tormented feelings.

Our separation and subsequent divorce did eventually happen, but not without some very bleak times which I had to get through. Throughout this difficult time, however, my daughters' needs remained paramount and any thoughts of my shying away at this most dire time were never an option. Instead, I was forced to confront some very testing situations as our new family circumstances gradually became public. Although those times were tough, together, we did eventually come through them.

We had told the girls that David would remain in situ and I would find accommodation elsewhere ,but I waited until after the festive period before disclosing news of my new partner, Paul, to them. In the meantime I had found a house to rent, close by to the family home and moved in just before Christmas. Although their immediate reaction to the existence of a new man in my life was, as expected, not good, it was only a matter of days before both Annie and Nancy, out of sheer curiosity wanted to meet him. Rosemary on the other hand remained steadfast in her reluctance. She had clearly given some thought to the situation and explained that she realised that if I liked Paul, then she too would certainly feel the same way and that wasn't something she was ready for just yet. However, her reticence was short-lived and Paul's natural charm and easy-going nature won the girls round very quickly. His subsequent involvement in each of my daughter's lives has proved to be an extremely positive one for them all. As I witness his standing within the family and the continual fun and laughter between us, I remain convinced that I have acted in the best interests of everyone. I can only hope that they will still reflect on their childhood favourably and with affection.

I adore my children. My love, support and encouragement for them have, I hope, provided an environment where they feel safe and secure and have enabled them to develop into happy, self-assured individuals. My approach to each daughter is distinct, as I appreciate their strengths and weaknesses in seeking out their specific needs, determined to help each of them achieve their own goals and ambitions. They are healthy, attractive and bright individuals with many skills and talents between them. Their engaging manner is always guaranteed to leave others captivated and that in turn fills me with a tremendous pride.

Rosemary is diligent and hardworking with an amiable temperament. Through sheer determination she has already accomplished a great deal. Her interests are many and varied: a talented musician, she plays the piano, clarinet and violin all to a high standard and since a very young age she has continued with her ballet. At nineteen she is now committed to a career in engineering, much of which has been inspired and supported by Paul. After her initial interest in the construction industry whilst still at school, she snapped up every opportunity that Paul could provide to gain some firsthand knowledge and understanding. This even included a desire to learn bricklaying shortly before her departure with a school group on a charity mission to Tanzania. Her determination paid off, as she proudly displayed her new-found skills, much to the annoyance of her very eager but uninitiated male companions. At the school parents' evening the following month, David and I heard little about her academic ability from the teacher who had led the mission. Instead he chose to enthuse about her building expertise. I am exceedingly proud of her, as she embarks on a four-year degree course in civil engineering.

Annie, my middle daughter, is a most vivacious and extremely passionate individual. The best way to describe her is as an all action girl, who ensures that her life is full-on at all times, busy organising her social life and keeping abreast of the latest fashions and trends, sometimes at the expense of all else. She has not only a charming and endearing personality, but often one which is also quite demanding. Her occasional angry outbursts are very wearing. However, whilst they are a fault which I am very quick to deplore for the sake of all those around her, regrettably it is one that I recognise only too well in myself. Like Rosemary, she too is a very able musician, playing the piano and flute, but her great loves are skiing and scuba diving.

She has already discovered a great aptitude and love of the retail industry, which she is intending to make her career choice. Just as I had done at BHS, her goal is to work in a buying office of a major retailer. Unlike me, she has the opportunity to study at university. Her current part-time job in the local Waitrose and prior to that, two-and-a-half years voluntary work in a local charity shop will undoubtedly stand her in good stead for her forthcoming course in Business and Retail Management.

My youngest daughter, Nancy, is a sweet-natured child. Seldom cross or angry, she floats along in a somewhat innocent fashion but with a great sense of humour and insight for someone so young. At just five years of age, having completed her first year of mainstream school, she was at a loss to understand why there were so many years of school ahead of her.

'Mummy, I've learned my alphabet and I know all my numbers, so when will all my work be done?' she asked. An amusing and interesting question from someone so young.

She is demonstrating a creative flair and one that I am keen to encourage, as I ensure that she too is steered down the most appropriate path. At eleven she is still exploring a variety of interests, and is already a keen violinist. It is particularly satisfying to witness her enjoy her music with the support of Rosemary – always eager to play duets with her at every opportunity. Unfortunately an asthmatic, as well as having a nut allergy, she is not always quite as robust as her two older sisters. Nevertheless, she continues to enjoy her ballet lessons and has taken up golf.

For Rosemary and Annie, news of another sibling on its way came as quite a surprise. The considerable age gap enabled them to voice their own thoughts concerning the forthcoming arrival and they were adamant that under no circumstances could it be a brother. For them, the prospect of football posts in the back garden was out of the question. Fortunately, the scan confirmed their greatest wish.

They both embraced Nancy's arrival and for Annie in particular, there was an added excitement. Already in possession of a fine doll's buggy, her existing and most placid passengers were now redundant as she pleaded with me to allow her to trundle Nancy around the garden. Predictably, it wasn't long before Annie wanted to go further afield. Determined to walk alone pushing her buggy with her precious passenger, I watched anxiously as she bounded along the pavement to meet her daddy, walking back from the office. Needless to say, he was more than a little taken aback to discover the identity of the passenger tucked-up snugly inside. Although only six-and-a-half herself, she showed remarkable confidence with her baby sister and passing Nancy to Annie momentarily, if the need arose, soon became second nature to me. In particular, one occasion sticks in my mind, when I needed to settle the bill at the hairdressers and handed my tiny offspring to a very able Annie. This completely natural gesture caused an audible sharp intake of breath from a salon full of elderly ladies.

As I watch my daughters grow up, it has been inevitable that I have pondered on our unknown family traits. The girls' facial resemblance to me is remarkable and I never tire of hearing people remark on it.

This reassurance of a visible connection is always guaranteed to fill me with the most overwhelming joy, which few could ever really understand. Annie has a great presence, taller than either Rosemary or myself, at almost 6' and size 8 shoes. These physical characteristics stem, I am convinced, from my own heritage, rather than her father's family. It is not just Annie's physique that I have attributed to my genetics, but also my daughters' considerable musical talents are unexplained. At school, I learned the recorder and although I showed great promise, nothing was ever pursued.

David, however, was determined to convince me that our daughters' inherent talents stem from his side, and he tried to prove this by pursuing his own lifelong ambition to learn to play the piano. Unfortunately, after weeks of repeated practice, (something that he refused to condone with any of our daughters) he had to concede that maybe he did not have the musicality that he had hoped for.

Today, without any doubt, I am a far more contented and happy person. After many years of suppression, I am able to think independently and that makes me a better mother to my children. I have instilled in them the confidence to make their own decisions, whether good or bad. After encouraging both Rosemary and Annie to seek more financial independence, each of them has found a part time job locally. For Rosemary it has been during vacations and for Annie it is regular employment each Saturday. Most importantly they each found environments where their own talents have been valued and suitably rewarded. I believe it is important for them to have some financial independence and an understanding of the value of money and budgeting at an early stage. Although I have encouraged them to save a little of their income, at the same time I also persuaded them to indulge themselves. In stark contrast to much of my own life, I want them to understand how vital it is to value yourself.

I freely admit to being consumed by an unsurpassable pride in my offspring that will never diminish. My love for them and my commitment to them is unwavering, I would do anything for them. Even during the most challenging of times, as tempers flare and patience is pushed to the limit, my devotion to them is unequivocal. My daughters have given me a sense of love and connection that I had never before experienced and it was this remarkable depth of feeling which ultimately triggered a turning point in my life, sending me on a journey that would inevitably change my life forever.

16. Are You My Mother ?

Saturday, 16th December 2006

I woke early after a second restless night. Two days had now elapsed since the contact details of my birth mother, Margaret Coleman, had come into my possession and I was faced with a dilemma. Should I contact her directly or should I first visit John, a possible brother, in person and disclose everything to him? There was one thing I was very clear about and that was to remain resolute in my decision not to abide by the adoption agency's schedule. The search for my birth mother had unexpectedly revealed some findings of considerable importance, namely three brothers and under no circumstances could I be expected to wait patiently for the appropriate time to elapse.

Lying there in bed, remembering that I now had Margaret Coleman's telephone number, I was thinking just how easy it would be to pick up the phone, punch those all-important digits and in seconds speak to the one person who held the knowledge needed to explain everything to me. I was both terrified and enthralled at the idea of communicating with her. Just days earlier and unbeknown to her son John, she had chosen to send a very clear message to me: KEEP AWAY! Her decision to deny any knowledge of the very specific details of my letter left me facing the realisation that she had no desire to communicate with the daughter she had given away.

My dream of a long-awaited reunion had been destroyed.

Moreover, it appeared that Margaret had no intention of informing her sons of the existence of their additional sibling. No matter what Margaret believed, she was not the only person affected by her actions and although her reaction towards me was devastating, it would not prevent me from seeking answers to my many puzzling questions. Fighting my desire to uncover the truth against a reluctance to act too hastily, the words of the adoption support agency still rang in my ears and did little to alleviate my anger and frustration:

'You have to consider all the individuals involved, not just your birth mother.'

Their concern seemed only to refer to Margaret and those around her, with little thought given to the effect on my own family and me.

However, I now considered the most important individuals at this very unsettled time: my three daughters. Their lives had been, and continued to be, very much affected. As I struggled in vain to maintain some sort of normality and with our preparations for Christmas sidestepped, I felt compelled to focus solely on achieving my quest to locate my birth mother. Life for us was in turmoil.

The events of the last few days had been appalling. I had given Margaret every opportunity to communicate directly with me, but instead she had chosen to reject me once again. How naïve she had been. Unlike the situation in 1962, this time I had a voice and the opportunity to question and challenge her. If Margaret hadn't considered the impact this might have on her own sons, then why should I? She had knowingly left John, her eldest son totally exposed; this woman was heartless. Consumed with rage, I made my decision.

Waking Paul early on a Saturday morning in mid-December, I was resolute and utterly focused.

'Are you awake?' I asked, in a loud enough voice to stir

anyone in a deep slumber. 'We are going to John's this morning,' I announced, triumphant in my decision as I switched on my bedside light and walked around the bed to place a large mug of strong tea beside Paul.

There was a groan from beneath the duvet and he finally appeared, shielding his bleary eyes from the sudden glare of artificial light.

'What time is it?' he muttered, realising it was not yet dawn.

'5 o'clock.'

I ignored his cries of displeasure and encouraged him to regain full consciousness, as I set about explaining my well thought out plan for the day.

'How long have you been awake?' he asked.

'Oh, I don't know – ages.' Although it was still dark outside, this momentous day was well under way for me.

Paul, sensing my determination, finally relented, realising that there was no other option other than to sit up in bed, drink his tea and remind me of all the pitfalls, should I choose today to confront a totally unsuspecting man in Stanmore.

'Are you really sure it's what you want to do?' asked Paul.

'Yes I am, this whole situation is affecting me badly. I'm not sleeping and I feel so angry, I've been treated appallingly and I'm not prepared to be just brushed aside like this. How dare she behave in this way towards me? Don't you agree?' I asked, eager to seek reassurance.

'I will support you in whatever you decide to do,' he said comfortingly. Paul's unequivocal commitment towards me was a new-found experience and one from which I drew great comfort. Never before had I felt that anyone had truly ever stood by me the way that Paul has been prepared to do.

Paul agreed that we would drive to John's later that morning. Today would be life-changing. I was so optimistic that once John got over the initial shock, I would meet with a positive reaction from the man who would appear to be my brother. Filled with a heady mix of apprehension and excitement, the imminent prospect of finally disclosing my identity to him was emotionally overwhelming. My feelings had been particularly painful during the last telephone conversation with him earlier in the week, when he believed there would be no further communication between us. This morning all I could do was envisage us sitting face-to-face, as I shared my remarkable story with him.

Thinking back, Margaret and Patrick's reluctance to face the situation was what made me so mad. I had, in my opinion, handled the matter with care and sensitivity and still they behaved in this way; their lack of thought for John at this time was also quite astounding. They had absolutely no idea how I might react once John had reported their position to me and they were taking a great risk.

The girls were with David and I decided to call them and relay my plans, as we were expecting to be absent for most of the day. It was David who answered the call and on hearing my intention I detected an air of caution in his voice.

'If you have really decided to communicate with somebody today, don't you think it should be Margaret?' he asked.

'No I don't, she's had every chance, I'm absolutely furious with her behaviour towards me. I don't care who I upset now: I'm so cross! How dare she deny all knowledge of Jim Donovan and Herbert Road?' I retorted, irritated that he was trying to dissuade me from carrying out my intentions.

'If you don't care, then it makes more sense to contact her, she is the one that you're angry with and the one whom you want to contact most of all. You have a lot of unanswered questions,' he added.

'I don't know, I'll think about it,' I said begrudgingly, annoyed at the prospect of reconsidering my entire day.

After ending the call, I discussed David's view with Paul. I was in turmoil, full of rage and at a loss to know where to direct my venomous feelings. Should I communicate directly with Margaret rather than John? David was right, I had nothing to lose. Perhaps she was expecting a telephone call from me? After all, John had told her that I had her number.

The day had started extremely early and despite much deliberating and discussion it was still only 8.00 am. Reluctantly, the idea of going to John's was shelved, but if I were to telephone Margaret I would have to wait a little longer. Paul and I sat patiently as we watched the hands on the clock slowly making their way beyond 9.00 am. Paul decided it would be wise for him to make the initial contact, I agreed.

My heart was racing as we sat together in the study and I watched him carefully dial the international number.

I felt sick, my stomach was churning and although my skin was clammy, I felt very cold and rather shaky but there was no turning back.

'Hello,' said a brusque sounding woman with a very strong Irish accent.

'Hello, is that Margaret Mary Coleman, formerly Hennessy?' asked Paul.

'Yes,' she replied, guardedly.

'Hello, my name is Paul Southon and I am calling you on behalf of a third party. I would like to ask you a few questions.'

'Yes, OK,' she said.

'Did you live at 13 Herbert Road, Ilford, in March 1962?'

'No, I lived in Ilford, but not Herbert Road,' she said evasively. Paul hesitated as he considered his response to her obvious untruth. He knew that through John, Margaret had already received warning of this impending communication, thereby giving her the opportunity to prepare herself.

'But I think we both know that you did,' he said pointedly. Despite her instant denial we knew that we had the right person.

There was no response.

'I am calling on behalf of Karen Brazel. She was born on 23rd March 1962 in St Margaret's nursing home, Hackney. I believe that you know whom I'm referring to, she's sitting here beside me now,' he said calmly. There was a pause as Margaret realised the caller could not be deterred.

'She shouldn't be contacting me like this,' she barked, confirming her identity.

'Karen needs to talk to you, preferably in person. She's prepared to fly over to Ireland and meet you,' Paul explained.

'No, no, I'll talk to her now,' she insisted.

'Would you prefer me to call you back in, let's say an hour, to give you some time to gather your thoughts before you talk to Karen?' Paul asked considerately.

'No, I'll talk to her now,' she said quickly, as if she had every intention of concluding this most intrusive matter at the first opportunity.

'Are you sure you wouldn't like a bit of time?' he emphasised, giving her a final chance to reconsider.

'No, if she's there, I'll speak to her now.'

Paul held out his arm to hand me the telephone. About to hear the voice of my birth mother for the very first time, I braced myself, sensing this was going to be hellish. My entire body flooded with emotion, as the tears welled up in my eyes and my entire body trembled. I tried to take a deep breath but all I could muster was a short laboured intake of air.

'Hello, Margaret,' I said, my voice wavering.

'Hello,' she said sternly. I was met with a harsh gravelly voice, evident from a lifetime of smoking. Her brusque response confirmed there would certainly be no rapturous reunion. Immediately, any intention I had to quiz her and obtain answers to my inexplicable findings suddenly diminished. Her obvious animosity towards me left me struggling to think, speak and even breathe. My total inability to communicate at that moment gave Margaret the opportunity to seize control of the call.

'Can I say that I am very annoyed that you have telephoned me? You had no right to contact me in this way. I thought the social services dealt with this sort of thing,' she said vehemently.

'No, I had to search myself,' I explained, remembering some of the difficulties I'd faced during the past year. She had obviously been expecting a call from a third party and clearly had every intention of denying all knowledge of me.

'Well, I am very cross about this,' she stressed again. 'And, you had no business to contact John. We've hardly slept since he called us with news of your letter, asking us questions,' she continued furiously. As I had expected, the inquiry from John had left her in no doubt who was attempting to make contact.

'Have you told him anything?' she asked angrily.

'No Margaret, I haven't. I've spoken to him a couple of times but I have not told him who I am,' I reassured her. I clung on to the hope that with each sentence we exchanged there might be signs of mellowing from her. I desperately wanted her to realise that I was simply someone that needed and deserved answers to a situation that had bewildered me.

'You shouldn't have involved John, he is coming over in a few days for Christmas, he might start asking us more questions now,' she said fuming.

'I haven't told him anything.' I stressed again. I was irritated by her insinuation that I was the sole cause of this dire situation that she had found herself in.

'But Margaret, it was always going to be John that I would make contact with first, because he is in this country,' I explained.

'Paddy and I are furious, we're very upset about this, he's got heart trouble you know and this worry has done him no good whatsoever,' she continued, still only referring to the effect this had had on them both.

'Why are you ringing me and what do you want?' she asked angrily. I looked down through the tears at the many documents and scribbled notes spread across the desk in front of me.

'I have a number of questions to ask you, I have information that I just don't understand.'

'OK, go ahead,' she said in a cavalier fashion, as if ready to deflect each of my anomalies one by one. I had one very crucial question to ask her before any other and I didn't know how she would respond.

'Margaret, are you my mother?' There was a brief pause.

'Yes of course,' she snapped, but with so much conflicting information, I was intent on pressing her further. There was certainly no warmth and without the opportunity to see a reaction from her, I needed further reassurance.

'It's not Catherine, then?' I enquired gingerly.

'No,' she said firmly. 'What's Catherine got to do with any of this? Leave her out of it,' she said furiously. Margaret was incensed. Shocked that I should even have knowledge of her family members, it was difficult to gauge a true reaction to my enquiries.

'Catherine's not well, she was involved in a fire a few years ago and she's never fully recovered. I don't want you contacting her. Do you understand? She's got nothing to do with this.' Despite her insistence that Catherine had no connection with my adoption, I was determined to challenge her further. I talked of my meeting with Jim Donovan and how he had spoken so very fondly of Margaret and recalled how helpful she was towards his wife and young family, but how he had stressed having absolutely no recollection of her being pregnant during the time with them.

'It all happened a long time ago,' she insisted, avoiding my question. 'Now let me tell you, I've watched a lot of programmes about adoption and seen how people go in search of their families

153

and nothing good ever comes of it. When I signed you off, you weren't supposed to come back!' Her venomous response hurt me immensely and provoked feelings of complete worthlessness. She displayed no maternal instinct towards me and although the call had been at my instigation, I was unprepared for the consequences. The tears had been trickling down my face throughout the call but her spiteful outburst made it impossible for me to contain my feelings any longer. I broke down. Margaret intervened.

'Have you had a good life?' she asked curtly. I had no intention of relaying to her the brief, positive response that she was hoping for and thereby easing her conscience.

'Well, not entirely,' I snivelled. 'It's not been easy.' It was hard to speak, I felt desperate. The woman who at last admitted to having brought me into the world had every intention of ensuring that I regretted ever searching for her and the answers to my mysterious beginning.

I wondered if, throughout the last forty-four years she had ever given a thought to me, as I had done her? Was she ever curious as to my whereabouts, my health, my appearance or what I'd become? Now all she could do was reprimand me for even considering making contact with her. She was keen to tell me how her life had been affected since hearing news of my letter through John but what of me, and my life as an adopted person?

Any idea of challenging her over the various documents that lay before me was slipping away. Trying to convince her that I needed to understand was a thankless task. I got nowhere. Her only concern was for herself. All I had found was an angry, frightened woman full of threats and abuse. In a final attempt to appeal to her I brought up the subject of my three daughters, her granddaughters, giving her their names and ages one by one. There was little reaction.

I asked about her sons and their families. She confirmed my findings: there were only three. Michael was the only son with children, a son and daughter age eight and ten but she chose not to elaborate.

'Stop crying,' she said impatiently. 'You have got to understand that this has been quite a shock for us. Do you want to call me back later in the week?' she asked. It was a surprising gesture considering her manner towards me.

'Thank you, Margaret, yes I will.' I said, relieved at the opportunity to talk to her again under perhaps less traumatic circumstances.

'No, on second thoughts, you'd better leave it until the New Year. I have the family coming next week for Christmas, I don't want you ringing then.' She was of course referring to my family.

'Perhaps we could think about arranging something. Maybe we could meet you in the summer,' she said rather surprisingly. The suggestion was most unexpected. I could hardly believe what I was hearing. Furthermore, it hadn't escaped me that she had been referring to both her and Patrick throughout our conversation. I was perplexed.

'You must never come to Thomastown,' she insisted. 'But perhaps we could meet you somewhere else.'

'Yes please,' I whimpered.

'This whole business has upset Paddy terribly,' she stressed, keen to reiterate just how much trouble I'd caused.

'I'm sorry.'

'It's Christmas, it's a very bad time to cause all this upset,' she continued. I didn't respond. I was slumped over the desk with my head in my hand weeping. I was mentally exhausted and at a loss to know what to say. There was an uncomfortable silence.

'So you'll leave it until after the New Year to ring and we'll talk again,' she said eager to seek reassurance from me that I wouldn't act impulsively and thereby cause her any further disturbance. I agreed to her plans.

'Like I said, maybe we could think about meeting you, perhaps in the spring?' The idea of a meeting had suddenly moved forward from the summer to the spring. Perhaps curiosity was finally getting the better of her.

'I've got to go now, I have to go to Kilkenny, shopping,' she explained, keen to force an end to this uncomfortable association.

'OK, Margaret, goodbye,' I said, also relieved that this ordeal was about to end.

'Goodbye and God bless you,' she said before placing the receiver down and ending the call.

Completely drained and desperately emotional, I somehow found the energy to write a brief note to Margaret, determined to build on the shaky beginning of our first conversation. I thanked her for talking to me, acknowledging the difficulty for us both and took the opportunity to enclose a recent school photo of Nancy, age seven, in the hope of it appealing to a cold, frosty, grandmother. I said I looked forward to speaking to her again in the new year and included my home address and phone number.

I sat quietly for the rest of the day contemplating the morning's events. Although I was saddened by her manner towards me, I remained satisfied that I had made the right decision in contacting her today. I was now a step nearer to finding the answers I so desperately needed. My next call to Margaret would be different. After the initial shock of talking to my birth mother and aware of her reaction to me, I was determined that any subsequent conversation in the new year would be at a time when I felt able to withstand her wrath.

It was early evening on January 2nd 2007 and our house was full of visitors celebrating Annie's fourteenth birthday the following day. When the telephone rang on the dot of 6 pm I broke away from the party to answer what was to be a very unexpected call.

'Hello, is that Karen?' said a harsh sounding Irish voice that I had heard once before. I was totally unprepared for this call. It had been left that I would telephone well after the festive season had ended.

'Err, yes, hello, Margaret, . . . Happy New Year to you.'

'Well, how are you?' she barked, although perhaps not quite as ferociously as the previous call. I closed the door of the study. I didn't want to alert my guests to the nature of this call.

'Margaret, I've got a house full of visitors at the moment, they're leaving shortly, they've been here celebrating Annie's birthday tomorrow. Can I call you back once they've all left?

'Yes, OK, I'll wait to hear from you,' she said. Her manner was surprising, almost as if our communications were a regular occurrence. Once all our guests had departed I was eager to return Margaret's call and discover her reasons for telephoning me. Surely it could only be a good sign.

'Hello, Margaret, it's Karen.'

'Well, how are you?' she asked again. 'Did you have a nice Christmas?'

'Yes thank you, how about you?' I asked, perhaps not quite the best question to put to her. I was at a loss to know quite what to say to this somewhat mellower sounding woman.

'Not really, I've lost weight, people have started to notice and Paddy's not been feeling too good either, it's all this worry you know.' Still she was intent on ensuring I took full responsibility for this massive disruption to their lives.

'I'm sorry to hear that Margaret,' I said half-heartedly.

'You have to understand, to have this news out of the blue has been very difficult for us,' she explained. Feeling little sympathy,

157

I turned the conversation to a more light-hearted note and told her briefly of the events surrounding Annie's birthday celebrations. She listened intently and to my utter amazement suddenly asked if I would like to speak to Paddy. It struck me as a strange request as I wasn't entirely convinced that Paddy was my birth father. So confusing was the information surrounding my adoption that nothing appeared to be what it seemed. I also didn't want to subject myself to any unpleasant retaliation from him also. After being informed of Paddy's poor health due to my actions, I declined the offer, insisting that I had no intention of making Paddy's condition any worse.

'No, no, he'll be fine, here he is,' she said adamantly, passing the receiver to her husband before I had a chance to respond. Why was she so keen for us to speak to each other? Totally bemused by the whole event I prepared myself for the unknown. He obviously knew of my existence, but to what extent?

'Hello,' muttered a quietly spoken Irish man. There was a pause; I sensed he was waiting for me to instigate the conversation.

'Hello, Patrick, Happy New Year to you. I'm sorry to hear that you've had a difficult Christmas and that you have been feeling unwell. It was never my intention to cause you such upset and difficulty,' I explained.

'Me ... no ... I'm all right,' he said in a carefree, throwaway fashion as if this whole business was no more than a storm in a teacup. His reaction surprised me. I warmed to this man immediately.

'How are you, have you and the girls had a good Christmas?' he enquired. Obviously nervous himself, he was polite and gentle. Unlike Margaret he had no intention of challenging or reprimanding me.

'Yes we have, thank you,' I replied. There was another pause. I was tense but keen to appear pleasant and communicative. I sensed he was not a great conversationalist but I wanted to try and allay any fears and concerns that would have arisen since my initial contact with them. They had obviously thought of little else over Christmas and had been curious enough to make the next move.

I talked to Patrick about my three daughters, describing their musical abilities and taking the opportunity to enquire of any musical background in the Coleman family. He listened carefully and was clearly impressed by their skills, but was unaware of any musical genes in any past generations.

'Well, Karen, we'll speak again, I'll hand you back to Margaret, here she is, look after yourself, goodbye.'

Margaret spoke immediately. 'Paddy and I think that we'll meet you in April, can you come to Dublin?'

'Yes certainly,' I said. April seemed a long way off but I was delighted that they had instigated a meeting. I would just have to be patient.

'You can't come here to Thomastown, but we can travel to Dublin on the bus and meet you somewhere there. We'll speak again,' she said.

'Thank you for ringing me, Margaret,' I stressed.

'God bless you,' she said, before ending the call.

Paul returned shortly after and I was keen to report the surprising event to him.

'You do realise that she's thought of nothing else for the entire Christmas, she has been dying to call you and hear your voice again, she couldn't resist it,' he said smiling knowingly at me.

From that point on, calls from Margaret, whilst regular, became erratic in their content. Having decided they would meet me in Dublin in April it wasn't long before the whole idea had been abandoned.

'I've lost even more weight and I've had to buy smaller clothes,' Margaret reported. 'I really don't have that much to lose. Paddy says that we won't plan any meeting at the moment, not until I've gained a bit of weight. The worry has been too much. We'll keep in touch and arrange something sometime,' she explained. Building up my hopes of a chance to meet them, only for it to be deferred indefinitely was exasperating. All I could do was wait patiently for an update on her wellbeing. I desperately wanted her to fix a date. I was keen to book the flights and finally determine a day, a day that I had thought about for much of my life, the prospect of finally coming face-to-face with my birth mother.

In the hope of building some sort of relationship with her during the calls that followed, I took the opportunity to enquire after various family traits within the Coleman and Hennessy families. First and foremost I was keen to know with whom in the family I shared my left-handedness.

'No, I can't think of anyone. I'm just trying to remember if anyone in Paddy's family might be, but no there aren't any,' she said. Interestingly she had made reference to my relationship to Paddy, I was starting to believe that he must be my father. Despite no left-handed person in the family, I struck lucky with my bunions. They had caused me severe discomfort most of my life, leaving me destined to a life of 'sensible' footwear. I discovered that I had Margaret to thank for this hereditary condition. Another interesting fact was her need to visit the hairdressers religiously every five weeks; this was indeed an identical schedule to my own. After a lifetime apart it was intriguing to learn just a little about her. She questioned me relentlessly wanting to know more of my personal circumstances concerning Paul and David, but what interested her most was the size of my house. How many reception rooms were there? How many bedrooms? Was it detached? I had made her aware that our home was under major refurbishment, which provoked her into sharing news of her own home improvements in readiness for a planned family gathering later in the year.

160

During this time I gained just a little more insight into the lives of my three brothers and, although they were unaware of my existence, they remained very much in my thoughts. John had no children and was married to Helen. I would later discover that the mysterious Lisa Murphy listed on the electoral roll, was Helen's sister who had lived with them both for just a short time.

Michael and his wife Helena lived in Ireland with their two children. Oliver was unmarried and lived with Margaret and Paddy.

Eventually, to my relief, they finally relented and came round to the idea of a meeting. The date was set for Saturday 28th April, at Bewley's Hotel, Dublin Airport, at 12.30pm. I booked the flights immediately.

On the afternoon of 21st March the telephone rang. Yet another call from Margaret. On this occasion Nancy was sitting beside me as she had just broken up for the Easter holidays. As I exchanged pleasantries with Margaret including news of our imminent holiday to the Far East, Nancy was signalling to me an urgent request to speak to this new-found granny and hear her voice for herself. I asked Margaret if she was happy to talk to Nancy and to my surprise she agreed. I passed the phone to the eager little person beside me. As they talked it was clear that Nancy was struggling to understand the unfamiliar accent.

'Pardon,' said Nancy at regular intervals. After a brief and laboured exchange, Nancy said her goodbyes and passed the phone back to me. With disappointment I noted that having conversed for the first time with her youngest grandchild there was no enthusing response. Bringing the call to an end, she surprised me by insisting that I call her on our return from holiday to report our safe arrival home.

Throughout the call, something else had been preying on my mind. In two days it would be my forty-fifth birthday, surely she would know that and couldn't let it pass without comment? After three months of regular contact it would have meant everything to me if she could have acknowledged it. Sadly it went unmentioned. It was a crushing blow.

17. Paul

Paul's support for me throughout the year-long search for my birth mother was unequivocal and it was no coincidence that my decision to have a second shot at tracing Margaret Coleman coincided with the start of our new relationship together.

I had first met Paul many years earlier in November 1993. A fabulous, once-in-a-lifetime, opportunity had arisen for David and me to have our own house built in Sevenoaks, close to both the town centre and David's office. Paul was chosen as site manager and was to oversee the project.

Much had changed in my life since leaving my high-flying job in the world of retail three years previously and my role was now that of housewife and devoted mother to our two young daughters. However, sadly I was also having to cope with many underlying difficulties.

David and I had been living in a rented property since selling our own home almost a year earlier in mid-January, just two weeks after the birth of our second daughter Annie. This move was only ever seen as a short-term arrangement while we searched for a new place big enough for our growing family. The decision to build our own house was not part of the original plan and meant we had to spend a second winter in what was really entirely unsuitable accommodation. The terraced house was significantly smaller than our previous home and even though it had at some point been extended to the front and rear, it created an oppressive, dark, tunnel-like space. Even on the brightest of days it was necessary for the lights to remain on throughout the day. An infestation of earwigs in the bathroom did nothing to improve our situation.

Bound by my husband's strict financial regime and with very little support from family and friends, I had become lonely and isolated. There was never any time out and my only respite from the daily routine was the regular weekly visits to the group of mothers with babies of a similar age.

David's reluctance to take any time away from the office, other than for scheduled holidays, meant he spent very little time in this tiny, dreary property, where I felt cooped up and almost trapped with two small children. He didn't sympathise with my need to get out and away and, ironically, the only holiday we did take together during the entire eighteen-month period was one-week's self-catering in the UK. And this in the middle of winter! It was doomed to failure from the outset.

Feeling miserable, lonely and lacking any support, my earlier attempt to trace my birth family had been firmly spurned and quashed. David could not understand why I should want to do such a thing. There was no alternative but to succumb to the continued drudgery. However, things were about to change. I saw the prospect of building our own home as an opportunity to revitalize my life and relieve me from the monotony and boredom. Here was a project to give me a focus away from my world of children and household chores.

The first meeting with Paul was encouraging. His extensive knowledge of the building industry was reassuring, the almost daily discussions to finalise specifications and the schedule of work for this project was exciting.

No sooner was our exciting project under way, however, than I realised building our own home with two infants in tow would prove problematic. Left to deal with numerous day-to-day matters, my tasks would have been unmanageable without Paul's caring and understanding nature. Battling to have a conversation with an array of trades people and needing to make so many important decisions, all the while coping with the demands of my daughters, was impossible. Paul's often practical offers of help were always much appreciated. Whether it was distracting the girls with a picture book or offering to collect samples of materials, thereby saving me fractious visits to builders merchants 'en famille', it was all extremely welcome. It was also a new experience for me. In fact a revelation of sorts, as nobody had ever shown me such consideration before.

This tall, dark haired, attractive man in his mid-thirties with appealing hazel eyes made a lasting impression on me. In fact, I had warmed to him instantly. He had a friendly, engaging manner and most of all, he made me laugh. His empathy and kindness was captivating and very soon I found myself looking forward to seeing him; he had quickly become a true lifeline. With him around to support me and bring some fun into my life, it meant that the pressures of my day-to-day grind could be temporarily forgotten.

Not only were my days relentless but also the evenings were fully occupied too. After preparing and cooking the evening meal and with the children in bed, I utilized my skills as a seamstress to produce all the curtains we would need for our new home. Keeping our rented home running whilst building another, and with two infants to manage, stretched me to the limit.

Our new family home was finally completed in the summer of 1994. By this time Paul had become a very valued friend and the fear of losing someone so crucial to my life was unthinkable. It seemed he felt the same way and needed little encouragement to continue calling by occasionally. Invariably there was the odd outstanding repair or modification to be seen to and he was always happy to oblige. On one occasion this even extended to the assembly of a Barbie horse-drawn carriage that Rosemary had acquired as a recent birthday present.

The friendship continued until the end of 1995 when I finally found the courage to confess to Paul how I felt about him.

Our affair spanned exactly one year. I truly loved Paul. He was so different from my husband. From a large working class family of ten children – six sisters and three brothers – he had, like me, grown up on a council estate. Although he passed his eleven plus exam, unfortunately for him, his twin brother did not. Faced with having to buy an expensive uniform, and having their two sons at separate schools, his parents made the decision to send them both to the local secondary modern school. Paul left school at fifteen without taking his O levels, gaining an apprenticeship as an electrician, working at the Chatham dockyard re-fitting nuclear submarines. Later he changed to working in the house building industry and rapidly set about understanding and learning the many other trades associated with construction. He was however, a married man with two children of his own.

The more I learned about Paul, the more special he became. Not only was he amusing and caring, but he was also a good listener and although I didn't fully appreciate it at the time, he had a great understanding of, and insight into people. He had a good grasp of my own, very complex, personal situation. Even at that time he stressed the importance of delving into my true family heritage. Although I was immensely happy with Paul, I was also plagued with guilt and worry for what lay ahead. As 1996 drew to an end, I was in turmoil. Paul pleaded with me to leave David, but for me this was just inconceivable. Never could my own daughters be subjected to the trauma of a broken home. They were safely cocooned in a life that I had ensured was a million miles from my own upbringing. I had no intention of turning their world upside down, they meant everything to me, I had to put them first.

So, after much anguish and in complete despair, I eventually confessed to David the events of the previous year. He was devastated. Unable to explain my actions at that time, neither to David nor to myself, I assumed the position of the guilty party. There was no alternative but to end my relationship with Paul and to do my utmost to rescue my marriage and focus once again on my family. Paul's sadness at my decision was evident. I pleaded with him not to contact me, to which he reluctantly agreed and after reminding me that he would always be there for me, we parted.

Many years later, in 2004, during one of my regular sessions with Maggie, she raised the subject of Paul. It was totally unexpected. I had mentioned him only once before. I had been so keen to receive help in

166

making sense of my very troubled life, that during my first session the previous year, I had blurted out everything. I had no intention of keeping anything from Maggie.

'You mentioned in one of your very early sessions, your affair with Paul,' she said, carefully introducing this highly sensitive subject. 'You haven't spoken about him since and I wondered if you would like the opportunity to talk about it a little more?' she asked.

Flooded by an immediate rush of emotion, I was reminded of the man that made me feel so loved and very happy and yet I felt so sad. He had remained locked away at the very back of my mind and now just the mention of him brought back overwhelming feelings of grief for what I'd lost. It was heart-rending. It was here after more than seven years and within Maggie's safe confines, where I began to explore my feelings for the man that had made such an impact on my life.

'In your mind you have never really ended this relationship,' she explained. 'It is still very much alive. You have held onto him. For you time has stood still and you haven't moved on. It's important that you find closure and we need to think about this together,' she added. I sat bewildered. My head hurt and my heart ached. The fragile veneer that I'd created had crumbled, leaving me with unbearable feelings of sadness and loss. She was right, I realised that my feelings for Paul were as strong as ever.

'It's been a long time, his life could be very different now, you have no idea,' explained Maggie gently.

'But I know he's waiting for me,' I said with total assurance.

'How do you know this?' she asked.

'I just do,' I replied with certainty, remembering the intensity of our relationship and his parting words. Maggie reiterated just how much time had gone by, but despite this I knew differently somehow.

Over the weeks that followed it became easier to discuss Paul in my sessions with Maggie. After the initial outburst of emotion, I could explore the reasons that brought Paul and me together and exactly what he meant to me. I was beginning to have an understanding of the cause for my feelings of unhappiness and worthlessness. I had hit upon a fundamental problem in my life. My marriage was a mess. To the outside world it appeared perfect, too perfect, but in reality I was at rock bottom. The man I had been married to for over nineteen years could never make me happy and eventually, after months of deliberation, I made the life-changing decision to call Paul.

Although a little guarded, his response was extremely positive and our first reunion after almost eight years was arranged. That morning at school it was almost unbearable as I watched the minutes and hours tick slowly by until eventually it reached 1pm. The short drive to the lunch date was so exciting, knowing we were just moments away from each other. Seeing him again, even after so many years, was wonderful. It felt so right. There was some inevitable catching up to be done. I had given birth to a third daughter, Nancy, and Paul had been promoted and was progressing within the construction industry. After some intense studying he had become a member of the Chartered Institute of Building. I was delighted for him.

We were both left in no doubt about how we still felt about each other. I knew that I could only ever be truly happy with Paul. I realised now that staying in a loveless marriage was ultimately not the best environment for my daughters. So I finally made the life-changing decision to end my marriage. In November 2005 Paul left his wife and David and I finally parted. Although for me there was no acrimony, David was at pains to point out that Paul had no interest in our three daughters and that their lives would be compromised as a result of my actions, but he couldn't have been more wrong.

In just a short time the girls were very comfortable in Paul's company and had grown extremely fond of him. Sadly, his own grown-up son and daughter had chosen to stand by their mother, and his relationship with them, was all but non-existent. However, my daughters had discovered a man very different to their own father and with those same qualities I had found so attractive many years earlier. He has wit, wisdom and patience. He is immensely generous both with his time and his money,

168

what little he has, and possesses a wealth of highly practical skills. Paul was equally overwhelmed by my daughters' response towards him and after a successful week's holiday together in Center Parcs, he made the decision to relinquish his one bedroom flat and move into our rented house. As I have watched the relationship between them all develop, it is evident that Paul treats my daughters as his own and I know that there isn't anything he wouldn't do for them. In fact, his utter devotion to them never fails to astound me. Long ago I was drawn to a man who was sensitive and kind, and in my heart I was in no doubt that Paul's love and consideration for me would extend to each of my daughters. He has become central to their lives too.

Paul's suggestion to introduce a pet into my daughters' lives proved most canny. The concept of a house rabbit was something that initially I found difficult to grasp, but Paul had past experience of such creatures and after some convincing, a dear little bunny was purchased. It was to be an overwhelming success on many levels.

Mr Bunny was a beautiful, dark grey, lop-eared rabbit but that was not how his life began. Born on Christmas Eve, give or take, we collected this tiny animal in early February, confidently informed it was a female of the species. Holly was to be its name. Unfortunately it wasn't long before the vet informed us all that it wasn't a Holly but a Wally. Unable to agree on a suitable name for our new addition to the family, the term Bunny was soon given some suitable reverence and so he became Mr Bunny.

Mr Bunny had some difficulty behaving like a rabbit, preferring instead to conduct himself more like a cat or a dog. Given the run of the whole house and – to my surprise – reliably using a litter tray, he soon became a very important member of the family. Whether stretched out in front of the television, sleeping each evening under our bed or eagerly following Paul throughout the entire refurbishment programme of our new home, he never missed a thing. A stickler for routine and order, he could be relied upon to point out anything out of the ordinary. He would never go to bed until each of my daughters was safely in theirs with their lights off. On one occasion he refused to settle. The sound of a restless rabbit pacing around the bedroom floor was not conducive to a peaceful night's sleep. I got out of bed and turned on the light. He was anxious for me to follow him downstairs, where, to my surprise, I discovered that one of the lamps in the lounge had been left on. Once sure that all was well, Mr Bunny and I could settle back down.

Sadly Mr Bunny's life was short lived. At three-and-a-half years old he was diagnosed with an inoperable tumour, but fond memories of him remain with all of us. Unwittingly Mr Bunny played a tremendously important role in our family. He brought focus, comfort and joy at a most difficult and highly transitional time in my daughters' lives. And amazing as it may sound, the shared interest that Mr Bunny created amongst the girls also played a part in smoothing the way for David's integration into the new family unit. One day, soon after Mr Bunny's arrival, David accepted an invitation to visit my rented home, ostensibly to meet our remarkable pet, but with Paul also present it was to be their first meeting for many years. As time has passed, David has established his own relationship with Paul and this almost unthinkable development has indeed reduced many of the inevitable traumas associated with separation and divorce.

Paul, with a little help from Mr Bunny, has helped transform my life. I am undoubtedly far happier and more content. As I continue to discover more about my birth mother and her family it is in the safe knowledge that Paul will be with me every step of the way.

18. Pooling our Resources

I'd begun married life determined to create a home and a lifestyle very different to anything that I'd experienced before. Unfortunately, and with the benefit of hindsight, I can now see that from the outset, my preconceived ideas only served to compound a fundamental flaw in my relationship with David.

David and I met at Peggy Spencer's Dance School in Penge, South East London.

At the time he was living in Bromley with his parents, and having finished Law School was about to begin his articles with a law firm in Sevenoaks. I had spotted an advert in the local paper encouraging newcomers of all ages to consider ballroom dancing and didn't think twice. I'd enjoyed dancing with a passion as a child and this was too good an opportunity to miss. Most of the other dancers were considerably older than me and so it was inevitable that David and I would become regular partners. He was a tall, slim, shy, quietly spoken, intelligent man and after eighteen months of dancing together and getting to know each other, we started dating. Two years later, on my twenty-third birthday we were engaged, followed by our wedding on the 19th October 1985.

David's family had been very warm and welcoming towards me and genuinely delighted by our marriage, which helped to ease my feelings of self-consciousness in surroundings so unlike anything I had previously encountered. His father was the finance director of a leading pharmaceutical company and his mother a housewife. Both David and his brother had benefited from a very different childhood to my own, including a private education followed by university. Despite these differences in background, I very quickly established a good relationship with them all, particularly David's mother Gill. With just two sons and a love of shopping and all things girly, she was delighted to suddenly have a new companion.

After returning from our honeymoon, we moved into our well-appointed and spacious two bedroom flat in a leafy avenue in Beckenham, Kent. Owning our own property was just one of the many significant changes to my life at that time. I'd entered the marriage with no savings, just a lingering Barclaycard debt. Being freed from the financial burden that had dogged me whilst living at home was a tremendous relief. David and I also had the joy of furnishing our home in a way that would have been unthinkable within my own family – lined curtains, fluffy towels, matching linen and china. A holiday abroad was to be a regular occurrence. However, it was the calm, peaceful environment that I instantly welcomed and which provided such a stark contrast to my former life.

At this time I was also excelling in my career at BHS, my highly demanding job often meant 12–14 hour days. Despite this, once at home I would assume the role of all things domestic, compelled to maintain the standards that I believed were necessary to create the perfect home life. Initially, my own domestic skills were very limited, but I wasted no time making sure they reached a high standard.

Towards the end of our honeymoon, I was beginning to feel daunted by the prospect of a mountain of laundry and using an unfamiliar washing machine for the first time. However, sensing the domestic side of running a home was of little interest to David, I found solace with a kind, understanding middle-aged woman sitting around the pool and I shared my anxiety with her. Such was my eagerness to get things right, that after arriving home in the small hours and with her reassuring words still ringing in my ears, I woke early to sit quietly reading the instruction manual while David slept soundly.

David managed all things financial. Initially his controlling financial influence had been a lifeline but it soon became extremely suffocating. Although my job required a high level of numeracy, I knew absolutely nothing about mortgages, interest rates, investments or pensions. My new husband came to the marriage armed with a cashbook, a practice instilled in him by his father. It would become a symbol of our marriage, something I grew to hate intensely.

My instructions were to present every cheque stub and debit slip to David, so that he could log and monitor outgoings. Nothing was allowed to slip through his system. Under his meticulous regime my sizeable earnings were paid directly into our joint bank account, to which I had only a limited access, namely for paying supermarket bills. David would then organise a modest sum of money to be paid into a separate account for my sole use, convinced the amount would easily satisfy my needs. My limited purchases needed to be carefully considered, to match David's idea of a wife's spending allowance. The enjoyment of a shopping trip, impulsive or otherwise, was out of the question. David's mother would often buy me various items of clothing and I came to rely on her generosity.

Inevitably, David's frugal ways would have a seriously detrimental effect on our marriage. As well as restricting my use of the joint bank account, he would monitor the length of my outgoing telephone calls, tapping his wristwatch and waving his hand around in a circular motion, as if to wind up the conversation, which was highly infuriating. A tentative request for a video recorder, to prevent me missing favourite television programmes due to my long hours of work was rejected.

'No no, we can't do that, it would mean buying a new television,' he explained.

He was referring to the ancient, wooden cased television set that his parents had donated. He had not planned to purchase a new TV and his solution to my dilemma was to recount the content of any programme to me on my return, while I busied myself preparing our evening meal!

David was always more than happy to justify 'his system'. He had the education and the training and could make a point and defend an opinion in an intelligent and articulate manner, all without raising his voice or a cross word being used.

Unfortunately, I remained compliant and allowed major issues to remain unchallenged, whilst continuing to provide a comfortable and welcoming environment. I performed my household duties admirably, even after an exhausting long day at work and David was naturally happy to maintain the status quo. During the early years of our marriage the idea of any paid help in the home was never an option. Not only did I feel I had something to prove, but more importantly, I had only recently come from that strata of society which did not hire but actually provided cleaners and domestic staff. Looking back now, I can clearly see that my actions only served to exacerbate what was for me an unfair situation.

However, I certainly had no misgivings in leaving David to do the washing-up each evening, even though the process could be highly tedious. Adamant that he'd complete the task in his own time, invariably it would be tackled late into the night. Amongst David's own family, his lack of domestic skills was openly acknowledged and when we finally moved from our second floor flat to a detached house, David's mother immediately came to his rescue and provided a dishwasher. Tormented to hear of comments from our neighbours regarding David's late-night washing-up activities in front of the kitchen window, proved too much for his mother. The thought of her son toiling away at domestic work was unthinkable.

Throughout his life David's mother had provided admirably for him and even whilst at university he managed to remain in halls for the entire duration. Indeed, during his time at Law School in Guildford he found an eccentric, single, middle-aged woman happy to dote on a handful of needy students. Unlike his mother, I had a demanding full-time career. Each weekend became a marathon, as I raced singlehandedly to complete a never-ending list of chores. There was very little time for me to relax or take time out, whilst for David, most Sunday mornings meant a game or two of tennis with his father, weather permitting.

Even when expecting our first child and still working long hours, there was no suggestion that I should reduce any of my duties. Late one evening, leaning over the sink, struggling to peel potatoes and feeling weary and exhausted, I expressed my concerns to David.

'Oh dear,' he said sympathetically, leaving the room only to return with a dining chair. 'There you are, sit on that,' he insisted, as he placed the chair close to the sink to enable me to continue preparing the supper. This 'caring' approach remained unchanged throughout each of my pregnancies. The prospect of David ever providing me with any real help or support had become a real bone of contention. Any suggestion from me would invariably guarantee a mock-weary reaction, as he sighed and raised his eyes to the ceiling.

David's hold on all aspects of our finances continued to dominate our relationship and any thought of frittering away or possibly wasting money was not to be contemplated. He needed to have every piece of expenditure accounted for and justified. His strict regime made little allowance for fun, treats, luxuries, or any spontaneity. Saddest of all, for me there were never any lavish gifts, as all Christmas and birthday presents had to be practical. Seldom were there ever any surprises.

After my year-long relationship with Paul came to an end, David arranged for some Relate counselling for us both. Despite the regular, weekly sessions lasting for more than a year, I believed the counsellor lacked the necessary expertise to address the many underlying issues, which remained unresolved. I was vulnerable and racked with guilt, while David remained sanctimonious throughout. With much use of the word 'empathy', by the counsellor, I was encouraged to change my approach towards David, in an effort to rekindle our relationship. David, however, made no effort to change his dictatorial and complacent ways.

As the counselling came to its unsatisfactory end, I took the part-time job at my daughters' prep school and eighteen months later our third daughter Nancy, was born. Our marriage remained seriously flawed and, in fact, David's vice-like grip on our joint finances had actually tightened. Although I continued to work, my extremely modest salary was not entirely my own. By now I did have some established help in the home, but it was me who had to fund this out of my meagre income. In addition to this, I made a monthly contribution towards the family holiday fund, thus ensuring that I paid my own way towards any holiday. Once again, despite working part-time as well as running the family home and looking after David and the children, things were much like the arrangement early in my marriage. I was left with very little to meet all my own personal needs.

I never knew exactly what David's income was and only after our divorce proceedings were under way did I discover an accurate picture of his earnings. I was astounded. In sheer disbelief I called into question his reasons for putting me under such a financial strain. As always, I received a calm and measured response.

'We were simply pooling our resources,' he explained.

Raising a family and running a home as well as a job, without the full support of my husband, left me feeling used and unappreciated. Within the marriage there was never an equal partnership and I never felt truly cared for or loved as a wife. Even when writing his own Mother's and Father's Day cards, he failed to include my name. I was never considered, let alone spoilt occasionally: my life was relentless. Any change to our routine to perhaps inject some family excitement or interest, was always instigated by me. I felt no more than an over-worked, unpaid housekeeper with little reward. Adhering to my husband's stringent rules was impossible. Often he gave the impression that we were living life on the bread line. The joint account debit card would occasionally be rejected as David strove to juggle his precious finances and we had to call upon my own frugal account to alleviate the predicament.

In an effort to replace our worn and dated kitchen china, I even took on some curtain-making in the little spare time I had remaining. Looking back, whilst I am extremely angry at David's attitude towards me throughout our marriage, it is indeed within myself that my true anger lies. I was complicit in allowing myself to become completely subservient to his domineering ways.

Constantly told by those around me, including David, how lucky I was, my feelings of despair seemed unfounded. As my self-confidence waned, I no longer felt capable of making any decisions and I found myself referring everything to David. Still troubled by my poor education, compared to David's superior one, it would be a long time before I came to the realisation that whilst undoubtedly valuable, education and qualifications do not necessarily provide essential life-skills. Examination results have little bearing on the truly important qualities in life.

It was the brief times with Paul, many years earlier that had given me a glimpse of how my future could perhaps be. Indeed, the combination of Paul's love and kindness, together with Maggie's tireless efforts to delve and explore my very troubled existence, finally gave me the strength to make significant changes to my life. When I first arrived at Maggie's door, full of despair, I genuinely had no perception as to the magnitude of my troubles, particularly within my marriage. Months turned into years as together we slowly unravelled the many complex issues.

Finally, in my early forties and deeply unhappy, I came to the conclusion that my marriage had reached its end. Although the prospect of what lay ahead was utterly terrifying, my responsibility was to my three daughters and their having a happy future. Thus, with my very few accumulated personal possessions, I moved out of the family home and into the rented house in the centre of Sevenoaks. It was mid-November 2005, after twenty years of marriage.

David was devastated by our separation and desperate for a second chance. However, I was determined not to be won over and was in no doubt that I'd given him a second chance years before.

19. The Bow Tie

November 2006

When faced with my own broken marriage, it was imperative that my children would never encounter the trauma and the misery that I had known during my childhood. Ironically, such tough and sad situations can also have a comical and quite bizarre side to them, even if one doesn't necessarily see it at the time.

It was Friday evening and the end of another busy week. Paul and I were still living in the rented house and relaxing with a glass of wine whilst making plans for our forthcoming move to the home that we were about to purchase together. Unlike most other Fridays during the past year, David, my estranged husband, was not collecting Annie and Nancy for the weekend. Instead he was attending a Law Society black-tie event in Tunbridge Wells.

Since our separation, my eldest daughter Rosemary had chosen to live with David in the family home during much of the term time. For her, the short walk to school was very convenient, particularly with compulsory Saturday school to consider and at fifteen she was content to remain there alone for the occasional evening.

Our own evening was soon disrupted by an urgent call. It was Rosemary.

'Mum, Daddy and I have got a problem,' came a desperate plea from the other end of the line. From the tone of her voice I ascertained that this was not life threatening. Since David and I had separated, the girls' living arrangements were split between two homes and calls at all hours of the day or night had become commonplace. Invariably it was a matter of items of mislaid clothing, forgotten homework, an unexpected request for a car with a driver or a sympathetic ear during times of conflict either with Daddy or an intolerable sister. Paul and I were never off duty.

'Yes,' I asked tentatively. 'What is it?'

'Well, Daddy can't do up his bow tie, I've tried and I can't do it either and the trouble is, he's late.' The late was heavily emphasised and intended to stir up some concern in me.

'Mum, do you think that you can come and do it?' she pleaded.

'I can't really drive, I've had a couple of glasses of wine,' I explained.

'Paul can bring you,' she responded desperately. It was the extremely good relationship that had formed between Paul and each of my daughters, which enabled Rosemary to confidently make this demand. In no time at all they had discovered Paul's caring, good nature. He would happily do anything for them and they knew it. Rather unexpectedly, even David had succumbed to Paul's affable manner.

David seemed reluctant to call on one of several neighbours, all very capable of assisting him in his predicament, not least the wife of his business partner with whom he had arranged to drive to the venue, hence the rush. Instead though, he turned to me for help. After a year's separation, I still hadn't been relieved of all my previous wifely duties.

I refrained from making any alternative suggestions. There was a more important consideration. Rosemary was in a dilemma. David had been unable to resolve his own problem and the onus had fallen on her. Faced with a difficulty she called me, her mother. I couldn't let her down. It was paramount that Rosemary, as with each of my daughters, knew that I would always be there for her --whatever the situation.

'OK Rose, I'm on my way.' Fortunately, Paul had picked up the gist of the conversation and was in a position to drive.

'Thank you,' came a very relieved response, 'but don't forget Daddy's late.'

I relayed the extraordinary conversation to Paul. Only a man with his remarkable attributes could readily jump into his car, chuckling to himself as he did so, for the five-minute dash across town. Feeling like the fourth emergency service, a temporary flashing light on the roof of the car wouldn't have gone amiss.

It was a dark November evening and as we pulled onto the driveway the car headlights lit up the entire house. Two figures could be seen each standing behind the glass panels, one on either side of the solid oak front door. Rosemary, clearly relieved at the speed of our arrival rushed to open the door. Her father was standing patiently in his dinner suit, hands down by his sides, his tie hanging around his neck ready to be miraculously transformed into a smart black bow.

Paul remained in the car with the engine running and I jumped out to attend to this helpless individual. Stepping just inside the house, leaving the front door wide open, I performed the urgent task in a matter of seconds. It was gratefully received.

Mission accomplished, I returned to Paul in the waiting car as David gave him a wave of gratitude. Together we had averted a disaster.

20. Bewley's Hotel

Saturday, 28th April 2007

It was a warm spring day and dressed in smart comfortable summer clothes and accompanied by Paul, I left for the airport to fly to Dublin. My mood was sombre and withdrawn as I prepared to meet, for the first time, the woman who had brought me into the world. Somehow I anticipated this wasn't going to be a joyous reunion. More than four months had passed since I first made contact with Margaret Coleman and although she had been calling me regularly, I'd heard nothing from her for the past two weeks. My own heightened emotions had prevented me from contacting her so close to the event. I could only hope that after Margaret's meticulous planning there would be no question of her reneging on our arrangements. She had been very specific about timing and location, adamant that any meeting between us would have to take place far away from their hometown thereby guaranteeing their anonymity.

'Are you coming on your own?' she'd asked during an earlier phone call.

'No,' I had replied, taken aback that she could imagine I would undertake such a traumatic meeting without any support, especially after her initial reaction and her subsequent lack of empathy towards me.

'Are you bringing your husband David or will it be Paul?' she asked in a rather derogatory fashion.

'Paul of course,' I'd replied, more than a little bemused that she could suggest such a thing. I'd also enquired as to whether she would like to meet my three daughters, but she had been quick to dismiss the idea.

The journey from their home in Thomastown, Kilkenny, to Dublin would take approximately two and a half hours. This was considered too much of an undertaking for Paddy to drive and therefore they had decided to take the bus which would deliver them directly to Bewley's Hotel at approximately 12.30 pm. Paul and I had been instructed to catch the hotel's complimentary bus service from the airport terminal to the hotel. I had booked a flight that guaranteed us an arrival time at the hotel some 30 minutes ahead of them.

During the flight I spoke very little to Paul, my thoughts were consumed by what lay ahead. As well as meeting my birth mother, there was the curious question of Paddy. Was he or was he not my father? Up until now I had refrained from quizzing Margaret as to Paddy's relationship to me. Armed with such conflicting information I had no intention of provoking her and jeopardising our rendezvous. Arriving at the hotel prior to Margaret and Paddy was paramount. I wanted to have the advantage of observing them, albeit briefly, before making myself known. Appearance was everything. What would they look like and would I spot any resemblance?

Margaret had ignored my plea to send a few photographs of herself and her family and sadly she'd also refrained from requesting one of me. However, I had brought several photographs along regardless, together with photocopies of relevant paperwork – or evidence, as I liked to think of it – relating to my adoption. Today was the day I would finally discover the answers to the many questions which had puzzled me for so long.

Margaret was sixty-eight and Paddy sixty-six. I knew very

little about them. Margaret spoke with a decidedly gravelly tone, suggesting a lifetime of heavy smoking. She seemed devoted to the smooth running of her home, claiming on several occasions that you would never find so much as a teaspoonful of dust in it. Paddy was a tarmacker who worked on an *ad hoc* basis. I'd only ever spoken to him once on the telephone but according to Margaret, he presided over everything.

It was my first visit to Ireland and once outside the busy airport terminal, I could hear the unfamiliar accents of the airport staff, ushering waiting passengers into vacant taxis. Thinking about my newly discovered connection with this country was still a strange notion.

Conscious of the time, I waited anxiously for the courtesy bus to take us to the hotel. After what seemed like an age it finally arrived and I sat on the bus in silence as we circumnavigated the airport to reach our destination. The realisation that I was soon to meet the woman who, forty-five years ago, had brought me into the world was all too much to bear. The radio was on and the DJ introduced the next song, it was Boyzone and their version of a Tracey Chapman hit, 'Baby Can I Hold You Tonight'. As I listened to the words they were so poignant, nothing could prevent the tears from rolling down my face.

We soon reached the hotel. As I climbed out of the bus I suddenly felt a tremendous urge to hide away and wait for my overriding feelings of sheer terror to subside. Paul, sensing my agitation took my hand and led me towards the entrance.

The automatic doors opened. We tentatively stepped over the threshold and stood on a sizable entrance mat. Clutching Paul's right hand tightly, I could feel my entire body shaking with a nervous anticipation. We were faced with a busy, cavernous foyer, furnished with numerous sofas and a throng of people, many of them seated, conversing in their own respective groups. Any plan that I had devised to strategically position myself in order to observe them from afar, quickly evaporated. However, conscious of my red, puffy eyes, a visit to the ladies was urgently needed. My head was bowed and I was relying on Paul to determine our destination and promptly guide me there. He swiftly scanned the entire space.

'There they are, that's them!' he whispered, looking towards the far left-hand corner of the vast reception area.

'It can't be them, they're not arriving yet, we've got about half and hour,' I reminded him anxiously. A feeling of absolute panic came over me. Impossible, I knew the timings. Margaret had explained them to me so very clearly.

'I'm telling you, that's them,' he insisted. I gripped Paul's hand ever tighter as I glanced across to where he was indicating. Across the crowded seating area I could see two people standing looking directly at us. There was a strong possibility that Paul could be right. I felt welded to the spot.

'Come on, let's go,' said Paul tugging gently on my hand to encourage my first tentative step.

'That's her!' said the well-dressed woman to the man standing anxiously by her side. Margaret had spotted me. Was it a mother's intuition or did she know what to expect? With some 30 metres between us, it would have been impossible for her to spot any similarities.

'I don't think so,' said Paddy, looking across the busy foyer towards the doorway and making his own judgement. 'She's not forty-five.'

'I'm telling you that's her,' said Margaret confidently.

Still clutching Paul's hand, my every step was leaden. As we crossed the foyer, weaving amongst the acres of seating, Paul was obliged to use a certain element of force in order for us to make the perilous journey towards the waiting couple. I had positioned myself just a shoulder's depth behind him, creating a much-needed shield. My gaze had been fixed very firmly on the ground in front of me, but realising I was just moments away from meeting my birth mother, I decided to take a discreet look. I could see a very smartly dressed couple, as if attending a wedding. Margaret was wearing a cerise pink jacket and dark skirt with high-heeled black patent shoes and her hair had been set for the occasion. I was most surprised by Paddy. Quite wrongly, I had a preconceived image of a man with little regard for his appearance, but I found him to be most dashing. He was tall and dressed in a jacket and tie with smart trousers and highly polished shoes. Unlike his wife he had a large, friendly, welcoming, open sort of face. Margaret on the other hand had a face that showed no warmth whatsoever. Once again, I felt the tears start to trickle down my face. Margaret reached out, grabbed my hand and pulled me towards her. Keeping hold of my hand she kissed me on the cheek.

'No tears now,' she said tersely before releasing me from her grasp. Paddy then approached me and putting his arms around me gave me a warm embrace. They each greeted Paul.

'We changed our minds and decided to drive,' explained Margaret, justifying their earlier arrival. I should have guessed that despite the length of their journey, like me, she too needed the satisfaction of presiding over this highly charged occasion.

We sat down at the small round table close to the bar already taken by Margaret and Paddy. They each had a drink in front of them. To my astonishment, they immediately raised the subject of a most extraordinary incident that had occurred in Folkestone that same morning. An earthquake had rocked the town and had made the news headlines. I struggled to respond to their conversation. All I wanted was the opportunity to sit in silence and study them both intently, particularly Margaret. Here at last was the woman to whom I was so connected and yet had never seen. I wanted to see her hands, her bone structure and her skin. I was interested in her mannerisms, searching desperately for similarities between us.

What a strange scenario! Margaret talked nervously, punctuated by the occasional word from Paddy, whilst I had little interest in anything other than having time to scrutinise the woman who had taken up so much of my thoughts these past years.

'Paddy,' said Margaret, in a curt tone. 'Get Karen a brandy, look she's shaking.' Paddy jumped up.

'Do you want a brandy?' he asked gently.

'No thank you, I don't drink brandy.'

'No brandy, what do you want?' asked Margaret, insistently.

'I'd like a glass of white wine please.'

'Paddy, get Karen a glass of wine and whatever Paul wants,' she instructed, emphasised by a great deal of arm waving. Paddy headed over towards the bar and returned promptly. Despite her nervous disposition, Margaret had every intention of controlling the proceedings. She was sitting upright in the leather armchair, leaning on the armrest with her legs crossed. She tried her best to appear relaxed, her shoulders down and swinging her foot whilst holding her folded glasses in her hand.

'You're very thin,' she exclaimed, studying me intently, catching sight of my slender wrists. 'You look as if you could carry a few more pounds,' she suggested pointedly. 'How much do you weigh and how tall are you?' she asked abruptly. 'Get up and stand next to Paddy. Paddy stand up next to Karen,' she ordered, as he returned with our drinks. She was waving her arms around directing Paddy and me into position. I'm five feet six and standing alongside Paddy I guessed he must have been a little over six feet. Margaret, I had noticed, was considerably shorter than me, even in her high heels. She looked me up and down, as if assessing a height to weight ratio.

'Yes, you're quite tall,' she concluded.

They briefly asked after my daughters and I took the

opportunity of producing a photograph of me with all three, but rather surprisingly there was little reaction. I had expected Margaret to take hold of the picture and like any other proud grandparent bombard me with questions relating to each of them, but nothing was forthcoming. I felt awkward and I found myself making conversation, giving details of their names and ages, but as I did so sensing a total indifference. It had been my intention to present them with the photo, but instead I tucked it away despondently into my folder. Margaret had made no reference to any similarities between us or her own family and even when I quizzed her, she was unable to recognise any. However, Paddy thought I bore some likeness to his own mother. Paul, having analysed us all, was keen to point out that Margaret and I were extremely alike. Still there was no response from her.

Determined to take a firm control of proceedings, she was keen once again to seek reassurance that I'd had a good life. This remark really irritated me, how could I sum up my entire forty-five years? I sensed there was only one answer, any talk of difficulties and problems, great or small were not what she wanted to hear. She was seeking reassurance for her actions. I told her that life for me had not been easy and that I had grown up surrounded by some pretty difficult circumstances. Clearly she felt uncomfortable at this reply and was keen to move on and talk of other things.

'Well,' said Margaret, 'what is it you want to know?' This was the true purpose of my visit, answers to questions and an understanding of the circumstances that led to my adoption. I took my birth certificate from the folder but before placing it on the table in front of us, I looked at Paddy.

'Are you my father?' I asked.

'Yes,' he whispered without any hesitation, before bowing his head. It was the question that had foxed me since the start. So Patrick Coleman was indeed my father, I was in the most remarkable position of being in the company of both my birth parents.

'Did you know you were pregnant on your wedding day?' A question I directed at both of them. They confirmed that they were both aware. 'And Paddy, have you ever seen me before today?'

'No,' he said quietly. He looked forlorn. Although I sensed that he was intent on meeting me, he was certainly uncomfortable with any pointed questioning. Still clutching my birth certificate I posed a question to Paddy.

'Do you know when my birthday is?'

'Yes,' he said immediately.

'When is it?' I asked staring directly at him. He started to think, a very deep sort of thought. He looked up to the ceiling for a few seconds and back to the floor, he continued to do this for some time, as I sat quietly waiting for the answer. Margaret refrained from intervening. As his head moved up and down, he appeared to be trying to recall and calculate in his head, his lips were moving as if to talk to himself although nothing could be heard. Suddenly something registered and he prepared to speak.

'I can't give the date, just the month,' he declared. I stared, waiting for the result.

'February or March,' he announced.

'Which one are you going to plump for?' I asked, keen to maintain any pressure. He returned, briefly, to that state of floor to ceiling calculation.

'March,' he said confidently. 'But I can't tell you the date,' he added. I turned to Margaret; she had remained silent throughout Paddy's intense questioning.

'Do you know the date?' I asked her.

'Yes of course,' she said with a slight hesitation. 'March 22nd.' Her words were devastating. Throughout my whole life I had assumed that she was sharing my important milestones with me. Surely any mother would have the date of the birth of a child engraved on their heart. How, despite giving me away could she erase me from her mind in such a callous way? I had spent my life wondering if she was ever thinking of me. She was one day out. It may as well have been a week or a month out. I was mortified. I hated her.

'No,' I said instantly. 'It's the 23rd.' Margaret looked unperturbed. Paddy appeared emotional. He was finding the meeting exceedingly difficult and had pulled a handkerchief from his pocket, using it to dab each eye in turn. The hanky remained in his hand and in constant use.

I placed the birth certificate on the table.

'Why does it say that Paddy is deceased?' I asked, pointing to the inexplicable information in front of me. Sitting in her seat she barely moved to look at the document. She thought for a moment.

'Um, I've no idea, I don't remember that,' she said uncomfortably. Her response was pathetic. I was infuriated with her. Paddy leaned forward to study the document.

'Margaret, why does it say I'm dead on there?' he asked curiously, pointing towards my birth certificate. She claimed to have no memory of the circumstances of my registration, cunningly leaving my question unanswered. Her attitude irked me intensely. I sensed that she had no intention of disclosing anything to me, but this day was too important an opportunity to let anything pass. I wanted to come away from this meeting with a complete understanding of the events that led to my adoption. In the absence of Margaret volunteering any information I posed the ultimate question to them.

'Why did you give me away?'

Margaret prepared to speak. 'We wanted you to have a better life. Times were very different then, Irish people living in London were not welcome. There were signs everywhere stating no blacks and no Irish. If you were Irish and you had children it was

189

even worse,' she said. Her manner was cool and phlegmatic but I remained unconvinced, none of her reasons seemed remotely adequate and came anywhere close to explaining my adoption. I decided to challenge her.

'But you did have somewhere to live, you lived with Jim Donovan and his wife Mary. He's spoken very fondly of you and your kindness towards his wife, telling me how fond you were of his daughter and your willingness to help them.'

'You've got to understand that money was very difficult then,' she concluded in an effort to provide a reason that I couldn't dispute. Through sheer frustration and utter despair, my eyes filled with tears. She was clearly lying to me and I was immensely angry with her.

'You know, you're just like Paddy, you hang on to too much, you keep it all inside and that's not good,' she said.

'Well I'm glad to hear that I'm like somebody,' I snapped. I was irritated by her ineffectual attempt to console me. Throughout this time Paddy had kept his head bowed and continued to dab his eyes. The same could not be said for Margaret. Sitting there confidently with her legs still crossed, leaning slightly on the arm of the chair towards me, she was moving her elevated foot around in a casual, circular and up and down fashion. Not only had I not received a satisfactory explanation as to why I was adopted, but also there appeared to be not one ounce of remorse in her. Curiously, her callous attitude seemed to give me renewed energy and I battled on regardless, determined to present all of my findings.

'Jim Donovan has no recollection of you being pregnant, how could that be when you were living in his home and helping his wife with their young daughter?' I asked pointedly.

'I didn't really show,' she replied.

'But how did you continue to work on the buses?' I asked. My patience was waning. She quickly dismissed my question, claiming to have little memory of any detail at that time. Infuriated by her responses, I decided to change tack.

'How was it that if you had no money, I was born in a private nursing home?'

To my surprise, Paddy quickly intervened.

'Ah,' he said, happy to oblige in solving one of my many queries. 'There were lots of adverts in newspapers at that time asking for babies for adoption. They were everywhere,' he stressed. He may have been correct in his account of adverts but this didn't answer the question of payment.

'But this was a private nursing home, the money would have come from somewhere and I know that my adoptive parents certainly didn't part with any money.' Paddy looked puzzled.

'I think we knew one of the nurses,' interrupted Margaret.

I was getting nowhere.

'How did you get from Herbert Road, Ilford to the nursing home in Hackney? That's eight miles away, not easy when you're in labour.'

Again, Paddy was eager to respond. 'I had a car,' he announced proudly. Beaming as he was reminded of his younger years and how thrilled he must have been to own a car at just twenty-one years of age.

'It was an old banger,' he added, still delighted at the thought. 'I drove her there,' he declared. 'I remember the insurance on that car was eight pounds a year,' he added, impressed by his own memory recall. Paul responded immediately.

'If you can remember the cost of your insurance forty-five years ago why is it that you can't remember things of far greater importance?' he asked, referring to Paddy's apparent reluctance to assist Margaret in her vague recollection of events. Paddy looked nervously at the ground.

'Did anybody know that you were pregnant?' I asked, turning back to Margaret.

'Nobody.'

'Not even your sisters?' I asked.

'No, they didn't.'

In an effort to reveal to them the extent of my search, I described the visit to the church where they were married and our conversation with the priest who provided me with a copy of their entry in the marriage register. I also queried the home address given by Margaret at the time of their wedding. After checking it on the electoral roll, we could make no connection with either family. It had left us baffled. Paddy chuckled nervously, recalling something long since forgotten.

'Ah, that was the address of my driver on the buses – George Whytock. We gave that as Margaret's address because it was close to the church,' he explained. I pulled out the document relating to Margaret's appearance at Ilford County Court in October 1962 and placed it in front of her. It stated that Paddy was not dead; I was illegitimate and that she had no knowledge of my true father's whereabouts. After the briefest of glances, she categorically denied that she'd ever been to Ilford County Court, insisting that the signature on the document was not hers. Turning to Paddy to seek clarification and support of this fact, it has to be said he was more non-committal than affirmative.

No doubt weary with the relentless questioning, it was at Margaret's suggestion that we move into the restaurant for lunch. It was a self-service arrangement and as we each took a tray Margaret was quick to voice instructions. A starter was considered unnecessary, we would each take just a main course only and as we approached the payment desk Paddy was ordered to settle the bill.

We selected a booth where we were able to continue talking freely. I was seated directly opposite Margaret and next to Paul. The roast beef dinner that we had all chosen was mediocre. Margaret poked and prodded at her meal making very negative

192

remarks as to its quality before pushing it to one side. After our table had been cleared away, Paddy unexpectedly reached out across the table and took hold of my hand and held it tightly for some considerable time. I was moved by his genuine display of affection.

Conscious of the time, I still had a great deal to raise, namely the subject of my three brothers.

'When are you going to tell the boys about me?' I asked. My question succeeded in riling her, she was furious.

'Although we've agreed to meet you, you have to understand that we shan't be telling the boys about you. The boys must never know that you exist,' she said curtly.

Her announcement was ridiculous and totally unacceptable to me.

'But Margaret you can't say that, the boys have a right to know that I am on this planet. They have to be told they have a sister,' I pleaded.

'I've said, absolutely no. You'll have to wait until I'm dead and then you can tell them. You can do what you like then. You've only got four years to wait, seventy-two is when I'm going, seventy-two,' she stressed. I was totally exasperated.

'How do you know that you are going to die at seventy-two, where did that come from?'

She reeled off a list of family members, including her mother, all, she claimed had died at that age.

'I don't think that I really want to hear this,' I said, realising that I was now privy to some family medical history.

'Ah, well you have to be careful then don't you, careful what you come looking for,' she replied, with an element of sarcasm in her voice. I brought the subject back to my brothers.

'Margaret, you know that I have all John's contact details and —'

She interrupted. 'I know that and I am furious, you had no

right to contact him.'

I ignored her remark, I did have rights, and my patience was wearing thin.

'I know exactly where he lives and I have his phone number and you know that I have already spoken to him several times. I didn't disclose my identity but I could have. Can't you understand that I am giving you the chance to tell your sons? I'm trying to be sensitive. I could have contacted him at any time, and told him everything, but I haven't, they need to hear this from you.'

Her face was searing with rage.

'If you tell the boys, I will commit suicide,' she announced, throwing her arms into the air once again. Her reaction was ridiculous. I had no intention of allowing her shocking threat to deter me.

'You have to understand, I'm well respected in the community, I know a lot of people and they can't know about you,' she explained. 'So there you have it, I've made myself very clear,' she said vehemently, turning to Paddy. 'Paddy, I think we should go, there's nothing more to discuss.'

I was furious with her wanting to leave, just because the conversation wasn't going her way.

'No,' I said firmly. 'You can't just leave because it's difficult, we need to talk about it,' I insisted. I could feel my emotions surging once again. I was desperate, thinking about all my unanswered questions. Would I ever get this chance again?

Paddy was still clutching my hand and had been listening intently to our heated exchange.

'You know Margaret, we could always move, we don't have to stay living in the same area,' he suggested. His attitude was a complete contrast to Margaret's. She was steadfast in her beliefs, whilst he was prepared to consider the prospect of forming a new relationship even at this stage in his life. Needless to say his proposal was instantly rejected.

'Margaret, if you commit suicide, how are Paddy and Oliver going to cope? You have told me how dependent they are on you. You do absolutely everything for them.' I said, reminding her just how indispensable she thought she was.

'Yes I do.'

Paddy looked on earnestly. I sensed that he was keen to know where his next meal might be coming from should she take her own life.

'Do you intend to fill up the freezer before you go?' I asked flippantly. My impudent manner angered her, but it did have the desired effect. She thought for a few moments.

'If we are going to tell the boys we will need time to think about it,' she announced. I was relieved by her apparent change of heart, but feared it was simply a diversion. I needed her to be more specific.

'But you've had since December, it's now April,' I reminded her.

'We will do it but you must give us a year,' she said looking to Paddy. He nodded in agreement.

'No,' I said. 'It's too long.' I sensed this was merely a delaying tactic.

'Six months then,' came her next offer. Still not content with her latest offer, I remembered her talking of major home improvements for a forthcoming family gathering this coming June. I reminded her of this occasion and suggested that they take the opportunity to speak to the boys then. This notion was immediately rejected. Conveniently, her memory was rather vague as to the family event in question. I removed myself to take a much-needed break and went in search of the ladies, leaving Paul alone with Margaret and Paddy. Paul had also become increasingly rattled with Margaret's impossible behaviour and in particular her need to seek reassurance that I'd had a good life.

'Don't expect Karen to tell you she's had a good life. You have

195

no idea what sort of life she's had. She's had to face numerous traumas and difficulties,' he told them firmly.

I had so wanted to connect with this woman. I had hoped that as the day progressed she would warm to me. Instead, during our time together, things had steadily deteriorated. Why was she so reluctant to answer my questions and why did she make me feel so guilty for asking them? At this stage I had no intention of sparing her feelings. Returning to the table, I had every intention of antagonising her.

'Margaret, tell me how, just three years later, did you take John home from hospital as your supposed first born? How did you feel with your friends and family around you, knowing what you'd done just three years earlier?'

'No trouble at all,' came her measured response, verging on the insolent. Nothing I could say seemed to affect this woman. Her cold and calculating manner astounded me.

'Let me ask you this. Over the years, if any of your sons had needed any sort of medical intervention involving a donor, would you have tried to find me then?'

'No,' she said firmly. 'I would not.' It was a truly shocking response. As a mother I know that I would do anything for my children. It seemed that Margaret was prepared to put her own interests before the well-being of her three sons. We were so different.

'Why don't you talk to John first?' I asked. 'John is in England and away from the close community where you live. I have spoken to John and it seems to me that he could be very understanding and supportive.'

Paddy was nodding. Margaret was non-committal. It was so important that they went away from this meeting understanding what needed to be done. Annoyingly for them, I wasn't going to go away. Margaret refused to be pinned down. She was vague; although she hinted that she would tell the boys at a time convenient to her, I sensed that she would say anything in the heat of the moment. Reminding me of their long journey home, Margaret was keen to leave.

Before returning to their car in the underground car park, Paul suggested that we take a couple of photographs outside the hotel. Much to my surprise, they were happy to oblige. With a record of the day to present to my daughters, we walked with them to their car. Margaret kissed me goodbye and insisted that we would meet again. Paddy whispered to both Paul and me that we were to leave everything to him, he would speak to John. They got into the car and I watched as Margaret continued to wave frantically until they were out of sight. Paul could only see it as a very positive gesture. Deeply upset by the day's events, I begged to differ.

We returned to the airport for our journey home. Once back in the car at Gatwick we telephoned Rosemary, Annie and Nancy to give them an account of the day. With so much to report we were still talking to them twenty-five minutes later as we pulled onto David's drive to collect them.

I spent the following day reflecting on events, recalling the conversations over and over in my head. I was left firmly of the opinion that Margaret had carefully planned her account of forty-five years ago and Paddy, I believed, had been under strict instructions to say very little. Despite this, my long awaited desire to meet my birth parents had finally come to fruition and for that I was truly grateful. After all, they could have refused to meet with me. I began to feel a little more favourable towards this elderly couple. Most of their lives must have been affected by their actions and the prospect of our meeting must have been equally daunting for them, but what next? Margaret had implied that we would meet again. What did she mean? The following morning I had an overwhelming urge to telephone her and as we had already established telephone contact over the past several

197

months, I decided to take the plunge.

'Hello, Paddy, its Karen.' I hadn't expected him to answer my call; on the few occasions I had rung he had never once picked up the phone.

'Hello Karen,' he sounded guarded.

'Paddy, I just wanted to thank you both for meeting me yesterday, I know it was difficult, but I really appreciated it. I also wanted to thank you for lunch.'

Paddy muttered a brief response. I sensed that all was not as it should be.

'Could I talk to Margaret?' I asked.

'Um, no, no you can't, she's not well.'

I hadn't expected to hear that, she hadn't appeared ill the day before. I enquired further.

'What do you mean, what's the matter with her?'

'All that business yesterday has upset her; we should never have met. She doesn't want to talk to you.'

'I'm sorry to hear that, it wasn't my intention to make Margaret ill,' I explained.

'I think we'll leave it there for now and see how she feels in a while,' he said.

'I'll tell her you called,' he added.

'Yes please do, goodbye.' I went to find Paul and report Margaret's sudden downturn.

'I'm not surprised, not surprised at all,' he said knowingly.

'What do you mean, not surprised?' I asked. How did he know she'd be unwell?

'The box has been opened,' he declared. 'There's no going back, not now she's met you. She's got to face all those difficult feelings that she's kept locked away for forty-five years. It's impossible for her. She's struggling alright.'

'What do I do now?' I asked.

'Nothing, she'll ring you,' he said confidently.

'I don't think so, Paddy didn't sound very happy and somehow I didn't get a good feeling from the conversation.'

'She'll definitely call you I'm sure of that, you've just got to wait until she's ready,' he insisted. He was right. I didn't have to wait too long. Just two days later, as I was about to leave for work the telephone rang. The caller display indicated an international call.

'Hello,' I said gingerly.

'Is that Karen?' said the harsh gravelly-voiced woman. She had the ability to fill me with an instant dread.

'Hello Margaret, I hope that you're feeling better. I was sorry to hear from Paddy that you were unwell on Sunday,' I said immediately, in an effort to moderate what I anticipated to be a difficult conversation.

'Yes, and I need to talk to you about that. I have a few things to say and I want you to listen, OK,' she said curtly.

'Yes Margaret, I will listen to you providing that when you've finished, you'll listen to me, because I also have something to say.'

'Firstly, we should never have met,' she declared, in a most hurtful tone. 'I told you before, that no good comes of these reunions. Some things are best left alone. Next, we didn't like the way in which you've been poking and prying into our business. Finding out all those details, Paddy and I are furious. Also, we certainly didn't like the way Paul interfered. This whole business has nothing whatsoever to do with him,' she said venomously. 'And finally the interrogation that you put us both through, was something akin to being in Guantanamo Bay,' she declared indignantly. Her onslaught complete, it was my turn to respond.

'OK Margaret, I have listened to you and now would you please listen to me,' I said confidently. Much had changed since our meeting four days ago. I was no longer the quivering wreck that I had appeared in Dublin. I felt better able to deal with Margaret's ridiculous nonsense. She begrudgingly agreed.

'I'm sorry that you feel the way you do about our meeting but I don't feel the same. Despite everything, I'm glad we met.'

'Oh... right... um, yes, OK,' she said, unsettled by my response. I continued.

'We didn't poke and pry, most of the documents that we discovered during our search are public documents and anybody can access them, the rest were made available to me as the adopted person. It's the only way to trace a birth mother,' I explained. 'Paul was there on Saturday to support me. It was a very difficult day for me and he stepped in when he knew I was struggling.' I waited for her reaction.

'Yes... OK... I see. Well... um... yes. She was momentarily lost for words. My efforts to stand up to her bullying had worked.

'How are the girls?' she asked, suddenly changing the subject to something more affable.

'They're fine thank you, they were very interested to see the photos of you and Paddy.'

'Are you off to work soon?' she asked.

'Yes, I'll leave just before eleven.'

'How's Paul?'

'He's OK,' I said, surprised that she'd enquired after him.

'Will you say hello to him, he's not so bad you know,' she said in a distinctly light-hearted tone.

'We'll speak again,' she said. 'Goodbye and God bless you Karen'.

She left me bemused. Where exactly did I stand? Perhaps she really was mellowing and I just needed to give her more time. I needed to be patient.

21. Bollocks

2nd June 2007

A call from Margaret the previous weekend had not only left me seething but also facing a difficult dilemma. Ever since our meeting in April, Margaret had been telephoning me regularly. Whilst her preference was to keep the topic of conversation to mundane matters such as daily chores, household waste collections and the weather, mine was always to turn our exchanges to the subject of her three sons, my brothers. They remained completely unaware of my existence and I was waiting patiently while Margaret pondered on how best to break the news of their unknown sister to them. It was a cruel game of nerves she was knowingly inflicting on me. How could she, the one who had given me away and who needed to account for herself, keep the upper hand like this?

'You've got to give me time,' she'd insisted each time I broached the subject. I was desperately hoping that she would succumb to my plea and divulge to them the events of more than forty years ago, thus paving the way for a much-awaited introduction. Weary and frustrated by her constant deferrals, I feared that Margaret's 'friendly calls' were nothing more than a way to string me along indefinitely. Six months had elapsed since I'd made my initial contact with her and five weeks since our meeting in Dublin.

Then, in the last week of May, she dropped her calculating bombshell.

'I've decided after careful thought not to tell the boys, I don't want to disrupt their lives. John's very busy and Michael's got his two children to take care of, one of which has recently been diagnosed with a sight defect. It's best if this entire business stays just between us. We can keep in touch occasionally but there will be nothing more. Oh, and I've also been talking to a doctor friend of mine recently who agrees with me. Establishing contact in situations such as these is never a good idea and she also reminded me that Paddy and I have rights,' she stressed, insinuating that any further pressure from me would be firmly rebuked.

'So I've decided that we'll leave it at that,' she announced firmly. This heartless and totally unfeeling remark had infuriated me beyond measure. I would not allow her to dictate to me. I had no intention of remaining a secret indefinitely. However, I was nonetheless faced with a quandary, ever mindful of Margaret's earlier suicide threat. It was one of the reasons why I had not simply resorted to contacting my brother John directly and had put up with Margaret's cat and mouse phone calls all this time.

For my part I had tried hard to be understanding and put myself in Margaret's position. Was I perhaps expecting too much, too soon, should I remain compliant and respect Margaret's wishes, rather than my own deep needs? Was I acting too hastily under these very difficult circumstances? Perhaps time would eventually bring me the results I so desperately sought.

I was longing to meet with each of my brothers and was hopeful of maybe even establishing some kind of a relationship with them. John, in particular, as he lived only an hour's drive away and having already spoken to him, had become a real person for me. Even more so now that I had gleaned further titbits, inadvertently disclosed in Margaret's conversations and additional information via the internet, thanks to the invaluable help of David Trill.

John was married to Helen but they had no children. Although John had a full time office job in Watford, his passion had always been sport and he was in the process of establishing his own business as a personal trainer during the evenings and at weekends. David Trill's most impressive find was a picture of John on the internet, advertising as a personal trainer. At last, I could put a face to a voice. My earlier request to Margaret to send some snaps of the family had been totally ignored. Sat at the computer, I was able to scrutinise this image, avidly looking for similarities between us.

Michael was her only son with children. He lived in Waterford, Ireland, with his wife Helena and their son and daughter. He worked as head green-keeper at a local golf course on a hotel complex, a beautiful eighteenth-century mansion in magnificent surroundings. I even discovered an article reporting on a recent golfing event, which was very complimentary about Michael, specifically mentioning the quality of the greens. With this information I was easily able to locate Michael's contact details both at home and at work.

Oliver was somewhat an enigma. Their youngest son, age thirty-five, was single and still lived at home. Margaret explained to me how he'd been deprived of a complete education due to ill health caused by severe asthma and frequent chest infections. He worked part-time on a Government scheme that primarily involved grass cutting. With the remainder of his time taken up carrying out various tasks within the home and ferrying his mother around in the family car on shopping trips and her regular hairdressing appointments, I detected signs of complete subordination to a strict regime.

All this information served only to make me more impatient than ever to meet my brothers. Margaret had already alerted me to the impending family gathering in June, her grandson's first communion. Clearly it was an important event and there had been much talk of home improvements in readiness. With each of her sons present, I saw it as an ideal opportunity to enlighten the boys on news of their unknown sister. However, for reasons known only to Margaret, she had no intention of ever disclosing my existence to them. The suggestion that they had rights greatly angered me. I knew that with regard to my adoption, they had none.

After dwelling on these very emotive feelings for an entire week, I bumped into a friend at the supermarket. Penelope or Peps as she was known to everyone, whilst not one of my closest friends, was a very engaging, forthright individual, always fun and someone whose company I much enjoyed. Over the last few months she had been riveted by the events surrounding my search and was always eager to catch up with the next instalment, invariably shedding a tear at my account. On this occasion after reporting my latest dilemma to her, I received a somewhat unexpected reaction.

'BOLLOCKS,' she announced. I giggled at her frankness, whilst hoping nobody else in the shop had overheard. Peps never held back. I braced myself for a reprimand.

'You're not going to listen to her are you?' she challenged. 'You have three real brothers out there and they have every right to know of your existence. Margaret has no right to say these things and you mustn't feel that you're doing anything wrong by contacting them. She's had her chance. She's trying to frighten you off. Don't allow her to dictate to you. I don't understand why you haven't contacted your brothers before now. You've given both Margaret and Paddy plenty of time to tell them, what are you waiting for? Go and do it, now,' was her forthright response.

To my great relief, Peps stopped to draw breath. Despite such a sudden onslaught, I had to admire her thinking. She was absolutely right. This was just what I needed.

'Yes, you're right. Bollocks,' I repeated in defiance of this entire ridiculous situation and with huge relief. 'I'll go home and do it now.'

She wished me luck and asked to be kept informed. I raced home with a spring in my step and butterflies in my stomach, full of trepidation at the prospect of finally making contact with my brothers. They were about to get the shock of their lives. I would make the initial call to John.

I raced into the house laden with shopping bags, dropped them immediately in the hall and broadcast my intentions at the top of my voice.

'Today, I am going to telephone John,' I bellowed. Much to my dismay there was no sudden reaction from inside the house. 'Paul,' I called, eager for a response.

'Yes,' came a muted reply.

'Did you hear what I said? I'm going to telephone John, today.' It had been six months since I had spoken to John and unfortunately Paul had witnessed similar scenes. Each time it would come to nothing as I resolved to handle the situation a little more delicately. In all fairness to Paul, he had no reason to suspect this would be any different.

'Today I'm serious, I'm really going to do it,' I insisted. Paul knew me well. Somebody had to be responsible for provoking me today.

'Who did you meet in Waitrose?' he asked knowingly. I disclosed the name of my collaborator and reiterated my plans.

'Have you decided what you're going to say?' asked Paul. I brushed his question aside. The moment was too exciting to consider any details. Whilst extremely anxious I had no fear. I had convinced myself John would be receptive, after all, we'd already spoken. He would be sympathetic to my plight and appreciate my considerate nature. I also held on to the real prospect of meeting him this weekend. Surely this was inevitable, curiosity on his part would see to that.

'How about we have some lunch first?' suggested Paul, keen to slow things down and inject some thinking time. I reluctantly agreed.

An hour later I was still determined to make the call but I was feeling less optimistic. The bravado had vanished. How do you tell someone that you're his or her unknown sister? The prospect of the forthcoming call was truly daunting and here I was about to make it. Rosemary and Paul had settled in the lounge to witness this momentous occasion while I paced around the room deep in thought, clutching the handset tightly in my hand.

'Am I doing the right thing?' I asked. It wasn't so much a question but a plea for support.

'Yes you are,' said Paul reassuringly.

'Do I ring his mobile number?' I asked.

'Yes.'

'Do I arrange to meet with him or do I tell him everything over the telephone?' I asked frantically.

'Try and arrange to meet him,' advised Paul calmly.

After several failed attempts to punch the correct number into the phone, I eventually heard a ring. My body was trembling. I sat down next to Paul.

'Hello, John Coleman,' he said rapidly. This was the voice of my brother. Unlike the telephone conversation six months earlier, this time I was certain. I was indeed his sister.

'Hello?' he repeated, impatiently.

'Hello is that John?' I was flustered.

'Yes,' he said brusquely. I turned to Paul for reassurance before taking a deep breath and engaging in this most terrifying conversation.

'My name is Karen, I don't know if you remember me but we spoke last year around Christmas time. I was trying to find somebody?' My tone was diffident. All my efforts to appear eloquent and composed had evaporated.

'Yes Karen, I do remember you.'

'Is it convenient to talk to you now?' I asked.

'Yes, go ahead, but as I said then, I don't think I can be of any more help to you,' he added. I ignored his remark.

'I was trying to locate a Jim Donovan and you very kindly contacted your parents to see if they could help me.'

'That's correct.'

'They told you they didn't have any information.'

'Yes, that's right.'

Although his answers were brief, I sensed he was listening intently.

'Well, I believe that your parents do know something about this matter and there is a good reason why they have chosen to deny any knowledge of this man.' I waited while he digested my statement.

'I'm surprised at what you're telling me. I know that if my mother was able to help in any way I'm sure she would have done so, but OK, as it happens I'm returning home next week and I will discuss it with them again then.'

Any suggestion that he should raise this subject with them had to be averted. She would instantly realise that I'd made contact and I just couldn't discount her threat of suicide, should any of her sons learn of my existence.

'John, I don't think you should mention this to them, I'm worried what might happen if you do,' I said earnestly.

'With respect, you have to understand that I have a very good relationship with my parents and like I said, I will speak to them about it. If I discover anything more I've got your number logged in this phone and I will contact you.' His mood had changed. He had made no attempt to enquire after my involvement in this matter or to learn more about my circumstances. Instead, I sensed unease in our conversation. He was not the same accommodating John Coleman that I had spoken to before. I once again stressed how important it was for him not to tackle them. He declined. The call was deteriorating. The thought of John's imminent meeting with Margaret filled me with horror. I sensed the need to act immediately.

'John, there's something I need to tell you, could we meet?'

'Karen, I don't want you to tell me anything, just leave it with me.'

'But I'm so worried,' I stressed again.

'I hear what you say but it's a risk I'm prepared to take. Maybe I will get back to you with further information when I return.' John was guarded and clearly irritated by the whole episode. The good feeling I had so anticipated never materialised. Saddened by the entire sorry affair I was unable to hold back my tears any longer. Paul sensed the change of mood and encouraged me to reveal my identity immediately.

'Just tell him now, tell him who you are,' he whispered. John overheard Paul's intervention.

'Karen, I don't want you to tell me anything,' he said firmly.

'Can we just leave it there, I'll get back to you if I need to,' he said adamantly. I managed a very feeble goodbye and ended the call.

I turned to Paul.

'That was terrible.' His arm reached out and drew me towards him. 'I know what's going to happen now,' I said woefully. 'He won't wait until next week, after that conversation he'll ring her immediately.'

'You don't know that, you'll just have to wait,' said Paul, trying desperately to comfort me.

'I'm really frightened.'

'You couldn't have done anything more,' he stressed.

'But Margaret will telephone here this afternoon. I just know it. It doesn't bear thinking about. I'm not answering the phone for the rest of the day. You can do it.'

22. Under the Duvet

June 2007

At times of great distress and anguish, I have often resorted to my bed to seek comfort and refuge. On this occasion it was mid-afternoon and I was still fully dressed, as I burrowed down safely under the duvet. I had no intention of moving. I pulled the bedcover up around my head and held it there to muffle the inevitable, unwelcome sound. As anticipated, the response was rapid. That trill sound of the telephone had to be the call I was most fearing, alerting me to the possible shocking outcome of my very recent actions. I tightened my grip on the duvet.

As Paul dutifully answered the call, I made no effort to listen to the conversation. It would be Margaret, enraged that I had defied her and carried out the very act she'd forbidden. Would she really take her own life, as threatened? Unlikely, but I'd witnessed her wrath several months earlier and although practically a stranger to me, perhaps because of our unique connection, her rage had left its mark. Paul tugged at the bedding. The call had been very brief.

'Well it wasn't Margaret.'

'Who then?' I asked curiously, lifting the duvet away from my head.

'Helen,' he said. 'She wants to talk to the woman who called her husband a short time ago.'

'Oh no,' I said despairingly. 'I just can't face a grilling from her too. This is turning into something really terrible.'

'No, I don't think she does want to give you a hard time. She sounds concerned. John has gone out for a run and she's taken the opportunity to pick up this number on his mobile phone. It doesn't sound as if he's telephoned Margaret.' Immediately a wave of relief washed over me. So Margaret was still unaware of the day's events.

'What do you think, should I ring?'

'Yes definitely. I told her you'd gone out but it doesn't matter. If you ring now you can talk to her before John returns.' I threw back the duvet and sat on the edge of the bed. How would she react to me and what exactly would I say to her?

'OK then, I'll do it. Are you sure she sounded OK?'

'Yes, it'll be fine,' said Paul reassuringly, before making me aware of his minor blunder. 'I may have slipped up though. Although she didn't introduce herself, I called her Helen at one point but I don't know whether she picked up on it or not.'

Over the last few months I had gained a great deal of information on John and Helen but still they knew practically nothing about me. I left the bedroom to retrieve the phone. Paul called after me.

'Oh and one other thing – she sounds just like Margaret.' His throwaway remark was intended as a jape and although I took it in the spirit in which it was given, I returned briefly to deliver a piercing glare. I found the prospect of talking to someone who sounded like Margaret, but wasn't actually her, particularly unnerving.

The events of the day had taken an unexpected course. Just hours earlier, I had fantasised about a sympathetic and positive reaction from John, leading to an impromptu and emotional meeting. Instead, before I'd even had the opportunity to come face to face with one of my much longed-for brothers, I was possibly on the brink of engineering the most devastating moment of his life. I felt wretched. It had never been my intention to create such bad feeling among this family, but Margaret's totally unanticipated behaviour had been quite absurd and she had put me in an impossible situation. I was ready to take the plunge. I collected the phone and address book and joined Paul. Looking up their telephone number under C, reminded me of all the contact information relating to the Coleman clan, which I had accumulated over the past few months. It was very satisfying and the secrecy gave me a strange feeling of power over the destiny of others for once in my life. Clutching the telephone, I punched in the number of the landline.

An Irish woman answered immediately.

'Hello, my name's Karen,' I said timidly.

'Hello,' she replied cheerily, as she thanked me for calling and to my relief took up the conversation.

'As I have just explained to the gentleman, (referring to Paul) my husband John is struggling. He doesn't know what to make of your call. He's feeling very stressed and agitated and has taken himself out for a run. I wondered if there was something I could do to help in any way?'

Once I had overcome the initial shock of her vocal similarities to Margaret, I sensed a very calm, controlled and caring individual, very easy to talk to. Unlike my conversation with John earlier, there was no resistance.

'I really do need to talk to John,' I stressed. 'I am worried what will happen if he talks to his parents before talking to me.'

'He's not going to call his parents, whatever this is about he realises that it may only concern one of them and he doesn't know which one. He knows he has to talk to you first, but he won't do it until he's ready and I can't make him. He's very worried at what you might tell him. All sorts of possibilities are going through his mind.'

There was genuine concern in her voice and I felt responsible, but tempted as I was to unburden myself to her, I just couldn't. I had to speak directly to my brother John. Margaret had failed to do the right thing by him and inform him of the existence of a sister, now it had to come from me. Hearing of John's anxiety, I wanted to ease the situation and rule out any sinister notions they may have formed.

'Let me reassure you, nobody has died.'

She gave a huge sigh. 'You don't know how relieved I am to hear that. It was certainly one of John's worries. Imagining something awful had occurred many years ago, perhaps in a car accident or something. But if it isn't that, it really can't be that bad. Most families have skeletons in the cupboard and at some point they have to come out. I have a good understanding of Irish families, all manner of secrets are hidden away. It's not right you know.'

These were comforting words under the circumstances.

'Let me tell you. There are things that have gone on in my own family that would really surprise you,' she said choosing not to elaborate.

'I think my story might really surprise you.' I said immediately. Determined to delve further, she pressed on.

'Well,' she paused. 'Let me think. If nobody's died that means it must be something like, um ... a family matter, a step-brother or sister perhaps?'

In a short time I had warmed to Helen, it was becoming increasingly difficult not to submit to her sympathetic ear. I considered my response carefully.

'Although you're on the right track, it's not that,' I confirmed. 'Are you sure that John's not going to mention this to Margaret and Patrick?' I asked anxiously.

Deliberately mentioning both of them by name, I wanted to emphasise my knowledge of them and to reiterate their close involvement in the situation in an effort to steer her away from any thought of step-siblings. I needed her to relay all this information to John in the hope of persuading him to call me. I desperately wanted to avert a possible tragedy.

'I'll make sure he doesn't,' she said. She was determined not to let the opportunity to try and uncover this dark secret pass her by.

'You know, I think that one of them must have had an illegitimate child. If it were Margaret then it would have been in a previous relationship before her wedding. But if it's Patrick then I suppose it could have been anytime,' she paused. 'I think it must be Patrick. Do you mind me asking how old you are?' This wasn't getting any easier. I chose to ignore the latter question and respond to the previous statement, averting any reference to my age.

'As I said, it's something like that but not that. Helen you're making this very difficult for me. I have been talking to you for just a short time and you seem so understanding, it would be so easy to tell you everything but it really should be for John to hear first,' I stressed.

'I can tell this is very difficult for you Karen. I'm a good listener. I've spent a number of years working in the caring profession and I just wish I could be of more help to you.

'Will you tell John that you've spoken to me?'

'Yes I will. As soon as he comes home.'

'Do you think he'll ring me later?'

'Karen, I will tell him about this call and I hope that he contacts you, but he has to do it when he's ready. I don't know if it will be today.'

'Helen, thank you so much for talking to me, this is so difficult, I'm finding this quite impossible at the moment. I have come very close to telling you everything and I don't even know you.'

'I'll do what I can Karen. Goodbye.'

'Bye Helen.' I switched off the telephone and turned to

Rosemary who had just joined me, ready to hear an account of the conversation. 'Rosemary you've got a lovely aunty.'

An hour later in the Coleman kitchen, John and Helen sat mulling over the curious events of the day.

John, I don't know who Karen is but I'm convinced she is related to you in some way. And I'll tell you something else – she's genuine.'

John gazed pensively into his mug of tea.

23. Helen

June 2006

The waiting game inflicted on me by different members of the Coleman family over the last six months was unbearable. And now John, too, seemed reluctant to contact me. Three days had now elapsed since my conversation with both him and Helen. My life had been dominated by this situation for too long and I wasn't prepared to wait a moment longer. Having spoken to Helen on Saturday and hearing her very sympathetic manner, I decided to call her again.

'Hello,' she said in an accent that had become remarkably familiar.

'Hello Helen, it's Karen.'

'Oh, I didn't expect to hear from you,' she said cheerily.

'I hope you don't mind me calling you, but I'm surprised not to have heard from John,' I explained.

'Karen, I know it's difficult, but I can't make him ring you. He realises he has to talk to you before he talks to his parents, but as I have already explained, he'll only do it when he's ready. There's nothing more I can do.'

'But how does he sleep at night, doesn't he want to know?' I asked desperately.

'I don't know. If it were me, I would have contacted you straight away, but John isn't me and he'll do things in his own time.'

'But Helen, I'm really struggling with this.'

'I know, but all I can do is tell him that you've called.'

I had given John every opportunity to communicate with me and, unfortunately, I could already see many similarities between him and his mother. Once again my caring and sensitive nature had gone unnoticed. I was tired of thinking of everyone else.

'I can't wait any longer for John to contact me. Helen, I've decided to tell you everything.'

'But Karen, only tell me if you're absolutely sure.'

'I am.'

'Maybe once I know, I can be of some help to John,' she added.

I was convinced it was the right thing. The decision to share my secret with Helen had brought a sudden wave of relief.

'Karen, I don't think there's anything that would surprise me.'

'Helen, I think this will,' I said knowingly. I was poised, ready for a shock reaction.

'I am John's sister.' There was a moments' delay.

'My God!'

'I told you it was something big, didn't I?'

'Oh no, I don't believe it.'

I waited patiently as she tried to absorb the startling news.

'So your father is Patrick, yes?' she asked hesitantly and making what she thought was an obvious assumption, perhaps believing me to be the result of a relationship between Patrick and an unknown liaison.

'Yes,' I confirmed.

'But your mother, it's not Margaret is it?' she asked warily.

'Yes, she is my mother.'

'Oh, no. Oh my God!' The confirmation that I was a full sister was most distressing to her.

'Karen, how old are you and when were you born?' she asked.

216

'I'm forty-five and I was born on 23rd March 1962.' Helen did a quick mental calculation.

'But they were married,' she whispered.

'Yes, that's right.'

'Oh no, surely not. I just can't believe it.' Battling with her tears, she bombarded me with questions. I gave her a potted history of my search, highlighting the points that, for me, were impossible to understand. She too was astounded by the facts I had uncovered and could think of no acceptable explanation. I described at great length my meeting in Dublin with Margaret and Patrick and told of Margaret's suicide threat if her sons ever discovered my existence.

As we talked, her sadness turned to anger. It was impossible for her to understand what would have driven Margaret and Patrick to give away their first-born child. Margaret and Patrick's actions appalled her. She was incensed as she recalled how she and Margaret had watched adoption programmes together over the years. Not only was Margaret highly critical of any women who gave up their babies, but she would also express great concern for those 'poor children' left to the mercy of the Catholic church.

'Margaret and Patrick's lives have been a lie,' she announced. 'I've known them for more than twenty years and I still can't believe it. John will be very shocked. He has a special relationship with his mother. I don't know how he's going to take this news. Since your call, we've discussed many scenarios but we've never imagined this.'

I sought solace in our conversation. The care and empathy she had displayed several days earlier was still evident. I sensed a connection between us. As Helen slowly absorbed the initial shock she began to delve and enquire a little more and so I explained my current personal situation and my location. She was excited to discover that we only lived an hour's drive away, but saddened to think that so much time had passed. This was the moment to introduce the existence of my three daughters.

'Oh my God,' she cried again. 'They are John's nieces! I didn't think to ask if you had any children. Doesn't Margaret want to know her granddaughters?' she asked despairingly.

'No,' I replied.

'What are their names and how old are they?' she asked eagerly.

'Rosemary sixteen, Annie fourteen and Nancy seven.'

The mention of each name produced another wave of emotion from her.

'Whatever happens Karen, I'll certainly come and meet you all.'

After talking for almost two hours, I asked Helen about her next move.

'I'm not going to tell John that you've called, he needs to hear this from his mother. We're going back home the day after tomorrow, for a week. John will be staying with his parents for the entire time. Margaret will have a number of opportunities to talk to all three of her sons.'

'She won't do it,' I said adamantly.

'Yes she will. I've known Margaret for a long time and she'll want to do the right thing, she knows she's got to tell them. This is the first time since meeting you that she'll have them all together. She'll do it.'

'I'm not convinced.'

'I've got to give her the chance and I'm not going to say a word to John about our conversation,' said Helen.

'But how can you keep a secret like this?' I asked.

'The next couple of days won't be easy, but once we're back home (clearly Ireland was still considered to be home) I'll take myself off to my parents and give Margaret as much time as possible with John, Michael and Oliver.'

'I still don't think she'll do it.'

'If she doesn't, then I'll have no choice but to tell John as soon as we return next week. God, I really hope I don't have to.' Unlike Helen, I knew it was a real possibility.

'Helen, I can't imagine how you'll keep it a secret?'

'Luckily, I'm not seeing John this evening as he's out. I shall look forward to the trip home and I will be looking at Margaret in a totally different light,' she said in a devilish tone.

'Look after yourself Karen and we will speak again soon.'

I had really warmed to Helen.

24. Father's Day

Three days had elapsed since John and Helen's return from Ireland and still I'd heard nothing from either of them. Although my assumption was that Margaret had chosen not to confess news of my existence to her three sons, surely Helen had found the opportunity to inform John of his parents' great secret? I'd been on tenterhooks all weekend, carrying the phone around the house waiting for those recognisable last two digits on our caller display, even reluctant to go out for fear of missing the call. I had to be the first person to speak to John. Finally, on Sunday morning at 11.00 a.m. the phone rang and I spotted the number I'd been hoping for.

'Everyone, this is it,' I called out, alerting both Paul and Rosemary as I answered the phone. I had no idea quite what kind of reaction I'd receive from the voice on the end of the line.

'Hello,' I said nervously.

'Hello, is that Karen?' It was John.

'Yes,' I said, my heart pounding. There was a brief pause.

'It's your little brother here!'

There was an immediate surge of emotion as the tears started to roll down my cheeks. Those words from John reassured me that this was not a conversation I needed to fear.

'Well, you know the secret now,' I said.

'And what a wonderful secret to discover,' he replied. I was completely overwhelmed. After so many months of negative feelings towards me from both Margaret and Patrick, I suddenly found myself faced with a positive reaction and it was truly uplifting.

'Did Helen tell you?' I asked.

'Yes, we returned home on Thursday and I could tell she had something on her mind. She eventually sat me down and told me everything on Friday evening. So after spending yesterday in a state of total shock, I decided that as it was Father's Day, today would be a really good day to contact you.'

It felt very strange. The previous conversations with him had been truly agonising for me and now at last with my true identity revealed, I was able to talk to my brother freely. It was clear that Helen had relayed much of the story about my communication with her and my dilemma concerning Margaret and her terrifying threat of suicide. Fortunately, he showed understanding and sympathy to my impossible situation and reiterated that he had not discussed any of this with his parents.

He was interested to hear more of the details surrounding my search and how I had coped throughout this impossible time. Then at last came the question I had been waiting for.

'Well, when can we meet?'

'Whenever you like,' came my immediate response, hoping desperately for sooner rather than later.

'Today?' he asked.

'Yes, definitely.' I was delighted to find that he felt the same way.

'I know you are in Sevenoaks,' he said, intent on pointing out that he too was capable of a little detective work. Prior to calling me he had searched my name on the internet and through our outstanding planning application on our new property, had discovered my home address.

'I can find my way there if you like – it's no trouble,' he said cheerily. I looked around and was reminded of the building site we had been living in for the past seven months. I didn't feel comfortable inviting him here for such a special moment in our lives. There was also another consideration. Despite my daughters being as eager to meet John as I was, I wanted to have some time with him alone first, before introducing them. So I quickly deflected his idea.

'Oh no, we're quite happy to come to Stanmore,' I insisted. 'Where can we meet you?' John thought for a short time and decided upon a pub at Stirling Corner, close to the M1. He gave some brief directions and we arranged to meet there in the car park at 1.00 pm.

'Is your partner's name Paul? I noticed his name on the building application – will he be coming?' asked John.

'Yes he will, and Helen: she'll be there, won't she?'

'Certainly,' he confirmed. 'I'll be driving a little blue Toyota, what sort of car will you be in?' Despite knowing exactly what car I would arrive in, at that moment my mind was unable to process any information. I rambled on quoting ridiculous model numbers and letters that bore no relevance to our car. Realising that I was getting nowhere other than making myself appear totally vague, I settled for the colour.

'Silver,' I said. Luckily it seemed enough to satisfy John.

'Great, look forward to seeing you there,' he said as he ended the call.

During my conversation with John, both Paul and Rosemary had both appeared at my side and had been listening intently. In my excitement and desire to keep them abreast of the conversation I'd found myself scribbling brief, garbled notes directly onto the soon to be decorated bedroom wall. Trying to talk, listen, reply and write messages had been quite a challenge, so I set about relaying the entire conversation back to them in full. Next I telephoned Annie and Nancy. Conveniently they were in Bluewater on a shopping trip with David. Had they been in Sevenoaks, judging by their sheer excitement at the news, I fear it would have been impossible to persuade them to remain behind.

With little more than one hour remaining until our rendezvous, including an hour's drive, I flung open the wardrobe to frantically search for something suitable to wear. I tried on endless items, rejecting each in turn, as the mountain of discarded clothes on the bed grew ever larger. It was a warm, sunny day and I wanted to look smart but casual, but alas nothing I tried had the desired effect. Conscious of John's commitment to fitness I wanted to look my best, remembering Paddy's comment in Dublin that I certainly didn't look my age. Whilst not entirely happy with my final choice, it was the best I could find. I grabbed the camera, the document wallet containing everything relating to my search and some assorted photos, before flying out of the house on this most extraordinary next chapter of my mission.

During our drive I made several calls to family and friends whom I knew were on tenterhooks this weekend, anxiously awaiting news of any possible communication from John. I also made a further call to Annie and Nancy, who by this time were beside themselves with excitement. Annie was desperate to know what I'd finally chosen to wear, which thankfully did receive her seal of approval. I had to promise to keep them in the picture for the rest of the day. All three of my daughters had shared every stage of this search and it was not only my family that I was about to be united with, but theirs too.

Looking back now, what a peculiar journey! There was little conversation between Paul and me, totally absorbed by my emotions which fluctuated between unbelievable excitement at the prospect of meeting a true brother and great sadness to have to wait for this union until this stage of our lives.

Pulling into the car park, we scoured the area but there was no sign of John. We parked and remained inside the car, monitoring each vehicle as it arrived. My heart was racing and my palms were clammy: at forty-five years of age I was about to meet somebody that I could never have dreamed possible.

It wasn't long before a little blue sports car sped into the car park and without hesitation drew up alongside us. I caught a glimpse of John at the wheel, he appeared red faced and rather emotional. Paul and I got out of the car.

John wasted no time, literally leaping out of his car and racing towards me. Without any exchange of words he reached out and threw his arms around me. Everything happened so quickly, there was little opportunity to really look at him. Locked in the clutches of my brother I immediately noticed that he was only marginally taller then me. Based on his father's height I had expected him to be at least six feet tall. This warm embrace was a far cry from any reception I'd received in Dublin. Eventually, after releasing me from his clasp he turned and hurried off back to his car, this time to the passenger side where Helen was still sitting. He bent down and reappeared with an enormous bouquet. As he turned to approach me, carrying the sizable display, his face was hidden and still I was prevented from studying the face of my sibling.

Not only was I looking forward to meeting John, but Helen too, having played a key part in this clandestine affair. Like me, John was extremely anxious, he stuttered and his sentences were unfinished. He looked around the beer garden nervously unable to decide where we should all sit, eventually he chose to leave the decision to Helen and me, while he and Paul went inside to purchase some drinks. I had so much to share with Helen, who had been such a comfort during those initial traumatic phone calls, but alas, I was dumbstruck. Together we sat in silence, waiting for Paul and John to return, barely managing to exchange the briefest of remarks.

Once together around the table, in the warm sunshine, I could hardly come to grips with the reality that the man sitting opposite me was indeed my true brother. I was greedy to take in his every aspect. His face, his physique, his mannerisms and even his voice transfixed me. The picture on the internet of a somewhat forbidding John, with short, severe haircut and his stern expression had given the appearance of perhaps somebody in the armed forces. In the flesh, however, he was warm, jovial and extremely amiable.

I realised how difficult it is to look at another person in such detail and see any likeness with yourself. Does anyone really know the intricacies of their own features and expressions? Something however that could be in no doubt, was our same freckly complexion. I was also quick to notice the protruding joints on his wrists and elbows and unlike me, John could make visual comparisons between his close family members and his new-found sister.

'Those hands are just like mother's,' he said pointing to the wrinkly, boney hands that I'd been ashamed of all my life. He could see similarities between his brother, Michael, and me and rather interestingly, just as Paddy had done in Dublin, his paternal grandmother. Helen was keen to point out how similar I looked to Margaret, but this wasn't something I cared to dwell on. However, despite this, talk of my resemblance to John's family, and particularly Paddy's, was certainly comforting. Margaret had refrained from making any comparisons, in fact when pressed she claimed not to see any.

After moving inside for our meal we continued to talk non-stop. Our plates of food had been barely touched when the waitress finally decided to clear them away.

John was in awe of my efforts to trace Margaret and most impressed by my detective skills. He was also keen to hear every detail of my time in Dublin, meeting Margaret and Paddy. but he expressed great surprise at my account of his mother. He was adamant that the woman I had met and described was not the mother he knew. Although the photographic evidence confirmed that I'd met with our parents, Margaret and Patrick Coleman, he was at pains to point out that there must be some good explanation for her reaction and her manner towards me. He was utterly convinced that his mother would always strive to do anything for anyone. Despite this, John was at a loss to know how best to tackle his parents. His mother's suicide threat was not one to be taken lightly.

John retrieved his laptop from the car, intent on showing me numerous images of the entire Coleman clan. However, it was impossible for me to retain any of the information, even pictures of my other brothers, Michael and Oliver – I had reached overload. The afternoon had been extremely emotional and physically draining.

After four hours sitting in the restaurant, John invited us back to their home. They lived just a short drive away and as we followed in convoy we made a quick call home to the girls. As expected, they bombarded me with questions; fortunately the short journey restricted the interrogation.

Arriving at John and Helen's semi-detached property with its narrow access road, I could see that I had made the right decision not to sit and stake out the property some months earlier. Inside, it had a contemporary feel and a tidiness that only people without children can achieve. We followed them into the kitchen. Paul sat himself down at the round table in the centre of the room, but I chose instead to sit in an inviting looking rocking-chair in the corner. Helen made a pot of tea while John disappeared upstairs, intent on finding yet more snaps to share with me. He soon returned with a comprehensive, historical photographic family record. I felt a little more receptive than earlier in the day and John's obvious enthusiasm was so clearly displayed, even providing me with a large number of assorted snaps to take home and study at leisure. I had truly warmed to his genial nature.

I reached out and took a photo from my own folder. It was the one of me with my three daughters, which I had originally taken on our first trip to Dublin. Sadly, at the time, it had stirred little interest from Margaret. John reacted quite differently, seizing it immediately and claiming it as his own, then instructing me to write each of the girls' names and dates of birth on the reverse.

Next I raised the subject of Michael. The prospect of meeting a second brother was now high on my agenda and made even more imperative with John's most remarkable news that Michael had always wanted a sister.

John explained how he'd kept Michael abreast of the curious communications from me: firstly my letter and calls to him the previous Christmas and then my recent telephone call, prior to his return to Ireland. Michael had been intrigued by events and had urged John to contact me to discover exactly how I might be connected to their family. However, I was more than a little taken aback to learn that John had refrained from sharing any of this weekend's revelation with him. Instead, he had chosen to wait several weeks until after Michael's return from his forthcoming holiday to Florida. He feared that news of a sister might be an unwelcomed distraction prior to Michael's holiday of a lifetime. Although I was more than a little disappointed by his decision, I refrained from challenging it.

John was eager to show us around his home, particularly his gym, located in a single-storey extension to the side of his house with direct access from the hallway. It housed an impressive array of hi-tech exercise equipment. Helen was also keen to point out how the gym had expanded into their former dining room across the way. Everything was exceedingly orderly and pristine, he was right to be proud of it.

After taking a multitude of photos between us, we finally said our goodbyes and encouraged John and Helen to come to Sevenoaks at their first opportunity to meet their nieces. It had been quite a remarkable day, from which there could be no turning back. At long last I had indeed met my true brother. Not surprisingly, Paul and I talked non-stop for the entire journey home. One point in particular came up time and again, John's reaction to my account of his mother's behaviour towards me. Furthermore, despite the good feeling that had developed between us throughout the afternoon, I was left with a lingering niggle. Why had John decided not to share the news of something so monumental with his brother Michael? I rather resented waiting for John to determine the next move.

Over the next few days I carried the digital camera around, proudly displaying a picture of me with my brother John. I soon printed off some good-size copies, rather than peer at minute images on the camera. It was only then that I saw the remarkable likeness between us both. Each and every feature was strikingly similar, right down to the matching individual creases on our faces. It was quite uncanny. There was no doubt about our blood ties.

There were frequent telephone conversations as I tried desperately to persuade them to come and visit us all in Sevenoaks, but John was invariable busy at the weekends with clients in his gym. I would have to wait until the opportunity arose. Finally, three weeks after our first meeting in Stanmore, on Nancy's eighth birthday, to my absolute delight, word came from John that he would come and join us for our family celebrations. He came alone, as Helen had returned home to Ireland for a prior engagement, although she was mortified to miss the occasion.

It was an enjoyable if a somewhat surreal day. As well as my ex-husband David, Dad and Eileen were also present and although

I think Dad understandably felt quite uncomfortable, he was welcoming and gracious throughout. John too, was nervous but made tremendous efforts to integrate with everyone. The day took on a more relaxed tone when we all set off to watch Nancy perform in an informal concert that afternoon. Sitting together in the beautiful garden belonging to Nancy's music teacher, drinking Pimms and listening to Nancy as she played a specially chosen Irish piece on her violin, I could see that John was quite moved by the whole experience.

Back at home after all the guests had left, John remained behind and stayed until late, taking the opportunity to talk further to the girls and to reflect on the recent events. He was still highly perplexed by the revelations of the past few weeks. I listened with interest to John's account of his conversations with Michael, who was currently away on his holiday. Before leaving for Florida, Michael had been most insistent that John should follow up the matter that had given rise to so much speculation just weeks earlier. He had even called John from his holiday for an update. John had continued to deflect his brother's enquiries.

25. Michael

August 2007

Although I was delighted with the regular contact John and I were now having, I felt somewhat uncomfortable that Michael and Oliver were still totally oblivious of what was happening. John had made it clear that the responsibility was his alone to determine the right moment to reveal to his two brothers the existence of an unknown sister. Feeling more than a little beholden to him, I soon became frustrated by another waiting game.

Oliver, the youngest, still lived with Margaret and Paddy and meeting him was always going to be a more difficult matter. Michael had returned from his holiday almost two weeks ago and still there was reluctance from John to share this extraordinary story with him. Michael was already aware of a woman keen to make contact with John. Having encouraged his brother to follow up this strange communication, Michael had quizzed John repeatedly to no avail. Armed with Michael's contact details, I was very tempted to bring this painful waiting game to an end for myself when, finally, almost six weeks since our first dramatic meeting, John called with the news I'd been waiting for.

'You'll be pleased to hear that I've told Michael. I talked to him a couple of days ago and, as you would expect, he was very shocked,' he announced. Although a little miffed to hear their conversation had taken place days earlier, I listened intently.

'As you can imagine, it was a very long call. I told him as much as I could remember about your search, but you'll need to fill in the gaps at some point,' he explained. 'One of the first things Michael asked for was a photo of you, so I emailed a couple to his office that evening. I've spoken to him since and he's been in turmoil. He was unable to sleep a wink the first night, there was so much going around in his head. At work the following morning he downloaded the photos and the first thing he noticed were your hands, he was in no doubt that you are his sister. You have mother's hands. He told me that he'd spent the entire day just glued to the computer screen, analysing the few pictures I'd sent. He wants to come over and meet you as soon as possible and is suggesting the weekend of the 10th August. He's intending to fly into Luton on Friday evening, stay with us and return Monday morning. He'll be coming on his own. Although Helena is aware of everything, they can't share it with the children at this stage as they both spend a lot of time with their grandparents. He's planning on telling everyone that he's away on a golfing weekend. Anyway, have a think about it and let me know. If you've got something else planned, then Michael's fairly flexible and we can arrange something for another time,' he said, casually.

'No, no, that weekend will be fine,' I stressed, desperate to confirm a date before ending the call. Another time was out of the question. As on my first meeting with John, I was prepared to cancel anything. Nothing else mattered more and I don't think that John could fully appreciate that.

It was difficult to understand why Michael hadn't contacted me directly. John obviously still saw himself as the go-between, asking for all arrangements concerning Michael to be passed through him. Despite this, to hear of Michael's sleepless nights, inability to do any work and an eagerness to meet me at the first opportunity could only be positive.

The rendezvous was just over two weeks away and checking the diary, I was delighted to find that Rosemary, Annie and Nancy were all available. The little knowledge I had of Michael just fuelled my desire to meet him even sooner. Unlike John, Michael had a family of his own and, as a parent himself, he would undoubtedly have a greater understanding of the acuteness of my situation. The news of Michael's lifelong wish to have a sister made the prospect of a meeting all the more appealing. I wondered how Margaret and Paddy had reacted to what was for Michael, only ever a pipe dream, but for them an absolute reality? I was convinced that I would find a special connection with Michael.

Clearly, this brother was as keen to meet me as I was to meet him and unable to contain my sheer delight, I decided to gauge his reaction for myself. Eight months had passed since my shocking discovery of three brothers. How patient I had been throughout this entire search! I didn't need John to now sanction any direct communication. So with a combined feeling of nervousness and excitement, I called Michael's place of work. A woman answered.

'Hello, can I speak to Michael Coleman please,' I asked, my heart racing.

'He's not here at the moment, in fact he's not in the office a great deal, I can give you his mobile number and you can contact him on that,' she added. I scribbled it down excitedly.

'Is it OK to contact him on his mobile, would it be a problem?' I asked.

'Oh no, that would be fine,' she said reassuringly. I thanked her for her help and ended the call.

I dialled again. Knowing that I would find a brother on the end of the line was utterly thrilling. As usual, in these most anxious of situations, it took several attempts to enter the correct digits.

Eventually, success: it was ringing.

'Hello,' said an unfamiliar, fast speaking, Irish voice.

'Err, hello, is that Michael Coleman,' I asked, nervously.

'Hello, Karen?' he asked. There was no doubt. I had certainly been on his mind.

'Yes, hello,' I said excitedly. 'I understand that John has told you all about me at last,' I said, hoping that he would seize the opportunity to lead the conversation.

'That's right, what a shock! It's been hard to get my head around it. He's told me a lot about you and your difficult time in Dublin, I'm sorry to hear that,' he said sympathetically. 'It's great to talk to you, but how did you get my number?' he asked curiously.

'Ah, there's nothing I can't find out,' I said mischievously. Unwilling to disclose my source, I liked the idea that my brothers appeared most impressed with my cunning detective skills and had no intention of disillusioning them now.

'It seems not,' he chuckled. 'I've heard a lot about your search from John, you appear to be capable of finding out anything,' he teased.

'I hear you're planning on coming over?' I asked.

'Yes, did John tell you? I'd like to come on the weekend of the 10th August, if that's OK with you?'

'Yes, that weekend is great, all three girls are around and so you'll be able to meet everyone.'

'I'm really looking forward to it,' he said sincerely.

He spoke far more quickly than John and with a very pronounced Irish accent. What a strange notion that someone so closely related to me could sound so different. John had shown me a photo of Michael some weeks earlier, but somehow his unfamiliar accent made it impossible for me to conjure up an image of him. His voice was reminiscent of my childhood, as I remembered the race commentator for the Grand National, Peter

233

O'Sullevan – an amusing thought. Michael seemed delighted that I had taken the initiative and made the first move. His manner appeared relaxed and jovial and I would have loved to talk for longer, but knowing he was at work and likely to be standing in the middle of a golf course, I kept it brief.

'I'd better let you go now. I look forward to seeing you soon. Goodbye,' I said reluctantly.

'Take care, bye Karen,' he replied and the call was over.

I had great expectations for Michael's whistle-stop weekend. It would require some careful planning and I was keen to make the most of our limited time together. Michael lived in Waterford, Ireland, so unlike John, he was never going to be easily accessible. With Michael's visit now imminent, the girls had yet to meet Helen, who had questioned John relentlessly after his trip to Sevenoaks for Nancy's birthday and was longing to meet my daughters for herself. With the school holidays now in full swing, we drove to Stanmore to spend a delightful day with her and, later, John who joined us after returning from work.

'Actually, they don't feel like strangers. It seems like we've known them for a very long time,' said Annie, on the journey home.

'Yes I agree,' added Nancy. 'But did you think it was difficult to understand what Helen was saying sometimes?' she asked.

'Yes, but she was so nice and John's so funny,' added Annie.

I called John to confirm plans for the coming weekend. By now I'd rather taken control, but John seemed quite unperturbed.

'Paul and I will come to you early Saturday morning, without the girls, as it'll be easier to talk,' I explained.

'Yes, that's absolutely fine, feel free to stay as long as you like, I'll be busy in the gym throughout the morning but I'll join you later. And Sunday?' he asked.

'Come to Sevenoaks and spend the day with us, but come early,' I stressed.

'We'll do what we can. I'm looking forward to it,' he announced cheerily. 'Oh, and I've heard from Helena that Michael is suddenly feeling rather anxious at the prospect of meeting you,' he added rather gleefully. I felt a little sorry for Michael. Somehow, I sensed that John was deriving a certain satisfaction acting as go-between and thereby relaying to Michael an already established relationship with me. Michael's feelings were to be expected, but it still concerned me that having already spoken to him, his fears had not been allayed. I had already picked up on his wonderful sense of humour and decided to call him once again and put it to the test.

'Hello,' he said cheerily, he'd spotted my number and knew it was me.

'Hello, how are you?' I asked.

'I'm good thanks and looking forward to the weekend.'

'That's not what John tells me. Apparently you're feeling rather nervous,' I teased.

He chuckled. 'Yes, a little I suppose,' he agreed reluctantly. I ran through the weekend's plans with him.

'Yes it sounds good, although I think I'll need a few beers with John tomorrow night in readiness for Saturday,' implying his nerves needed steadying.

'I don't want you with a hangover on Saturday morning, I want your full attention,' I exclaimed. 'We're coming early.'

'Better make sure I'm up then,' he said, jokingly.

'You talk too fast and I struggle to understand your accent. You'll have to slow down. It was the same for the girls when we visited John and Helen last Monday,' I said cheekily. He laughed again.

'O.K, I 'l l try. Is this any easier ?' he said in a slow, laboured and exaggerated fashion with every intention of provoking a humorous response.

'Yes, that's much better, thank you. Have a good journey and

I'll see you Saturday morning.'

'See you then,' he said, still chuckling.

The weather was glorious as Paul and I drove to Stanmore. It was hard to contain my excitement but once again my emotions were awry and I found my eyes spontaneously filling with tears at the prospect of the imminent meeting with my brother Michael.

Helen answered the door. I could see Michael hovering nervously behind her, his hands firmly in his pockets. He moved forward and placed his arm around my shoulders.

'Hello, how are you?' he asked embracing me and kissing my cheek. A surge of emotion prevented me from replying as my eyes flooded with tears. Michael greeted Paul and we went through into the kitchen and sat around the familiar table. After a quick coffee and pleasantries, Paul disappeared to attend to a maintenance matter.

Prior to our visit, John had asked Paul if he could repair their bathroom tap. Oliver had turned it off rather enthusiastically, during his last visit. He appeared to have the strength of an ox, refusing to ignore any resistance, as he continued to tighten the tap ensuring it was fully secure. As a result a new set of hand basin taps were required.

John was in the gym and Helen was discreetly supplying everyone with refreshments throughout the day. There were a wealth of feelings and emotions racing around my head. The sheer excitement of this union and the sadness of what may have been lost were overwhelming.

Unlike John, Michael was not such a talker. He sat and listened keenly, as I told him something about myself, sharing the various documents and photographs, which I had already shown John. Although Michael was aware of the outline detail, it was with disbelief that he sat holding my birth certificate, shaking his head in horror. I watched intently as he digested

236

the extraordinary details, the blank column headed Christian name and undoubtedly for him the most alarming entry: Patrick Coleman, his own father, declared deceased.

Faced with details of my birth and subsequent adoption, together with my account of meeting in Dublin with his parents, he was visibly perturbed. He had some recollection of that fateful day, which he wanted to share with me.

'I remember it well, they phoned to tell me that they were going out for a spin that day,' he recalled. 'I thought it odd at the time. They said they would be out for the whole day. It was completely out of character,' he added. The term 'out for a spin' was a very peculiar, old fashioned sort of expression and to hear Michael using it comfortably was extremely quaint. Added to which, for something so monumental to be referred to in a most throwaway manner was, even to me, a little humorous.

Michael got up and left the room, returning almost immediately.

'Here this is for you,' he said, smiling and placing his arm around my shoulders as he handed me a decorative carrier bag. I felt very special as I explored the contents of the gift bag. Inside there was a postcard depicting various scenes from Waterford, his hometown. A bookmark with the Coleman name and its origins. It had been my name once, albeit briefly. It derived from the word Colm meaning dove and there too was the Coleman motto 'Death is not to be feared;' I thought immediately about Margaret's suicide threat. Finally, I could see what appeared to be an item of Waterford Crystal, as I opened the box inside was a beautiful cut glass dish. I had accumulated very few treasured possessions throughout my life and it was very much appreciated.

'I've decided to start collecting this,' I announced suddenly, looking at Michael with a cheeky smile. His reaction was spontaneous.

'Great, I'll buy you another piece in forty five years.' The pair of us were reduced to laughter. Despite the reality of the sadness that was evident for both of us, it was a relief for the day to be interspersed with an element of fun.

Ever since my arrival I had been conscious of a television in the corner of the kitchen that had remained on throughout the morning. For Michael it had acted as a focal point as he sat listening to my account, which clearly made him feel ill at ease, but for me it was intrusive and any attempt to ignore it was impossible.

'Are you going to watch that all day or am I going to have your undivided attention at some point?' I demanded, believing this day to be far more important than anything the broadcasters could provide. He immediately reached for the controls and suddenly the screen was blank and the kitchen silent. He turned to face me.

'Thank you,' I said, triumphantly. With a stony look he drew closer to me and positioned his face directly in front of mine until our eyes met.

'My God, you're bossy!' he said pointedly. 'And we know exactly who you take after don't we?' breaking out into broad grin. There was devilment in his voice, as he dared after only a short time, to make comparisons between his mother and me. Once again we both dissolved into laughter. It came as a welcome relief from what otherwise had been a rather intense time.

His mobile phone rang. It was Helena. He disappeared to take the call.

'Helena wants to know everything,' he reported as he returned into the kitchen.

'What have you told her, did I get an OK?' I asked confidently.

'You certainly did,' he said, smiling.

'Doesn't she want to talk to me herself?' I asked.

'Yes she'd love to,' he said, quite surprised at my suggestion.

'Call her back now,' I suggested. I had some sympathy for Helena, for whom it must have been hard to miss out on such an eventful weekend. Although brief, the call did give us both a chance just to hear each other's voice.

To my absolute delight, Michael had loaded Margaret and Paddy's wedding photos onto his laptop. Taken in August 1961, I studied each picture intently. I recognised the church and talked about my recent visit there. It was strange to think that I could provide my brothers with completely new information concerning their parents' wedding. One photo in particular was most significant. It was of Margaret standing alone after the ceremony, looking radiant and extremely happy, her bridal bouquet in one hand and the open palm of the other shielding her stomach. She was, of course, hiding a deep secret. I analysed her joyful expression, wondering if it had always been her intention to give me away, even at that early stage?

Paul and John joined us for a late lunch prepared by Helen. We then moved out into the garden to enjoy the warm sunshine and remained there until late into the evening as Helen continued to supply us with a much welcome array of refreshments.

As the mood relaxed and conversation turned to more light-hearted topics, I thought about Margaret, oblivious not only to this meeting, but also completely unaware of the events of the last two months. How could she have been so dogmatic as to deprive me of such a wonderful opportunity to establish a relationship with my brothers?

The following day we prepared to welcome John, Helen and Michael to our home in Sevenoaks. A Sunday brunch was planned out on the patio. The previous evening Paul had talked of his love of guitars and both John and Michael had been most impressed to hear that his talents extended to making them. So it was with great pride and excitement that he arranged his collection of instruments outside, together with an amplifier for them all to amuse themselves strumming some tunes.

Michael had come armed with gifts for the girls: a cuddly Eyeore, shamrock between its teeth for Nancy, guaranteed to remind us all of our Irish roots. My daughters were happy to interact with their new family and even David, having delivered the girls earlier that morning, was keen to meet Michael and Helen.

'I can definitely see a strong resemblance between you and Michael,' he remarked.

'It's all in the eyes,' said Michael, winking at me slyly. I smiled. I loved that sense of connection – it gave me a warm, contented feeling.

David said his goodbyes, perhaps a little forlorn as he watched the joyous party, presumably knowing that he should never have denied my search, and thereby deprive both me and our daughters of such a marvellous occasion.

Later that day we visited Hever Castle, the home of Anne Boleyn. It couldn't have been a better venue. Its fantastic water maze caused great amusement for Michael, John and the girls as they chased each around, enjoying the occasional soaking. On reaching the centre point, I watched Nancy's obvious delight as Michael lifted her high above his head. It was inconceivable to imagine that their relationship had only begun just hours before.

By sheer chance, our visit coincided with a birds of prey display, something John had certainly never encountered before. I sensed that this family hadn't really seen or experienced a great deal of life. They watched in amazement as an American Fish Eagle named Annie showed a clear reluctance to fly over the seated crowd to collect her reward. Instead she chose to walk confidently across the lawn amongst the spectators, which made for some stunning photo opportunities as she ambled by.

A wonderful dinner at a local restaurant followed, before returning back to Sevenoaks to relax and enjoy the remainder of our time together. Even Mr Bunny felt the need to establish a good relationship, singling out Michael to sit alongside for the rest of the evening. It had been a most successful weekend for all concerned. Rosemary, Annie and Nancy engaged effortlessly with their new relatives, particularly enjoying John and Michael's frequent tomfoolery.

Whilst Michael had clearly loved the weekend's events, he was downhearted that it was necessary for his family to remain at home. The matter of his mother needed to be dealt with urgently.

It was hard to say goodbye to Michael. In just a short time we had discovered a real affinity with one another.

On his return to Ireland, Michael's life was very troubled. He wanted so desperately to share the news of his new family with his own children, particularly as they had inadvertently discovered a glorious picture of Mr. Bunny on his laptop. Explaining it away as being a rabbit he'd seen on the golf course, he had raced to shut down the computer hoping that they hadn't caught sight of the soft furnishings in the background. The prospect of confronting his mother and raising a subject that he knew would certainly be contentious, terrified him. The situation was exacerbated by John's reluctance to support his brother in this unenviable task. Michael had hoped that both he and John would tackle their mother together. He had, however, shared the news and photographic evidence with his younger brother Oliver, explaining to him as much detail as he thought he could digest before swearing him to secrecy.

Finally, after several weeks, the tension became too much for Michael to bear any longer. The realisation that the task of confronting his mother lay with him alone, caused him to act on sheer impulse and leave his place of work to drive to his parent's home.

Margaret was alone.

'What are you doing here?' she asked curiously, somewhat startled by his unexpected arrival mid-afternoon. Feeling anxious and frightened there was no turning back now.

'Mum, I need to talk to you,' he hesitated. 'Have you got anything that you would like to tell me, anything at all?' he asked as calmly as he could, emphasising his last three words.

'No,' she replied nonchalantly.

'Are you sure, I'm giving you this chance to talk to me about anything you think I ought to know,' he stressed again, desperately wanting his mother to take the initiative and not to leave him in this most unbearable of situations.

'No,' she said firmly, he could sense she was guarded. Michael feared the outcome.

'I know about Karen…,' he said shakily. Her reaction was horrifying. Without a moment's hesitation, she reached for the carving knife and brandished it in an utter frenzy. She dramatically pointed it directly at her heart, where it remained while she made shocking threats to carry out this and other appalling acts, including throwing herself off a bridge into the local river.

Michael was distraught. Never before had he witnessed such a display of rage. She was furious, shouting at Michael at the top of her voice.

'Ollie is not to know anything of this, do you understand?' she screamed.

'Ollie already knows,' said Michael, knowing that news of this would just fuel her anger. She demanded that Michael leave the house immediately. Concerned for her safety, he pleaded with her for reassurance that she wouldn't carry out any of her appalling threats.

'No,' she snapped. 'I've got a neighbour coming round for

a cup of tea this afternoon,' she announced in a surprisingly controlled and composed fashion. Michael was deeply upset and returned to his car and drove some considerable distance, reliving the traumatic experience over and over before stopping at the roadside to call his wife Helena, John and finally me, to report the shocking event.

26. Andrew

The prospect of siblings to share my life and that of my daughters from now on was incredible. Even at such an early stage in our relationship, my new-found brothers' genuine display of warmth and commitment convinced me that they would enhance my life in a way which until now would have been inconceivable.

Until recently, Andrew had been my only brother but there was never any possibility of us having a conventional brother/sister relationship. After many years fraught with difficulties, I had severed my relationship with him almost twenty years earlier. The longstanding feud between us had left me unaware of his whereabouts or his current circumstances.

Andrew was two years my junior and like me, he too had been adopted. However, despite our shared circumstances, it did nothing to bring us together. As a young child, I soon noticed how demanding and extremely difficult he could be. His odd behaviour was exasperating and intolerable. Our lives consisted of endless disputes and battles and I have no recollection of us ever really enjoying each other's company.

I noticed how Mum and Nanny seldom discouraged Andrew's wayward behaviour. Instead it was often justified and defended. He was reluctant to share his toys or play together. At the age of five or six, I remember him receiving a most wonderful shiny blue pedal car for his birthday. I was very envious and desperate to test out this magnificent toy for myself, but it wasn't to be. Any idea that I might try it out for myself was forbidden, for fear of upsetting Andrew. Furthermore, their willingness to respond to his every need and demand, however bizarre, was infuriating. Whether it was flapping his hot meals with a rolled-up newspaper until it had reached an acceptable temperature or putting on his shoes for him whenever he ordered, their over-zealous reaction to him only seemed to exacerbate his underlying problems.

Andrew's highly controlling influence on my Mum, however, would continue throughout the rest of her life and ultimately also had a detrimental effect on my own relationship with her.

Andrew's approach to life was very different from mine. An ardent nonconformist, he had no intention of complying with anything unless it suited him. As far back as infant school, at only five years old, there were issues over his timekeeping. School was just a short distance from home and like many children at that time, Andrew and I would go home for lunch. However, whilst I was happy to return in time for the afternoon session, Andrew would insist on remaining at home until after he'd seen 'Watch with Mother' on the television. Mum would walk me back to school, leaving Andrew in Nanny's care before returning with him a little later at his own convenience. Although Mum believed that those fifteen minutes or so were neither here nor there, allowing Andrew to flout the rules at such a young age, heralded a highly problematical situation, which would span his entire schooling and beyond.

Andrew was six years old when we moved from nanny's house to the large new council estate in Mitcham. Despite the abundance of young children around us, Andrew was never particularly outgoing and any friendships were short-lived. Instead he seemed to prefer his own company. It soon became apparent that Andrew had a tremendous knowledge of far-reaching global and national topics, many of them still of little concern to the public in the mid 70s. While still very young, his strong opinions made for a fractious time within the family.

He would challenge Dad's chain smoking, declaring it to be not only anti-social, but also highlighting the serious health implications. His anguish was evident as he battled to avoid being a victim of passive smoking, to the extent that whenever he travelled in the family car he insisted on having his window wide open, whatever the weather. Needless to say, this dramatic approach did nothing to endear him to Dad.

245

Andrew would talk frequently about pollution and the poor air quality and to protect himself in built up areas, he would tie his handkerchief around his face, covering his nose and mouth. My parents would find the unwelcome attention this caused particularly difficult to deal with. He was extremely concerned about all aspects of his health, even to the extent of querying the competency of our family dentist. He questioned the ease with which Mum would allow us to be subjected to frequent drilling and filling of our teeth and continued to blame her for the poor quality of his teeth even as an adult.

He also held very strong views about his diet. After announcing his concerns over methods of animal farming and the subsequent consumption of meat and poultry, in particular beef, he became a non-meat eater. This was the late 70s before the widespread health implications had made the headline news. His views extended to the use of pesticides on fruit and vegetables, making his diet very restrictive. The solution to his concerns over what he consumed was resolved with a daily mix of either boiled potatoes or pasta mixed with yeast extract and frozen peas. This very unappealing concoction would always be eaten directly from the saucepan.

His concern for the environment meant that he had no intention of ever learning to drive. He would speak knowledgeably about unsustainable fuel and the problems that lay ahead, trying his utmost to convince me that I would be mad to ever think of buying a car. (Although, he was always more than happy for me to chauffeur him around when the need arose.) His preferred method of transport was a mountain bike and he longed to own one. Unfortunately, once again he was ahead of his time and the idea of a bike claiming to be suitable for off road, rough terrain created much hilarity. Living on a council estate in South London, Andrew's request was considered highly peculiar. It would be many years before such bikes became commonplace.

The source of Andrew's knowledge was never really understood. Whilst patchy, many elements of his seemingly absurd theories were to become real issues in later years. On reflection, Andrew was highly intelligent

Four generations: Mum (No. 1 Nanny), my maternal grandmother
(No. 2 Nanny) cradling Rosemary, and me.

Rosemary, aged 3.

Rosemary, aged 4, reaady to attend her school's Spring Festival.

Annie at 7 weeks.

*Swimming lessons
commence for Rosemary
and Annie, c. 1993.*

Annie and Rosemary in their matching dresses, 1995.

Annie and Rosemary with their baby sister, Nancy, 1999.

Nancy aged 15 months, c. 2000.

Nancy aged 7.

Annie and Nancy paragliding in Borneo in 2007.

*A proud mum with her three daughters,
each in their school uniform, 2003.*

Nancy aged 7. This is the photograph I sent to Margaret immediately after our first telephone conversation in December 2006.

Nancy showing off her new teeth, aged 8,

The amazing Mr Bunny.

Paul and Me, happy and content, 2010.

Rosemary and Annie (above)
Nancy (left), 2011.

Karen, Annie, Rosemary, Nancy
and Paul in 2011.

and possessed many great skills. He was not yet five when he learned to ride a two-wheeled bicycle. If his intelligence and his abilities had been correctly channelled he may have achieved great things. Sadly, not only were my parents ill-equipped to deal with their gifted son, but also there was very little support available to them. Andrew's challenging attitude and forthright approach caused tremendous friction within the family. Dad found it difficult to relate to his son, whilst Mum continued to be devoted to him and responded to his every need. With hindsight, I can see that this must have caused a great strain on my parents' marriage.

Ironically, it was Andrew's own intelligence that would cause conflict with his education. Highly scathing about the quality of teaching he received at school, he had made the decision to spend as little time as possible there. His attendance became ever more infrequent, choosing instead to remain at home with the very misguided support of my mother. Although she was at pains to persuade Andrew to attend school, she was always armed with an alibi – either he would be feeling unwell or he would be arriving a little later. Nothing could convince Andrew that academic qualifications were vital. Instead, he saw the whole examination process as no more than a massive memory test. He failed to see how this system could measure anyone's true intelligence. Andrew was not wrong in his belief that our schooling was unacceptable, but his ill-considered actions would ultimately lead to the intervention of the local authorities.

With a certain amount of 'extra time' to fill, Andrew was very fond of travelling, in particular the planning element of the journey. He would spend hours, days and even weeks scouring maps, reading his extensive national railway timetable and most of all packing. For him it was a meticulous process and one that needed to be repeated over and over again, painstakingly emptying and refilling his backpack. Invariably many of these expeditions never actually transpired and after lengthy preparations for one particular journey, it was usually time to focus on another location. Any teasing from me on his numerous aborted expeditions was always met with an intense fury.

Occasionally his plans did come to fruition. His very first and highly successful trip was on the train from East Croydon to Hastings. At just eleven years of age, he had made the journey on what was then a 2d (1 new penny) platform ticket. The first my parents heard of it was a telephone call from the Hastings police, asking for Dad to come and collect his son. He quizzed him intently to discover his thinking behind this bizarre act, but it was for no other reason than to prove that he could.

Many of his adventures were further afield and for longer periods, involving the purchasing and preparation of food. Countless quantities of monkey nuts were shelled and bagged in appropriate daily portions for his epic adventures. He was in his late teens when my Mum received a surprise telephone call, reporting his arrival on the island of Guam! I never really understood how these trips were funded.

The one thing that Andrew did allow himself to excel at was athletics. A middle-distance runner, he belonged to an athletics club and often competed at national level. He was committed to the sport from a young age, through to his late teens, but with mounting mental and emotional difficulties he was unable to maintain the discipline required, sadly never reaching his undoubted full potential.

Andrew was also plagued by obsessive behaviourism, which became worse as he grew older. In the belief that he could enhance any product, he would seek out a flaw in almost any item and then attempt to eradicate it. Eventually he would abort the various improvements and thereby destroy the item irreparably. He would unpick the stitching on his trainers and running shoes, for instance, with the intention of re-sewing them by hand, but there was never a successful outcome. It was the same with his backpack and sleeping bag. Clothing, too, came under Andrew's intense scrutiny. As he justified his actions, all I could see was vast sums of wasted money. I was utterly mortified to discover that our family hi-fi system had become the subject of one of Andrew's improvement schemes. I watched in horror as he began to dismantle this valuable piece of equipment. My plea to Mum fell on deaf ears, as I received her usual

248

response to Andrew's unwelcomed antics.

'Leave him alone he knows what he's doing,' is a phrase that even now still fills me with dread. Needless to say the entire music system, in its many pieces, was dispatched to the local dump.

His obsessive behaviour also extended to his appearance. Andrew lacked confidence in others, including hairdressers, claiming their inability to cut his hair evenly on each side. Hell-bent on a perfect haircut, he decided to tackle it himself. Behind closed doors he would cut one side and then the other. Cutting from side to side, struggling for an even finish, his hair becoming even shorter until he felt he had no alternative but to shave his entire head. Once he had allowed it to grow back he would repeat the task again. Sporting a permanent woolly hat indoors and out, he became fixated on the growth of his hair and his head was regularly shaven.

Around the age of fourteen, Andrew ceased to attend school completely. Although letters were sent home warning my parents of the outcome, nothing had the desired effect. In a last ditch attempt, the school devised a plan. My parents received notification that the deputy headmistress herself would come each morning to escort Andrew to school. My brother had no intention of complying and made the appropriate (in his mind), preparations for her unwelcome visit. With the aid of just a screwdriver he gouged out a hole in his bedroom door and crudely installed a lock with a key. On the fateful morning and with Mum and Dad already out at work, it was left to me to open the front door and allow this poor little Welsh woman the humiliating task of persuading Andrew to attend school. It was most embarrassing, as I watched her tentatively calling up the stairs in the hope that Andrew would obligingly appear. Aware of her thankless task, she bravely took herself up the stairs and banged on his door, rattling the handle, demanding that he unlock it. Andrew, with quite extraordinary confidence, remained firmly on the opposite side, refusing to even acknowledge her.

It was around this time that dad left the family home, leaving my Mum to single-handedly cope with her delinquent son and the subsequent dealings with the court. Andrew was taken into care. He was sent to

249

Peper Harrow, a fine-looking period building in Godalming, Surrey, and although I didn't realise it at the time, it was a renowned therapeutic centre for the care of troubled young people. The local authority duly informed her that the decision to fund the vast expense necessary for him to reside there had not been taken lightly and that Andrew was extremely fortunate. He would receive one-to-one attention and many opportunities. Although Andrew remained there until the age of sixteen, his frequent attempts to abscond saw him returning home on numerous occasions, only to be collected by a member of staff just hours later. Nothing of any benefit came of his time at Peper Harrow, except a huge bill for the taxpayer.

Back at home again, without any pressure to do anything whatsoever, Andrew began to keep extremely anti-social hours. His bedroom transformed into a dark, murky, fusty environment with heavy blankets at the windows to ensure no daylight could seep through. The base of his bed was discarded and the mattress placed directly on the floor. He preferred to sleep for much of the day and at night adhered to his carefully chosen diet, whilst watching the television until the early hours.

It was hard to see how his nocturnal habits would enable him to meet anyone, but much to my surprise a Japanese girlfriend suddenly appeared for a short time in his life. Her name was Itchie, a curious individual. It was very difficult to guess her age, just over four feet tall and extremely solid, she seldom spoke. She would come and go at very strange hours making it impossible to know when she was under our roof, shut away in Andrew's gloomy quarters.

Andrew was placed on a variety of employment schemes in the community, but each time the story was the same. Unwilling to listen to, or take instruction from anyone else, his time was always limited. At some point his GP registered him as long-term unemployed and although a mental illness was diagnosed, Mum and Andrew's colluding excluded me from knowing any specific details. I understood that he was prescribed drugs to improve his condition but I remain in some doubt as to whether he actually took them.

Life for me at this time was not easy. Whilst Andrew wallowed at home, I was in regular employment at BHS and providing Mum with much needed housekeeping money. Financially, life was tough for Mum but still she didn't seek to obtain any of Andrew's benefits to help provide for him.

In view of this unbearable situation at home, meeting David my future husband was the break I had been longing for and the prospect of my forthcoming marriage and a new life was extremely liberating.

Despite everything, the relationship between Mum and Andrew continued to be very tight-knit, even though he was of very little help to her. However, when Mum was diagnosed with an incurable degenerative disorder at the early age of sixty-two, it was Andrew's reluctance to provide any notable assistance for her that finally made me crack and resulted in our heated exchange.

I was so infuriated, not only by his complacency but also his objectionable attitude to what might be best for our Mum, I decided I wanted no further dealings with him. The way ahead proved troublesome and exasperating. Mum was soon wheelchair bound and the council re-housed her in a warden assisted ground floor property, providing Andrew with a council flat nearby. Extraordinarily, Andrew still maintained a strict control over Mum's way of life. Spending long periods of time in Mum's flat, he would sleep in a sleeping bag at all times of the day and night. Although this arrangement was in breach of her tenancy, Mum wasted no time in gaining the sympathy of the care staff. However, he was aware of the anomalous situation and always chose to make himself scarce before any of my scheduled visits.

Needless to say, it fell to me to purchase Mum's weekly groceries. I would invariably include a treat or two for her, until I soon discovered that under Andrew's intense scrutiny certain items would be discarded. I was equally enraged to learn that Andrew had often consumed much of what I had purchased on Mum's behalf.

Even more maddening was the realisation that Mum allowed Andrew unlimited access to her finances, which I noticed coincided with a series of regular trips to Finland for him. Any attempt to quiz her on Andrew's need to visit this country got me nowhere. His return trips to the UK enabled him to continue to collect his own benefits.

When Mum's condition worsened, David suggested that both Diane, Mum's sister and I jointly be granted Power of Attorney. Andrew, however, vehemently refused to allow us to do this and Mum abided by his decision.

Diane and I, together with Mum's approval, made the decision to transfer her to a nursing home. However, the relocation was short-lived. In just under a week I received a telephone call from the nursing home manager advising me that Mum had been discharged by her son and returned to her flat. Tragically, the remainder of Mum's life was traumatic. There was no full-time nursing care available for her and much of her day-to-day requirements fell to Diane and me. Andrew remained in the shadows.

Many years earlier, soon after Dad's departure from the family home, Andrew had made the decision to change his name disassociating himself completely from his father. He dropped his middle name of Peter and changed his surname to that of Mum's maiden name. I did discover that at some point, Andrew had been in search of his birth mother and although successful, he hadn't met with a good reception. I believe she wanted nothing to do with him. Unfortunately, a combination of Mum's poor speech caused by her condition and her reluctance to share any of Andrew's affairs with me meant that I had very little knowledge of him and anything I did actually discover was always via Aunty Diane. However, I do know that he found half-siblings who were prepared to spend time with him, but whether he remained in contact, I have no idea.

All this happened many years before my own search. How sad to think that amongst all our hostilities was a profound subject that was unique to both of us.

When Mum died in 2002 I felt I needed to get a message to Andrew. With no idea of his whereabouts and with little to go on, I contacted the Salvation Army. My only clue was Finland and to my utter surprise they located him within a couple of days. I was amused at the idea that someone on my behalf had approached him. Despite the gravity of the news, he would have been furious that, after so many years, I had managed to make contact with him so efficiently.

Andrew made no effort to communicate with me immediately after Mum's death, and neither did he attend her funeral. Whilst Mum didn't have a great sum of money, she left the bulk of it to Andrew. It was several years before he made contact with David through his law firm asking for his monies to be transferred to a Finnish bank account.

27. A Weekend in Waterford

November 2007

It was with a great relief that we pulled away from Margaret and Paddy's home in Thomastown, Kilkenny and headed to Michael's home in Waterford. The flying visit had only lasted some fifteen minutes, but what most bizarre minutes they had been! Much to my relief, her outrageous threats of suicide had subsided but the awkwardness of the occasion, as Margaret nervously held forth, had made it impossible for me to engage with my brother Oliver.

Nevertheless, Margaret and Paddy had now met my three daughters, their grandchildren. However, the real purpose of our whistle-stop trip to Ireland on this cold weekend in November was for us all to see Michael again and meet his own family for the very first time.

Since meeting Michael three months ago, we had spoken frequently on the telephone and much to my delight, he had already arranged to return with his family for a few days between Christmas and New Year. Throughout these conversations, Michael made no secret of the fact that he envied John and his proximity to me. Hearing his truly heartfelt wish to see more of me demonstrated a sentiment that I had seldom experienced before and, touched by this display of affection, I'd proposed an impromptu trip to Waterford. He'd insisted that we stay at his home and late on that Friday evening we finally arrived. After some brief introductions the children all settled down to sleep, leaving Michael, his wife Helena, Paul and me to talk late into the night. Michael was particularly keen to focus on the finer details of our visit to his parents earlier that evening. Instigated by his mother, he saw it as real progress.

The following morning we all set off to visit the Waterford Glass Showroom. The impressive display was all the more stunning for its beautiful Christmas products and decorations. As I wandered around admiring the exhibits, I was conscious of some very powerful emotions and feelings bubbling to the surface. Michael and Helena had been most attentive since our arrival the previous evening and as I looked at the happy faces of those around me, I noted a genuine sense of good feeling. For anyone looking in, it appeared to be something so natural, but for me it was an experience that so easily may have never been. Michael and his two children were my blood relatives and something that up until quite recently was unimaginable. Not only had Margaret done her utmost to ensure that this union would never materialise, but David my ex-husband had also been instrumental in delaying my search. I looked at Michael's children, my niece and nephew and remembered how my initial attempt to trace my birth mother had been thwarted long before they were even born. Had I been successful in tracing Margaret at that time I could even have been part of their lives from the very beginning. The lives of both our families had existed completely oblivious to each other and as the sadness of the situation took hold, my emotions surged uncontrollably. I was overcome. Helena was quick to notice the tears trickling down my face and whisked me away to a sofa conveniently situated in the showroom. I sat and wept. It was impossible for me to convey such intense feelings of sorrow into words. Instead, Helena was left with the impossible task of comforting and consoling me.

Although her sympathy and support were most welcome, nothing could truly begin to alleviate my feelings of despair. After a short time Michael came to relieve Helena and sat quietly beside me. Neither of us could find the appropriate words to express the enormity of the situation, but somehow even through our joint silence I could feel a sense of unity. Eventually I felt able to rejoin the rest of the family. I had yet to face the rigours of the afternoon. Margaret had been shamelessly adamant that she and Paddy should join us all for tea at the Faithlegg Hotel, Michael's place of work.

Later that afternoon, poised ready on a sumptuous sofa close to the large open fire, I waited anxiously with Helena for an encounter that filled me with dread. Michael had disappeared with Paul onto the golf course for 'a couple of holes,' while all the children were together, exploring the hotel and keeping lookout for their grandparents' arrival.

They all duly appeared: Margaret, Paddy and Oliver in tow. Oliver was beaming, but Margaret and Paddy looked decidedly uncomfortable. Both of them were dressed quite formally, similar to our meeting in Dublin. Paddy sat himself down on the sofa directly opposite me and Oliver joined him, leaving plenty of space between them both. Rosemary immediately seized on the gap, much to the obvious delight of the gentlemen either side of her. Margaret, however, chose to sit in an upright carver chair facing the fireplace, from where she could control and assess at ease. Her body language was just as I had remembered it in Dublin, leaning to one side, resting her elbow on the armrest and swinging her crossed leg. As expected, the gathering was fraught. Margaret true to form talked relentlessly, directing very little conversation my way. This was most welcome, as her first remark to me on her arrival was calculated to undermine my confidence.

'What's happened to your hair, it doesn't look as good as it did last night?' she said rudely. Hardly the best way to ease any tension when addressing her long lost daughter.

Feeling rather sidelined, I concentrated on proudly watching my own daughters converse confidently with both Margaret and Paddy.

Michael soon returned with Paul and immediately sat himself down in the vacant space next to me, a most welcome gesture.

'How's it going?' he whispered.

'Not very well; is there an ejector button?' I whispered hopefully. I looked across at Paddy, I could see he had relaxed considerably since his awkward entrance. When the suggestion of taking a few photographs was mentioned he jumped at the opportunity to stand and embrace all his five grandchildren. Margaret, however, continued to appear somewhat uncomfortable, even after insisting Nancy sit on her knee. I looked on as numerous photos were taken. However, Margaret and Paddy pointedly refrained from inviting me to join them for any, choosing to restrict it to grandchildren only.

I turned to Michael, whose attention had been diverted to his mobile phone. It was yet another text from John. Even before my arrival the previous day John had shown a tremendous interest in my visit to the Emerald Isle, making persistent calls and sending messages to Michael at regular intervals, asking for updates on my reaction to events. This did little to ease my anxieties.

Margaret had been keeping a close watch on the time throughout the afternoon. Oliver had been instructed to drive Margaret and Paddy to the nearby bus stop for their journey home, thereby allowing Oliver to remain with us before returning home to Thomastown later that evening. The idea of Margaret and Paddy enduring public transport had already caused much merriment amongst the family. Eventually, after what seemed like an eternity, Margaret stood up and announced their intention to leave. Everyone jumped to their feet, as if to hurry them along and bring relief to this very tense situation. Paddy was the first to approach me to bid his goodbyes. I took a few steps forward to meet him. He reached out and took both of my hands, clasping them tightly in his. He looked at me earnestly.

'You are very welcome to come to Thomastown anytime. You can stay with us whenever you want to,' he insisted. 'Let's put any difficulty over recent months behind us,' he added, before putting his arms around me and kissing me on the cheek. His words were so sincere that it immediately brought a lump to my throat. He stepped back to make way for Margaret. Somehow this second encounter didn't feel quite so genuine.

As Margaret drew closer, in my mind, the space between me and the familiar bystanders was becoming evermore distant. Standing face to face with Margaret was like standing on a remote island, miles from civilization. My tears were evident.

'What's the matter?' she asked abruptly, without an ounce of warmth in her voice.

I couldn't speak.

'Do you want Paddy and me to stay with you for the rest of the day?' she asked decisively. It was a most surprising invitation and one that I was desperate to quash immediately.

'No, no,' I blurted.

'Are you sure you wouldn't like us to come out for dinner with you, we could you know, if it's what you want?' she persisted.

'No I don't, really,' I insisted. I wanted them to go. I wanted to bring this traumatic event to an end. Throughout the afternoon I'd felt forlorn and neglected. Margaret had made no attempt to talk to me or even sit close by. I certainly didn't need more of the same.

'If you're sure,' she said, kissing me goodbye. 'Keep in touch won't you?' she said before turning around to head for the door. As everyone else accompanied them to the main entrance to see them go, I remained rooted to the spot. My inertia was immediately interrupted by a firm grip on my elbow, followed by some gentle pressure to move forward.

'What did she say?' whispered Michael, escorting me with just a little more force.

'Try as we might, none of us could hear a thing,' he added, still maintaining his physical hold on me. 'Well?' he asked insistently, anxious to receive a detailed account of the exchange between Margaret and me. It was clear that he had no intention of releasing me until I had revealed everything to him. There was a momentary reprieve from Michael's intense questioning as we reached the entrance and stood at the top of the stairs with the rest of the family bidding Margaret and Paddy goodbye. I watched in faint amusement at Margaret's rather grand departure. Seated in the back of the car she launched into a rather regal wave as Oliver drove around the elaborate circular feature at the front of the hotel. Once they were out of sight, the attention focused on me again. This time, everyone was eager to know the content of the brief but intimate conversation that had taken place. However, Michael had no intention of allowing me to share any of the details and promptly placed me in the passenger seat of his four-wheel drive, under the guise of trundling me around his beloved golf course, where instead he gently interrogated me.

The afternoon's events had left me quite subdued as we all headed out for dinner. However, Oliver's obvious excitement at the prospect of spending some quality time with me, his sister, away from the watchful eye of his mother, soon lightened my mood. Once again it was wonderful to witness my daughters enjoying the evening in the company of their family.

We left Waterford very early the next morning to drive to Dublin and catch our return flight home. Despite the tremendous difficulties I'd encountered throughout the weekend, our visit had clearly delighted Michael. We could all look forward to our next meeting in late December, only this time it would be on my territory and I knew it would be a far more relaxed affair.

Later that morning whilst waiting at the airport, I received a most unexpected telephone call from Margaret. She expressed how good it had been to see us and wished us all a safe journey home. She was in a most light-hearted mood, insisting that I speak to Paddy who, she declared, was still in his bed. She also talked of sending Oliver over to stay with us sometime soon.

'Keep in touch and God bless you,' were her parting words. Was she beginning to mellow at last? After meeting me again, this time with my daughters in tow, was she at last warming to the idea that perhaps a relationship could be salvaged after so many years?

28. 'My Big, Beautiful Sister'

October 2007

Even before I'd first met Oliver, or Ollie as he was known, I had already gained a considerable insight from John, Helen and Michael. Even Margaret had provided me with a mental picture of her youngest son. However, I'd been left slightly puzzled about this particular individual.

Aged thirty-six and still single, he lived with Margaret and Paddy but unfortunately suffered poor health. After a traumatic birth, he was plagued with asthma and various related conditions causing him to miss a substantial amount of schooling as a child. This, Margaret claimed, was the reason why he worked just part-time on a local charity training-scheme, mainly grass cutting on large municipal areas. Margaret had implied that Oliver was somehow 'different', a description that appeared to be accepted by the rest of the family. He'd been described as a rather awkward, slightly clumsy man with a heavy hand, (Paul had recently replaced John's broken bathroom tap after his previous visit), who seemed uncomfortable and withdrawn in social situations. John and Helen also told of his unusual sleep pattern whenever he stayed with them. Always waking before dawn, he was compelled to rearrange and re-sort his belongings, guaranteed to disturb any household at such an anti-social hour. John had resorted to carpeting the wooden floors in their home.

Oliver intrigued me and I was keen to meet him for myself, a brother for whom I already felt some concern.

What struck me from the outset was that he seemed to live a very restricted life. Governed by Margaret and her very tight regime, he appeared to have no independence. He had no real interests or hobbies and any friendships had been actively discouraged. I was surprised to learn that his free time was taken up driving his mother around on shopping trips and hairdresser appointments and carrying out numerous household chores, such as gardening, washing the car, cleaning the windows and washing-up. For a man that had been described as less able, he seemed very capable.

Margaret had been incensed to discover that Michael had already made Oliver aware of my existence. He had even shared with his brother, the many photos taken on his recent visit to Sevenoaks, thus paving the way for a meeting between us both during Oliver's forthcoming stay with John and Helen. It was his second trip this year. His earlier visit in April had enabled that fateful meeting at Dublin airport to take place without his knowledge.

Sadly, Oliver's trip was to be fraught with difficulties. He was arriving on Tuesday and staying for one week, but as I waited expectantly for John and Helen to make plans for a much-awaited happy union, I soon realised that John had a very different agenda. Since learning of my existence, four months ago, John had been intent on playing a mind game with his mother. He was adamant that he would not broach the subject of me, his sister, until she chose to raise the matter with him, which of course she hadn't. So without the blessing of his mother, John had no intention of instigating a meeting between Oliver and me. Instead he'd chosen to play a similar game with Oliver and wait until he voluntarily expressed a wish to meet me for himself. If Oliver's demeanour was as everyone had described, I felt this approach was nothing short of cruel. Unable to intervene, it was becoming increasingly more difficult for me to understand this family. Their complete inability to speak honestly and openly with one another was both infuriating and deeply upsetting and certainly did nothing to help Oliver. However, with Oliver ensconced in Stanmore, all I could do was wait patiently.

The programme for Oliver's visits seemed remarkably dull. John and Helen lacked the desire to entertain him and inject some real excitement into his life. When they weren't whiling away the hours sitting at home, it was either shopping trips, visits to the local pub, or accompanying John on long distance motorway business travel. This was because Oliver loved cars and could sit quietly beside his brother, spotting an array of models as they drove the length of the country.

Several days had elapsed and Oliver had still made no reference to me, his sister, and although John was becoming increasingly irate, he had no intention of wavering. His discreet telephone calls to me each evening, reporting yet another frustrating day with Oliver, merely highlighted the dire situation between them. Before even meeting Oliver, I felt truly sorry for him. Surely, with a little encouragement, he would have welcomed the chance to talk openly with his brother, far away from the clutches of his parents. Life at home must have changed dramatically (probably for the worse) since the news of the existence of a sister. If Oliver was aware of Margaret's very negative reaction towards me and her threats of suicide, it must have been extremely distressing for him. Regrettably, John's handling of the situation was producing a deadlock and it looked as if the opportunity to meet with my brother on this occasion was in jeopardy.

Later in the week, on yet another motorway excursion and after many silent hours in the car, John's patience finally snapped. He pulled into a service station and erupted.

'Aren't you going to ask me about Karen?' he shouted angrily.

Oliver looked at John. He was uncomfortable.

'Err, yes,' he replied, warily.

'Well, when were you intending to mention it and do you want to see her?' he barked.

'I don't know,' said Oliver, turning to stare directly out of the window ahead of him. There was a lengthy silence as John sat impatiently waiting for something more from his troubled brother.

'Look, I've got a new T-shirt,' said Oliver eventually, tugging at his clothing and still staring out into the distance.

The following day, John and Helen delivered Oliver to Romford to spend the weekend with Margaret's sister, Theresa, a trip prearranged by Margaret. I was aghast to discover that although John and Helen had spent several hours with Theresa and her husband Tom, the subject of a secret sister once again was avoided.

Oliver was duly returned to John's on Sunday evening, leaving just one more day remaining before he returned home to Ireland. If there was any possibility of our meeting, I had to hear from John soon. To my relief he finally telephoned that evening to invite me for a fleeting visit to meet my brother, Oliver, in Stanmore the following day. John would be at work, but both Helen and Oliver would meet me at the tube station. An opportunity not to be missed. Sandwiched between work (thankfully David Trill insisted that I leave earlier than usual) and collecting Nancy from school later that afternoon, I took the train to Stanmore, accompanied by Rosemary, already on her half-term break.

As we emerged from the tube station, I immediately spotted Helen. Standing by her side was a very anxious looking man, fidgeting nervously and intently watching the exit. Having quickly greeted Helen, I turned my attention to Oliver. Although obviously agitated, there was no hiding his excitement and sheer

264

pleasure at our meeting as he embraced me with a great bear hug. I spotted tears in his eyes, as I too felt yet another surge of emotion. I had at last got to meet my third brother.

He was tall, trim and muscular with broad shoulders and long legs, not the physique that I had expected for someone so apparently ailing. His appealing face with its strong features made for a handsome young man, but his thick head of hair was prematurely grey and unfortunately made him look decidedly older than his years. It was styled with a precise side parting and heavy use of hair cream. He was also dressed beyond his years. A horizontal striped Yves Saint Laurent polo shirt was tucked firmly into a pair of high-waist, close fitting, black Wrangler jeans. On his feet were a pair of gleaming white trainers. I later discovered that not only did Margaret choose his attire, but she also insisted on cutting his hair.

After introducing Rosemary, we set off for the short walk back to John and Helen's home. Oliver and I led the way and Rosemary and Helen followed behind, chatting happily together.

Oliver's gait was somewhat awkward, as he veered along the path, beaming at me continually and shaking his head in disbelief at this astonishing occasion. His long, haphazard strides were all the more noticeable for the large mass of bright white leather on his feet. I was immediately taken with Oliver, I noticed how easy it was to engage with this strapping and very able man, who had not only travelled alone to the UK but also could drive a car and a tractor, to boot.

Sitting around the now increasingly familiar circular table, Helen had prepared for lunch. With John not there to monitor and analyse his younger brother's every move, Oliver was very relaxed and our time together was fun and easy going. Oliver certainly had a great sense of humour and enjoyed recounting the events, after learning of my existence.

'It's really great to meet you Karen,' he declared, half way through our lunch. 'When Michael told me about you, I just couldn't get you out of my head. At work the following day in the tractor, cutting the grass was impossible. My mind kept wandering and the tractor was going all over the place,' with his hand he drew a wavy line. 'I was expecting my boss to ask me why there were no straight lines today,' he said earnestly. He was so open and sincere, I wanted to do all I could to encourage my gentle but repressed brother to converse with us all. He surreptitiously informed me of a little private gardening job that he undertook. Unrelated to his community work, it was the garden belonging to a friend of Paddy's and he was clearly very proud of his efforts.

Conscious of the delicate situation surrounding his new-found sister, he described his recent difficulty whilst staying with Theresa and Tom.

'I almost gave the game away at Theresa's,' he suddenly announced. 'I had a couple of beers and I nearly let slip news of my sister Karen,' he paused. 'It was a close thing, but I stopped myself just in time,' he reported with obvious relief. How shocking that he had been burdened with such a responsibility, unsure how to deal with this family revelation. Margaret, and failing that, John, should have ensured that Oliver was not faced with such a predicament.

However, throughout our time together, it was his frequent, furtive glances that were so endearing.

It was easy to make him laugh. He was keen to tell me how much I looked like Margaret, to which I immediately responded.

'Oh, no surely not,' I cried in a tone of disbelief (knowing it to be true as this had already been pointed out to me on several occasions), but my reaction amused Oliver greatly as he continued to insist that this was undoubtedly correct. Our thoroughly enjoyable afternoon passed quickly. Rosemary too, gently engaged with her uncle, who had no difficulty in chatting comfortably with her. The conversation remained easy and uncomplicated. I had no intention of grilling him over Margaret's current thinking towards me. After taking a variety of photos, it was time to leave. Oliver tentatively asked if I would like his mobile phone number. I could see from his timid expression there was a fear that I might decline, but I accepted readily and as a self-confessed technophobe, I asked Rosemary to programme his number into my phone. He was delighted to take my details in return.

Walking back together to the tube station, the light-heartedness continued. Oliver responded to a bit of gentle teasing as I suggested he should consider roughing up his immaculate trainers a little before returning home. Clearly for Oliver that was not an option, as Margaret ensured that all his training shoes were as pristine as these. The goodbye was particularly emotional for him. He had no idea when we would meet again.

In less than two hours I had discovered that there was far more to Ollie than I had been led to believe. The regular texts from him began to arrive in abundance, all addressed to 'his big beautiful sister'. Although they contained very little information, they always enquired as to everyone's well-being, asking after each family member in turn and brightening all our lives. My reply was always immediate.

It was just one month later when we pulled onto Oliver's driveway on that bitterly cold November evening. His sheer delight at our arrival was evident. Waiting to embrace me in another of his suffocating bear hugs just confirmed this. Once inside the parental home, under the strict watch of his mother, the extent of his true feelings remained concealed. This time his furtive glances in my direction were his only means of relaying his sentiment towards me.

I'd suggested that the Coleman clan (excluding Margaret and Paddy) together with Paul, my daughters and me, might like to consider spending a long weekend away together somewhere. The idea was well received and I duly organised a weekend break to Center Parcs. There were twelve of us in total, and we all met in Longleat Forest, Wiltshire. Michael and his family, together with Oliver, took the boat across the Irish Sea and then drove the lengthy journey to meet up with the rest of us. Spread over two villas, side by side, we all enjoyed the most fantastic weekend, but no one more so than Oliver. I discovered that this was his first real holiday. John and Michael substantiated this, hard pushed to remember any time away as children. For Oliver, this memorable weekend had been in jeopardy. A bout of shingles on his face just prior to the holiday almost prevented him from joining us. Thankfully, the necessary treatment was successful and Oliver's absence was averted, although I was horrified to hear that Margaret had used hairgrips to keep her son's swathe of hair away from his face. This was indeed a step too far. The modern spiky hairstyle that I had already envisaged for Oliver would have been far more apt.

I'd had conflicting reports from both John and Michael as to Oliver's ability to ride a bike, an essential for this adventure holiday, so it was with some trepidation that I arrived at the bike hire centre. My concern proved to be short lived as I watched Oliver confidently mount his bike and speed off with both Rosemary and Annie. Throughout the entire weekend he cycled alongside them always at the front of the convoy, tackling the steep gradients with ease and demonstrating a natural ability.

The activities that I'd organised for us all were a new experience for everyone. The entire group took part in a team building challenge, beginning with us all standing balanced in a row, on a horizontal beam one metre off the ground. Our task was to re-position ourselves in order of age, without falling off. We shuffled cautiously, gradually rearranging ourselves along the beam. Paul couldn't resist the opportunity to make an observation to John.

'You do realise that you're not quite as far along the pole as you once thought you were,' he declared cheekily. John's face was a picture. A high-wire adventure walk through the forest was also on the agenda. If left to John and Michael, they would have probably insisted that Oliver sit this one out. However, much to their surprise and also Oliver's, he successfully completed the challenge.

Throughout the weekend it was evident that Oliver was having the time of his life. Unlike the routine at home, he was delighted to be able to take a shower or bath whenever he chose, announcing to us all as he did so and keen to show that he was able to make decisions for himself. He enjoyed a glass of wine or beer in the middle of the afternoon, no doubt behaviour that would have been frowned upon by his parents. I worried that, having experienced a very different routine to anything that had gone before, he would struggle to cope once back under the watchful eye of his mother.

My plan was to make our last evening together a truly memorable one. Oliver's birthday was just days away and with help from all the children we decorated one of the villas with banners and balloons in readiness for the birthday party. Oliver was overcome, he had never had such attention centred on him before and didn't remember ever having a birthday party. After a slow but enjoyable meal in one of the restaurants on site and a flurry of snow, we returned to the villa to continue the celebrations.

With us all involved in a raucous rendition of Neil Diamond's 'Sweet Caroline', it didn't matter that Oliver was unsure of the words, as he joined in waving his arms high in the air. The weekend had undoubtedly been a complete success.

The holiday now over, Margaret wasted no time in reporting to me how it had all been too much for Oliver. He was exhausted, she claimed, and it wasn't something to be undertaken again in a hurry. I felt very differently.

Despite the fractious relationship between Margaret and me, she had decided to entrust me with her youngest son again later that year. She had made it her business to enquire after my hosting skills on endless occasions and had received nothing but positive feedback from the rest of her family. During Oliver's scheduled visit in October 2008, to John and Helen, he would spend a couple of days with me in Sevenoaks. I relished the prospect of having Oliver entirely to myself, experiencing a different, more relaxed way of life.

Our couple of days together were delightful. He soon made himself at home, following me into the kitchen and perching himself on a high stool. I noticed how he watched me intently. Positioned adjacent to my large stainless steel fridge, he took it upon himself to open it in a robot-like fashion each time I approached.

'You look just like mother working away there in the kitchen,' he announced.

Once again, I disputed his claim. My reaction didn't surprise Oliver, but it did amuse him.

'Oh, but you do,' he said teasing me further. 'The way you move about and the things you do,' he explained.

Rather tongue in cheek, he explained his need to analyse everything in our home, knowing his mother would quiz him relentlessly on the finer details. I jocularly pointed out that the colour of the walls was not cream but linen. Oliver did have a great sense of fun, but I sensed much of it was repressed living under the same roof as Margaret and Paddy. Whilst in Center Parcs, he'd expressed displeasure at the girls' reference to me as Deirdre, a term of endearment that they used to describe my frustrating and often slow response to things physical and technical. He saw it as highly disrespectful. However, during his brief stay with us, whilst waiting impatiently with the rest of the family for me to finally leave the house for a trip to London, I heard an unexpected and exasperated cry from the hallway.

'Oh Deirdre, do hurry up,' cried Oliver, laughing loudly and provoking much hilarity from us all. Margaret and her straight-laced ways would never have understood.

A visit to HMS *Belfast* on the river Thames enthralled him.

'My brothers will be really envious when they hear about this,' he exclaimed repeatedly, as we explored every inch of the battleship, taking plenty of photographic evidence on the way. With them clearly on his mind, the chance for him to experience something that they had never done was inconceivable. A trip on the London Duck tour followed (something already experienced by his brothers and their families during a visit the previous Christmas), until finally landing up in the evening at the very buzzing Hard Rock Café.

Rosemary and Annie had meanwhile jumped ship, literally. After visiting the battleship, they had taken themselves off on a shopping spree. Ollie had insisted that he provide them with some spending money and as he sat enjoying a drink awaiting their arrival, he was eager to see them again, and the evidence of a successful shop. The girls had so warmed to, and totally embraced Ollie, it was hard to imagine that this relationship was still in its infancy. John and Helen also joined us at the restaurant. Later that evening they were returning back to Stanmore with Oliver, ready for his flight from Luton to Dublin the following day. The inevitable parting drew nearer and Oliver was becoming visibly distressed. As he hugged each one of us, I reassured him that he could fly over and visit me anytime. It was an extremely poignant moment, which was to remain in my memory, as subsequent events would ensure that the prospect of any future meeting between us was to become uncertain.

29. My Father's Funeral

June 2008

'That's his daughter Karen, with her partner Paul and her three daughters, Peter's granddaughters. Over there is her estranged husband David and behind him are two of her brothers, John and Michael, but they're not Peter's sons,' whispered a woman sitting at the back of the crematorium, trying hard to explain an almost unheard of scenario.

My dad died on the evening of Sunday 25th May, 2008, almost 25 years to the day since the death of his own mother, the nanny with whom I had lived until the age of eight. I'd received a call from the hospital and was advised to come immediately. On hearing the news, Annie had insisted on joining Paul and me. There was no deterring her, she was adamant. Although I wasn't entirely comfortable with the idea, there was little time to discuss what inevitably lay ahead and we arrived at dad's beside in time for his last moments.

On entering the single room, I immediately sensed the gravity of the situation. Steven, Eileen's eldest son who lived close to the hospital, had arrived earlier and was sitting beside my dad, holding his hand as he slipped away. Steven looked up and shook his head. I quickly approached the bed, aware of my father's imminent death.

'Dad,' I said clearly, reaching for his hand and leaning over to kiss his forehead, in the hope that he was aware of my presence during those final moments.

Annie was, of course, very distressed but determined to spend some precious last moments with her granddad. At my suggestion she held his hand. It was a terribly traumatic experience for anyone and at only fifteen, I think she had made a courageous decision. Moments later my stepmother Eileen arrived. She was distraught; there was no consoling her.

Twelve days later, Paul and I were in the funeral car with Eileen and Steven. As I sat in silence for the journey to the crematorium, my thoughts turned to my daughters. It had been entirely their own decision to attend their granddad's funeral, but for both Annie and Nancy it was their first experience of such an event. As their mother, I longed to be by their side to support them at such a difficult time. They were travelling separately with David, who had also volunteered to collect John, Michael and Helen en route and drive them all directly to the crematorium. Knowing that my daughters were in the company of their new-found aunt and uncles did much to help alleviate my concerns for them.

The funeral procession passed through the gates of the crematorium and came to a halt while we waited for the signal to proceed. In the distance I could see Rosemary, Annie and Nancy waiting outside the chapel, standing close to David, John, Michael and Helen. As the hearse came into view I noticed Annie struggling to hold back her tears. I felt helpless. Unable to console her, I was relieved to see Helen move alongside her niece and place a comforting arm around her shoulder.

John and Michael's decision to attend the funeral of my father had been deeply heartfelt. With our relationship still in its infancy, I was overcome by their demonstration of support and commitment towards me, their actions were truly welcomed not only by me, but also my daughters. The sight of Michael, who had travelled over from Ireland very early the previous day, was undoubtedly the most moving. And yet I still felt a tinge of disappointment that he had chosen to stay with John and Helen. I would have welcomed the opportunity to spend some time alone with Michael, away from John's watchful eye. I wanted to get to know each brother individually and only one-to-one encounters would allow each of us to form our own special bond. Nevertheless, the previous day I had accepted John's invitation to travel to Stanmore and spend the day with Michael, John and Helen.

I was thankful that John and Michael had each had the opportunity to meet with Dad. Although a very sensitive and highly emotive exercise, it was extremely important to bring them together. I felt very strongly that my brothers should gain a little insight into the family to whom I'd been entrusted, I needed to demonstrate to them my own sense of belonging. I also wanted to reassure my adoptive dad that something extremely positive had transpired, despite the very negative strength of feeling from Margaret.

John had met Dad the previous July at Nancy's eighth birthday celebrations. However, it had been Michael's meeting with Dad that had been the most poignant. Michael and his family had spent several days staying with us immediately after Christmas and I'd invited Dad and Eileen to join us all for lunch on New Year's Day. As both men greeted each other, firmly shaking hands, Michael's gesture extended to a warm embrace, placing his arm around Dad's shoulders.

Today, at the funeral of my father, the gathering of my new partner, my daughters, my adoptive family and my blood family gave me a tremendous sense of belonging and was in marked contrast to the funeral of Nanny Gay, twenty-five years earlier.

I had always had a special relationship with my paternal grandmother. I was just two years old when we moved into her home and twenty-one

274

when she died, by which time my parents had been separated for over four years and my mother's relationship with her in-laws had become non-existent. It was my Aunty Frances who had called one evening to inform me, not only of Nanny's death the previous day, but also the date and time of the forthcoming funeral.

Sadly, during the time leading up to the funeral, I heard nothing more from any other members of my family, not even my Dad. The prospect of Nanny's funeral would be a very lonely one.

Neither my Mum nor Andrew had any desire to attend the funeral and were away on a week's break in the West Country. Thankfully, my mother's sister, Aunty Diane insisted on accompanying me. At the cemetery I watched as Dad, with his family, arrived to pay their respects to his mother, my beloved Nanny – Ethel May Gay. My intense sadness for the Nanny I'd lost was accompanied by my immense feelings of loneliness and isolation.

Standing amongst the mourning crowd, I felt very much an outsider. Nobody from my father's family had offered any support and so Aunty Diane's company was even more appreciated. The burial was a short drive away and we both watched the committal from afar before returning to my car. The husband of my cousin Barbara noticed us turning to leave and ran over to invite us back to Nanny's house. I declined the invitation and we drove away. Dad never raised the subject of Nanny's funeral or offered an apology for his actions. Episodes such as these are destined to remind me not of who I am, but of who I'm not.

Today my former feelings of isolation and loneliness were furthest from my thoughts. Surrounded by family, I felt a true sense of belonging, something I had seldom experienced.

Into the sadness of the occasion, I wanted desperately to inject something of Dad's light-hearted spirit and carefree approach to life. Somehow I found the strength to stand and pay him a brief tribute, focusing on more recent happy times. I talked of my Dad and his humorous antics with his granddaughters, as

I believe that despite his poor health in later years, this was an extremely enjoyable period in his life.

I had tentatively asked Rosemary, Annie and Nancy if they would like to play something during the service and to my delight they agreed. Dad had always been very impressed with his granddaughters' musical abilities, monitoring them from their early beginnings to becoming accomplished musicians. They planned and rehearsed a couple of foot tapping pieces that my Dad would have loved, Rosemary and Annie each playing flutes and Nancy her violin. Sadly and not unexpectedly, the occasion was just too much for Nancy who preferred to remain seated with me. However, I was later to discover that together with her sisters she had indeed rehearsed the pieces perfectly in the chapel prior to our arrival. Rosemary and Annie were immensely brave and carried out their performance together and I was so proud of all of them.

It was a difficult service. Eileen, consumed with grief, felt that life could never be the same. However, the musical interlude provided by my daughters brought a little relief to a most sombre gathering. Once outside the chapel there were favourable comments by the volunteers from Dad's stroke club about my words. They admitted to guilty giggling in the back row, recognising my very accurate account of the man they knew and their comments alone made my unenviable task worthwhile.

With the help of the local community, Eileen had provided a fine spread at the local bowls club. Surrounded by the various elements of a now very complex family, I proudly introduced my new brothers to my existing relatives, who were amused that, despite our clear facial resemblance, they both spoke with marked Irish accents.

I couldn't help noticing how comfortably David was conversing with all around him and genuinely delighted at the opportunity to catch up once again with my family members.

Despite our separation, they continued to show genuine warmth towards him and I couldn't repress a tinge of envy, mixed with resentment that none of his family could bring themselves to show similar warmth towards me.

We returned to Sevenoaks in convoy, David delivered his passengers and then left us for the remainder of the evening. I'd booked a table for us all at a local restaurant, where despite the traumatic day, we spent a relaxed evening.

However, the easy-going atmosphere was suddenly marred by a text to Michael from Helena, reporting Margaret's view of the whole affair.

'What is Michael doing over there playing happy families, he should be here with his own,' read the message. Michael was visibly shocked as he relayed it to the rest of the table. The intrusion of such a very insensitive and unpleasant remark brought the evening to an abrupt ending. The message affected everyone, including the girls, who struggled to understand such a callous remark. Paul settled the bill and I drove a somewhat subdued John, Michael and Helen to the railway station. I waited on the platform for their train to arrive and waved them off, still shocked by a comment that I considered both cruel and heartless. Did that message really need to be sent at all?

30. Theresa

April 2008

It was one year since that fateful meeting in Dublin with Margaret and Paddy and any relationship, such as it was, with my birth mother remained unpredictable and emotionally charged.

Our infrequent telephone conversations were, at best, mundane and often bizarre, as she single-mindedly avoided any reference to my adoption. During the prolonged spells between calls, I heard from Michael that I am still referred to as 'that woman' and accused of being pushy and cheeky because I have continued to press her for information which I feel is my right to know. Alas, to no avail. The longer this situation has dragged on, the more convinced I have become that there is a deeply significant motive for Margaret's dogged refusal to answer my questions.

Despite this, however, the bond with my brothers has strengthened. Our recent, highly successful holiday together in Center Parcs was a wonderful opportunity for us all to spend valuable time with each other. The chance to enjoy shared experiences and establish what I believe will be a highly fulfilling relationship with lasting blood ties has brought a whole new dimension to my life and that of my daughters. The enthusiasm with which my brothers embraced our union was something that until now I could only ever have dreamed of. Introducing each of them and their families to my own family and friends has been a sheer delight. However, as our relationship deepens and we catch up on so many lost years, it has become apparent that my brothers are being hindered in certain ways by their mother's continued unexplained hostility towards me.

It seems to me that this unsatisfactory situation has been brought about by Margaret's unwillingness to reveal my existence to other family members. I believe that both John and Michael are waiting for their mother's sanction – which, I fear will never be forthcoming.

I have no intention though, of remaining the Coleman's unmentionable family secret. Having allowed everybody time and space to adjust to the reality of my existence and our new relationship, I believe that a suitable transitional period has now elapsed. By now I am well aware that both Margaret and Paddy have a sizable extended family. Both have numerous siblings, each with children of their own – my first cousins. I'm tired of hearing accounts of these many relatives of mine from my brothers – I now want the opportunity, if possible, to meet them for myself. Both John and Michael's stance on the matter, however, has been infuriating and had begun to impinge on our relationship. Even Oliver's last visit to Margaret's sister Theresa, could not entice either of them to pre-empt his scheduled visit and reveal the family's grave secret to her. Instead they opted to subject their unwitting brother to several days of heightened anxiety as he battled to conceal his thrilling discovery.

Much to my disappointment John had also just spent an evening in the company of Theresa's daughter, his and my cousin, Rosalyn, and again had refrained from disclosing news of a sister. It was particularly upsetting to hear John's own jovial account of the occasion. Seemingly Rosalyn had spotted a photo of my daughter Annie on John's mobile phone and after enquiring as to the identity of this unknown young woman, John had chosen to casually pass it off as somebody from his place of work. Bemused by his actions, I challenged him but his response was succinct. He didn't consider it to be the right time to make such a disclosure and that I would just have to be patient.

I was mortified, in such a short time we had become integral to each other's lives, speaking regularly on the telephone, organising frequent get-togethers and not forgetting our recent holiday. I also learned that Rosalyn not only lived in neighbouring Croydon, but also travelled frequently to Sevenoaks to visit friends. This only fuelled my discontent. I was fully aware that my brothers' reluctance to completely commit to our relationship stemmed from their mother. Unfortunately, Margaret and I had reached an impasse and I was still no closer to ascertaining the truth behind my adoption. I feared that, yet again, my sympathetic softly softly approach had been in vain. Clearly, left to her own devices, Margaret had every intention of preserving the status quo, keeping me at arm's length and maintaining only a superficial relationship with the daughter she had chosen to give away. Observing my brothers, as they embraced me and my own family, only reinforced my concerns and festered my natural resentment. With this situation set to continue indefinitely, I had to make a move.

I'd heard only good things from my brothers about their Aunt Theresa, who appeared to have a very different personality from that of her sister Margaret. John and Michael had each described her as a very approachable, understanding and caring individual, full of life, with high-spirits and a good sense of humour. Married to an Englishman with three grown-up children, she had lived in the UK for most of her life and worked in various sectors of the nursing profession. I was particularly interested to hear that she was also a trained counsellor. Despite the distance between them, the two sisters had remained close all their lives and although their get-togethers were infrequent, my brothers talked of a very different Margaret whenever she was in the company of her younger sister. She would suddenly transform into a giggly, happy, carefree young woman again.

The more I learned about Theresa, the greater was my desire to meet her. She seemed well equipped with the relevant professional skills to deal with this highly sensitive issue and could perhaps offer the support and understanding needed to overcome her sister's reluctance to face the past. Margaret's guilty secret was indeed weighing heavily over the entire family. Michael had already raised concerns about his mother's mental state and was anxious for her to talk to someone. I'd also learnt that Theresa was soon to be visiting Margaret. The timing was perfect. For my part, I was optimistic that I might find an ally in Theresa, someone that I could appeal to and who might, at least, show a little sympathy for my situation.

Contrary to everything I'd told John and Michael about Margaret concealing her pregnancy, they were both of the firm belief that Theresa had been aware of my birth. They thought it impossible for Margaret to have concealed the pregnancy from her sister, who they understood was also living in London at the time. However, I couldn't help wondering if, as they claimed, Theresa did have knowledge of my existence, then why had it not encouraged either of my brothers to approach her? I remained to be convinced. If she could have hidden her pregnancy from the very astute Jim Donovan and his wife, then she could hide it from anyone. Margaret had indeed admitted to me that, other than Paddy, nobody in the family was aware of her predicament. Somehow I believed her.

I had high hopes for Theresa's support, understanding and possible intervention with her sister. Her involvement could only be a good thing for me. She was probably the only one who could persuade Margaret to tell the truth. Theresa's approach to life seemed far more akin to mine than that of her sister. I'd also learned from my brothers that she had no grandchildren of her own. With our relatively close proximity, perhaps the possibility of meeting three of her sister's granddaughters would be irresistible. Excited by my plan, for me, it signalled the possible end of my torment. I was resolute that, during the next tedious conversation with Margaret, I would broach the subject of Theresa.

'Margaret, I need you to understand that at some point you have to talk to me about the past. It's been a year since our meeting in Dublin and I still have so many unanswered questions,' I was pleading yet again, mentally ready for the usual negative response. To my surprise there was no explosion, nor threats or outrage, just silence. I continued.

'If you fell under a bus tomorrow, I would be distraught,' I pointed out. Trying desperately to make her realise that our time on this earth was finite.

'I don't think you'd be distraught if I fell under a bus,' she answered calmly, dismissing my request as if it had no real importance.

'But Margaret I would,' I stressed. Although she hadn't actually responded to my plea, I was thankful that there was no hostility and as our conversation appeared reasonably positive, I decided to seize the moment.

'Margaret, there's something else I want to ask you,' I paused. 'I really would like you to tell Theresa about me,' I ventured, holding my breath.

'Why on earth would I do that?' she inquired, in a distinctly derogatory tone. 'Theresa wouldn't be interested in *you*; she has her own family and her own problems. She really wouldn't be bothered or even want to know you,' came the callous and insulting reply, which was immensely hurtful. Apart from my own feelings, I thought Theresa should be allowed to make her own decisions. I was undeterred by her vindictiveness, unwilling to be deflected so easily and remained determined to pursue my request.

'I know that Theresa is coming to visit you next month. Whilst she is with you, you *must* tell her about me, this has gone on long enough. It's ridiculous that John, Michael and Oliver are all afraid to mention my name to her. If you don't, I have her address and telephone number and I will do it myself,' I declared.

'OK, I'll tell her,' she replied blithely. 'But I'm telling you, she won't be interested.'

What a strange conversation. Although once again, Margaret had shown her familiar malicious streak, she had not refused my request outright.

Relaying news of this conversation to John and Michael caused them great unease. Such conversations with their mother were unheard of.

A couple of weeks later I received an unexpected phone call. It was 10 pm on Sunday evening. Rather surprised by the late hour, I raced to answer the phone hoping it hadn't disturbed Nancy who had gone to bed some time earlier.

'Hello?'

'Is that Karen?' asked the caller brusquely. I recognised Paddy's voice immediately although I thought it strange as he'd never called me himself before.

'Hello Paddy,' I replied, curiously. Without further ado he launched into a vitriolic tirade.

'Now what do you think you're doing upsetting Margaret? Why are you asking her to tell Theresa about you?' he demanded. I didn't like his tone, which made me most uncomfortable. I had a bad feeling about this call.

'Theresa is my aunt and I would like the opportunity to meet her and her family. Added to which, she doesn't live far away from me.' I explained calmly whilst refraining from disclosing my intention to appeal to Theresa in order to infiltrate their deep dark secret.

'Theresa has nothing to do with you,' he replied with unexpected venom.

'She's my aunt and I would like her to know that I exist,' I insisted.

'How dare you threaten Margaret by suggesting you will contact Theresa directly if she refuses?' This was not the mild-mannered Paddy I had known until now. His approach was unpleasant and he was almost shouting.

'She needs to know about me, I'm not prepared to be kept a secret any longer,' I insisted.

'And what about the rest of our brothers and sisters? Are you going to bang on each of their doors one by one?' he yelled, by now extremely irate. I had no intention of allowing myself to give in to his bullying, I too, was feeling very angry.

'Yes I just might,' I replied as nonchalantly as possible. As expected, this made him even more furious.

From the very start of this conversation I was aware that my voice was being relayed through the loud speaker on the telephone, allowing Margaret to overhear my response. I was conscious of her goading Paddy at every opportunity and thereby encouraging him to behave even more offensively, which was highly distressing.

'You have no business to tell any of these people anything. Just leave them alone, none of them would be interested in you,' he continued spitefully.

'This situation has arisen because of your actions 46 years ago,' I reminded Paddy

'Ah,' he said in a measured tone before bellowing his reaction to my statement. 'ALL THAT SHIT!' I was struggling to hold back the tears.

'Paddy, please don't be so rude to me, don't talk to me like that,' I quivered.

Unbeknown to me, Paddy had already passed the receiver to Margaret.

'Are you alright?' she asked abruptly. I didn't care for her sudden intervention either.

'No,' I sobbed. 'I've never been spoken to like that before, it's appalling.'

'Paddy didn't mean it,' she said as if to restore some civility.

'OH YES I DID!' Came an angry and very audible response in the distance.

'Stop crying now,' she insisted.

'I don't want to talk to you any more, I'm very upset.' I said and switched off the phone. I turned to Paul.

'How dare they behave like this?' I asked shakily. He did his best to console me. Their shame and guilt was obviously weighing heavily on their consciences, but that was not my concern. I was appalled at Paddy's outburst and quite convinced that this call had been initiated by Margaret. No doubt she had been provoking Paddy, encouraging him. And where was Oliver throughout this abusive call? Had he been compelled to listen to his own parent's verbal onslaught on his big, beautiful sister?

Although still resolute in my search for the truth, I needed to distance myself from this family for a while and this included my brothers as well. Margaret and Paddy knew that John, Michael and I all spoke regularly and I didn't want to be accused of rustling up any sympathy. Whilst they may have been prepared to tolerate their parents' dreadful outbursts, I was not. I had no intention of retracting my threat and, unlike my brothers, her controlling and callous ways would not deter me.

The following evening the phone rang again. It was an international call and I was in no mood to answer it, so I left Paul to field it. This time it was Michael – he was very subdued. His parents had subjected him to a triumphant account of their abusive call to me the previous evening. Their gleeful satisfaction that finally I'd been put in my place had left Michael appalled. I didn't want to re-live the whole ghastly episode and declined to talk to him. Paul thanked him for his concern and support, explaining just how I was feeling and that no doubt I would contact him in a day or so. Michael had also talked to John and made him fully aware of the dreadful incident. I felt guilty for rejecting Michael. He couldn't be held responsible for his parents' actions and it was very touching that he wanted to console me and condemn his parents' behaviour, but I was tired of considering everyone else's feelings. Right now I cared only about mine.

The following day though, I was caught off-guard as I reached to answer the phone. This time it was John.

'If you don't want to talk, I'll put the phone down and try another time, I do understand,' he said immediately.

'There's no need,' I replied wearily, still feeling rather fragile.

'Michael's told me all about the abuse on Sunday. I don't know what to say. I'm ashamed of them. There's nothing to say in defence of such dreadful behaviour. It was utterly shocking. All I can do is apologise on their behalf,' he said despondently. There was nothing to add. Without any intervention from me, Margaret and Paddy's own account of events and their obvious display of euphoria had unquestionably alienated their own sons.

'Hey, listen. Don't forget about Michael. He's quite upset that you didn't want to talk to him yesterday. He very much wants to talk to you as soon as you're ready,' he said reminding me of their support at this difficult time.

'I know, I'll ring him now.' I reassured him. I hated the thought of Michael feeling dejected and as soon as John's call was over I wasted no time in telephoning Michael.

'You had me worried. I didn't know when I'd get to talk to you again,' said Michael, breathing a huge sigh of relief.

'I'm sorry about yesterday. I just felt so miserable, I really didn't want to talk to anyone,' I explained. Like his brother, he too expressed utter shame at his parents' behaviour. For Michael, hearing their account first-hand had been deplorable.

Knowing I had the support of both John and Michael brought great solace. However, I'd made up my mind to respond to the appalling outburst myself. I composed a letter to Margaret and Paddy, one which was uncompromisingly direct and honest. Whilst I had every intention of sending my brothers a copy, I had no idea how they would react.

12th May 2008

Dear Margaret and Patrick,

Following our last conversation, I have decided to write to you telling you exactly how I feel at this time.

Never before have I had to endure such an outburst as the one I was subjected to by both of you a couple of weeks ago. Patrick's language, manner and tone were completely unacceptable. I am extremely upset.

When I embarked on my search to find my birth mother, I was advised to be prepared for anything. As my birth certificate clearly states, my father had died prior to my birth and therefore I had an image of a sad, lonely woman who had lost her husband shortly after their marriage. However, it came as a tremendous shock to find that not only was my father still alive but that I also had three younger brothers – one of whom has been living only a short distance from me for over 20 years.

I accepted this news without anger and it was without anger that I came to Dublin on the 28th April last year to meet with you, my birth parents. It was my hope that I would come away from that meeting with some understanding of the circumstances of my birth and subsequent adoption. In fact, I came away from that meeting feeling frustrated and bemused.

During our meeting I expressed the need to inform John, Michael and Oliver of my existence. You refused to consider this and made various threats. When it became clear to me that you had no intention of telling my brothers, I took matters into my own hands. Since then, the girls, Paul and myself have been overwhelmed by the warmth and acceptance of all three of them. When you did become aware of my brothers involvement in my life you reacted furiously, without any consideration to your own children.

There did seem to be a turning point when firstly, we visited Michael in November and then secondly after John had stayed with you last Christmas when you spoke to me having decided that it had to be an 'all or nothing' relationship and both you and Paddy had settled on 'all'. I took this to mean that you were starting to accept that I am your daughter, a real person with her own family – your granddaughters. Things appeared to be stable, although you still seemed to have no desire to talk to me about the events of 1962 and whatever made it impossible for you to keep your first-born child. That was until I insisted that you inform your sister Theresa of me on her forthcoming visit to Ireland. It is now almost eighteen months since I first contacted you. Surely in that time you must have considered the possibility of other members of your family learning of my existence?

It is now clear to me that I am not dealing with sensitive, caring people – just selfish, arrogant bullies who insist on having their own way. I am a focused, determined person and to be told that I am not to do something only makes me more determined.

You owe me the truth. You stated that one of the reasons for my adoption was because you wanted a home of your own. However, when you gave birth to John I believe you were still living in rented accommodation at 85 Cambridge Road. It is very important that I understand. I am your first-born child and only daughter. I have been extremely considerate and patient to date – too patient.

I believe you intend to speak to Theresa when she visits. I hope that this is the case and I do believe that by talking to

288

her, you may begin to come to terms with your shame and guilt. From what I am told, I understand that Theresa is a kind, understanding person who may be able to help you to face the difficulties of the past.

Over the last couple of weeks I have done a lot of soul-searching and I have come to the sad conclusion that until you're prepared to talk to me truthfully about the circumstances of my birth and adoption, I have no further wish to have any contact with either of you. I have not made this decision lightly, not least because of the effect on my three daughters. I will not put my children in a position where they are likely to be subjected to the kind of abuse that I encountered just to maintain a relationship with you in the hope that at some point in the future you will see fit to talk to me honestly.

Until now, everything has been about you. You have not considered my feelings at all. You told me last year that you have rights. You have no rights when it comes to the matter of my adoption. The law states that as an adopted person, I have the right to find my birth family.

As you are unwilling to tell me the truth about my birth, I can only speculate. I am therefore considering my options. One of those options is a DNA test, which can easily be arranged via the internet. This will confirm whether I am in fact a full sibling to John, Michael and Oliver.

My story has been astonishing to all of the people I have chosen to share it with. They cannot understand how anyone who was recently married could even contemplate giving away their first-born child. I think that this is possibly the reason that you are having difficulty in being open and honest with me.

You do not seem to appreciate that I have no restrictions upon me to prevent me from telling whomsoever I like about my unique story. This I believe would be a story worth telling to a much wider audience.

I am sending copies of this letter to John, Michael and Oliver.

Yours sincerely
Karen

Whilst both John and Michael had conceded that in principle they agreed with the sentiment of the letter, they nevertheless did find it a little too forceful. Their sense of unease only served to reassure me that I had pitched the letter just right. I certainly had no regrets.

As expected, my letter was not well received. Margaret and Paddy were incensed by my audacity.

'How dare that woman write to this address,' Margaret had exclaimed to Michael.

'She's far too cheeky and pushy,' she declared furiously.

'That woman has a name and she happens to be your daughter,' Michael had retorted.

Although Theresa's visit was imminent, Margaret had chosen not to share any details of her planned trip with Michael. The tension between mother and son was evident. At best their relationship was highly strained and at worst uncommunicative. It became apparent that Margaret had every intention of keeping Michael and Theresa apart at all costs. Theresa would be adhering to her sister's strict timetable of events, leaving no opportunity for her to spend time with Michael and his family. So, when Friday arrived and Theresa finally returned home to London, Michael remained completely unaware as to whether or not she had been informed of his new-found sister.

It was now Sunday and the last day of the Whitsun half-term break. Theresa had returned home to Romford 2 days ago and I was extremely restless. Did she now know of my existence and would I receive a call from her, or had Margaret acted true to form and avoided disclosing anything to her? How long should I wait before contacting her myself, just as I'd threatened? I was feeling extremely impatient and time was not something I felt predisposed to lavish on the Coleman family any longer. I sat down at the dining table opposite Paul. He was engrossed in designing and building a model Viking longboat. It had been Nancy's project for the half-term break but with my attention focused on events in Thomastown, her homework had been furthest from my thoughts. Suddenly Nancy's imminent return to school concentrated the mind and it was imperative that she be armed with the completed Viking vessel.

'Do you think Margaret *has* told Theresa about me?' I asked.

'Um,' he thought for a moment, deeply absorbed in his construction. 'Um ... no ... I don't think so,' he muttered.

'I don't think so either,' I concurred. 'Do you think I should ring her today?' I paused only briefly, giving Paul little time to respond. 'I think I'll ring her now,' I announced. 'I've got the number here.' Feeling more than a little apprehensive at what reaction I would have to deal with, I made the call.

'Hello,' said a woman with a soft Irish accent.

'Hello, is that Theresa?' I asked tentatively.

'Yes.'

I hesitated. The anticipation of discovering whether or not she even knew of my existence made me extremely anxious.

'My name is Karen and I wondered if your sister Margaret has told you about me?' I asked nervously. There was a pause.

'Yes Karen, Margaret has told me about you, but I have no intention of discussing anything with you today. I've had a long journey home, I'm feeling very tired and I don't want to talk to you now,' she explained. 'I do have your phone number, Margaret gave it to me and if you give me a couple of weeks I promise to call you and I'll be happy to arrange for us to meet somewhere.'

Although she made it clear there was to be no discussion today, her favourable reaction induced me to try and engage her a little further. I asked if it had been difficult for Margaret to confess news of a daughter. She reported that her sister had been very upset and, as difficult as it was for me now, I had to understand how things were back in 1962. Theresa spoke of a lack of money and housing as the reasons for my adoption. I listened without comment, deciding not to challenge her at this stage. Although she sounded a little disconcerted she gave the impression of someone genuine and caring. Theresa was all I had hoped for. She said she would call me and I believed her. There had been no anger in her voice. Delighted as we were that we had at last made contact, both Paul and I were nonetheless rather surprised that Margaret had actually carried out my request to reveal all to Theresa.

Mulling over our conversation, I sat watching Paul utterly engrossed in his project. Nancy's input would come later. Utilising Paul's beer bottle tops that had accumulated throughout the construction process, she would glue them to the portside and starboard after varnishing, creating a line of shields.

Less than two weeks had passed when Theresa telephoned to organise a meeting. There was a wave of excitement as I instantly recognised her number on the caller display.

'Hello, is that Karen?' she asked. Her voice was bright and cheery, very different to her sister's.

'Yes,' I said, thrilled that she'd rung back so soon.

'It's Theresa, I wondered if we could organise something?'

'That would be good,' I said enthusiastically.

'You're in Sevenoaks aren't you. Can you get to Lakeside Shopping Centre?'

'Yes, no problem.' Needless to say, I would have been prepared to drive practically anywhere.

'I can do tomorrow evening or next Wednesday or next Friday,' she suggested.

I was so disappointed not to be available the following day. It was parents evening for two of my daughters and I was already faced with the task of splitting myself in two. The thought much amused Theresa and we settled on the following Wednesday.

She asked for my mobile phone number telling me that she would call once she'd arrived at Lakeside and from there would organise a place to meet.

Although Margaret was fully aware that a meeting had been arranged between Theresa and me, I learned from Michael that, rather interestingly, Theresa had been evasive when quizzed by her sister. News that Michael too has been less than forthcoming with his mother was also particularly pleasing.

As I drove to Lakeside for our 7 pm rendezvous, I was very much looking forward to meeting Theresa. She seemed just what this reticent and troubled family needed. I arrived in time to purchase a small bunch of flowers for my aunt and as I did so my phone rang.

'Hello,' I answered expectantly.

'Hello Karen, it's Theresa, where are you?'

'I'm in Marks and Spencer.'

'So am I,' she chuckled. 'Whereabouts are you?'

'I'm on the ground floor. I'll stand next to the flower display close to the Food Hall.'

'Ok, I'm on my way.'

Within moments, I could see a woman looking very similar to Margaret, but sporting a beaming smile, heading towards me. She walked briskly and as she spotted me, she pointed.

'It's you isn't it, it is you?' she asked cheerily, still beaming.

'Yes, it's me,' I declared already feeling most at ease. She was taller than Margaret and dressed in denim jeans a floral blouse and a three quarter length mac, an outfit of which Margaret would never have approved. Theresa reached out and embraced me.

'Here, these are for you,' I said handing her some perfumed freesias.

'Thank you, there're beautiful, there really was no need for that,' she said politely.

After checking that I'd already eaten, she suggested that we should go and find a coffee shop. Once seated, I allowed Theresa to do the talking. She spoke eagerly about her years in nursing and the various counselling skills she'd attained throughout her career. The conversation turned to her visit to Ireland and I was delighted to hear that Oliver had spoken enthusiastically to her about our holiday in Center Parcs. I took the opportunity to show her some photographs of the holiday, which included my three daughters. She was interested to see us all enjoying the various activities, however, she was reluctant to be drawn into any discussion with regard to likenesses, claiming that she wasn't very good at spotting similarities. She was however, exceedingly complimentary on my 'lovely thick hair.'

Eventually she raised the subject of her sister, Margaret. I listened carefully as Theresa described how Margaret had revealed news of me during her recent visit to her home in Thomastown, Kilkenny. After sitting up one evening until the small hours, Margaret had beckoned her sister to join her out in the kitchen, leaving Paddy in the sitting room with Oliver and Theresa's husband, Tom.

'She urged me to step out into the garden – I've got something to tell you – she said, as she unlocked the back door and beckoned me out into the cold night air. She was very anxious we shouldn't be overheard. Once outside Margaret told me of you, her secret daughter,' she explained. 'Margaret was utterly distressed. She was crying profusely,' she added. An image of Margaret sobbing over me at this stage was hard to visualise, but I did my utmost to control my cynicism.

'They wanted the best for you. They had very little money and finding a place to live was impossible,' she explained. This account was sounding strangely familiar.

'You have to understand, the circumstances at that time were just awful,' she explained, as if to justify their actions. 'There was a strong prejudice against Irish people in London and finding accommodation was terribly difficult and made far worse if you were either pregnant or had young children.'

I listened with interest, as I thought about Herbert Road, Ilford. The electoral roll had shown a large Irish community in that area during the 60s. I thought also about Jim Donovan and how he'd described Margaret's friendly and helpful approach towards his wife, Mary. Theresa's words were unconvincing. It was clear she had fallen hook, line and sinker for Margaret's version of the situation. Furthermore, contrary to John and Michael's theory that Theresa would certainly have been aware of Margaret's pregnancy in 1962, this certainly appeared not to be the case.

'I don't think that you can *really* appreciate just how tough it was for them,' she stressed, perhaps sensing my incredulity. 'Margaret was so upset that evening, it was dreadful to see her like that,' she added. 'Paddy slipped out to join us a couple of times, leaving Oliver alone with Tom. He too has found this whole business very disturbing and was keen to support everything Margaret said.'

I could feel the anger welling up inside me. Did they really believe their story could be substantiated? I waited patiently for Theresa to finish this very skewed account of events more than forty years earlier.

'You've got to try and understand, Karen. Things are very different now compared to then,' she pleaded. 'This whole situation has upset both Margaret and Paddy immensely. Life has become intolerable for Margaret these past months, she's terribly unhappy. The reaction of her sons has also compounded the situation. She's received no support from them whatsoever.'

How did Margaret still have the audacity to stand by this story at this stage? I wondered quite what Margaret and Paddy were hoping to achieve. They knew exactly what information I possessed and their story certainly wouldn't tally with any of my documentation. How did they expect Theresa to correlate my records, against their version of events?

Satisfied that Theresa would not be able to provide me with any significant detail, I was poised, ready to give her my own findings on this sinister tale. I wanted to bombard Theresa with indisputable facts, determined to bring into question Margaret and Paddy's credibility.

'Theresa,' I said calmly. 'Although I have listened to all that you've had to say, I still have many unanswered questions and some paperwork that I think you may find rather surprising,' I announced confidently. The anticipation of Theresa's reaction was quite thrilling. As I reached for my envelope to reveal the documents, she suddenly placed both hands down onto my folder, momentarily preventing me from continuing.

'Um, do you mind me asking how old you are?' she asked hesitantly. It seemed a strange question. Surely the subject of my age would have been key and undoubtedly arisen during the conversation with her sister?

'Forty-six,' I replied.

She gasped. 'You look younger than that,' she declared, looking somewhat bewildered. I wondered just exactly how old did she expect me to be? At no time had she herself insinuated that my birth was out of wedlock and that it was the reason for my adoption. Furthermore, Theresa would have known Margaret and Paddy were married in August 1961 – she was there, as a bridesmaid. She also knew that John was born in August 1965. So where did she assume I came in the pecking order? I took out my birth certificate and placed it down in front of her. She reached for her glasses and I pointed to the most astonishing entry on the document: Patrick Coleman, bus conductor, (deceased). The shock on her face was instantaneous.

'Has Margaret seen this?' she asked immediately. I was flabbergasted by her remark. It confirmed my belief that Margaret had told her no more than she had me, just a year earlier in Dublin. Despite lecturing me on past times, Theresa had absolutely no understanding of my situation.

'Oh yes,' I said mischievously. 'However she claims to have no recollection of declaring Paddy dead,' I didn't even bother to disguise the glee in my voice. Theresa was clearly uncomfortable, her initial air of confidence had disappeared and she was fidgeting on her seat nervously removing and replacing her glasses several times, glancing furtively at the alarming information on my birth certificate.

'And,' I added in a measured voice. 'I know that Margaret and Paddy *did* have somewhere to live at the time of my birth. In fact I have met with the man who rented them rooms soon after their wedding.' I paused and looked straight at Theresa, who didn't respond.

'Interestingly, this gentlemen is also insistent that he has absolutely no recollection of Margaret ever being pregnant whilst living under his roof,' I declared.

'I really don't understand any of this, there must be some explanation,' said Theresa somewhat pathetically. I was almost revelling in blowing Margaret's would-be glowing reputation into little pieces. I had yet another card to play though. I paused for a few seconds and then posed the question.

'If, as you explained, money was indeed an issue, then how was it I came to be born in a private nursing home?' The deluge of questions had had the desired affect. Theresa couldn't disguise the fact that she was perplexed and ill at ease.

'Finally, look at this,' I said drawing her attention to my birth certificate one last time. 'Margaret didn't even give me a name. Why was that?' Theresa shook her head with a look of utter despair. Theresa's upbringing and devout faith, together with her lifelong vocational occupation made her sister Margaret's conduct incomprehensible and totally bewildering. At this stage I had no intention of relieving Theresa of her immense discomfort. I recounted some of the highly venomous remarks Margaret had made to me and the recent appalling conversation between Paddy and myself, just weeks earlier. Her face contorted. Totally unprepared for my onslaught, she sat dejected and speechless.

'Now perhaps you can understand why I must have answers to my questions,' I said firmly. 'This is why there is difficulty between Margaret, Paddy and me. It's because she refuses to tell me the truth. It's also why her relationship with her sons is now strained. Margaret and Paddy were already married when I was born. Their actions are shameful. Margaret owes me the truth. I need to know the circumstances of my adoption,' I stressed firmly.

I described the difficulty now facing my brothers. Without their mother's sanction, they are unable to truly embrace our relationship and share the news of the existence of their sister outside the immediate family. I reminded Theresa of Oliver's visit to her home last October and how awkward it was for him to hide the secret from her.

Her response to these facts was most unexpected. She didn't agree with family secrets, she claimed and believed something such as this should be brought out into the open. Furthermore, I was delighted to hear that she had every intention of sharing news of me with her three grown up children. However, intriguingly she did refuse to enlighten her sister Catherine, claiming her to be in poor health and that such news would cause her tremendous upset and distress. Still visibly shaken and somewhat reeling from my unexpected onslaught, she decided to challenge my own reasons for determining the truth. I very much resented her attitude and questioning, particularly as she pulled herself together sufficiently to suggest that I leave the past behind and concentrate solely on the future. Had she not grasped the importance of what I had been telling her?

'You've formed a good relationship with your brothers and looking at your photos, it's clear that you all had a great time together. Why don't you just focus on them and try not to dwell on the past?' she asked callously, picking up my snaps and glancing through them again. 'What good will it do at this stage harking back over something that happened such a long time ago?'

Although I didn't want to alienate her at this stage, I was nonetheless irritated beyond measure by her dismissive approach. Expecting me to justify my need to know the circumstances of my adoption was nothing less than offensive. She needed to be reminded of a crucial fact.

'How could I, as an adopted person, ever have expected to find full blood siblings when it clearly states my father is deceased?'

Theresa looked away and did not respond to this fundamental question. Clearly, she was keen to bring our meeting to an end. One last time I repeated how important it was for me to establish the truth.

Although she assured me that she would speak to Margaret again, she felt it wasn't something for the telephone and like the rest of the family played the waiting-game card. It would have to wait until her next visit to Ireland in September. However, having met with me, she now felt extremely compromised. She didn't want to reveal her knowledge of the catalogue of anomalies to her sister for fear of appearing disloyal. Instead, she would try to encourage Margaret to have a candid discussion on the matter. To me, Theresa's approach sounded futile, Margaret needed to be confronted, she had been evasive for too long. Once again, in this drawn out search for the truth, it seemed I had no alternative but to leave myself at the mercy of yet another individual.

We had been talking for over two hours before parting on

what appeared to be good terms.

'It's been nice to meet you Karen, I'm sure we'll meet again soon,' she said warmly, putting her arms around me and kissing me goodbye. 'Safe journey home and remember, I'll do what I can.'

Later that year, Theresa did indeed spend a week with Margaret. However, since her return, there has been no communication from her whatsoever. I had great expectations of Theresa, but I now have no plans to make any further contact with her. I left her in no doubt as to the importance of my plea and so I feel extremely let down. Any suggestion that I might contact her again has been ruled out, as my request would undoubtedly meet with yet more of Margaret's lies and deceit.

And I ask myself, in her everyday professional capacity, is this how Theresa chooses to operate when faced with a difficult situation?

31. Anger, Sadness and Disappointment

April 2009

Since my outspoken letter to Margaret and Paddy, almost a year ago, there has been no further contact between us. Although my feelings of anger towards my birth mother have not diminished and I remain resolute in my quest for the truth, sadly I have now come to realise, that anything I undertake in the future will be without the true support of any of my brothers.

More than eighteen months have now elapsed since John, Michael and Oliver learnt the astonishing news of the unsuspected existence of a sister. Since then, I feel I have been extremely patient and understanding, allowing them time and space not only to adjust to the reality of an unknown sibling, but most importantly, to the unfolding implications surrounding my entire existence in relation to their parents. During this time my brothers continued to enjoy their relationship with my family and me, spending many joyous family occasions together in each other's company. On the surface, these events and the frequent affectionate telephone calls between us appeared to establish a very enjoyable and fulfilling relationship for everyone.

However, my brothers' stance today towards my on-going issues with our mother is hugely disappointing and extremely difficult for me to comprehend. Ultimately, unless there is a significant change in my brothers' attitude towards my plight,

I fear that it will inevitably have a detrimental affect on our relationship.

I have learned from them that I continue to have a great impact on Margaret's life. Her anxiety is most evident. However, their regular and almost jocular reports of their mother's erratic behaviour do little to ease the ever-growing tension between us. I understand that in the company of her sons she maintains complete control of all conversation. Fluctuating between superficial chitchat, thereby ensuring that neither she nor they make any reference to me, or alternatively and only when she chooses, there is a tirade of abuse directed at me and, once again, I am referred to as 'that woman'.

Margaret has made it extremely clear to her sons that my adoption has absolutely nothing to do with any of them – it happened before they were born and she has no intention of discussing the matter. Regrettably for me, my brothers seem resigned to abide by this edict, citing their need to respect their mother's wishes. I find their acceptance of this situation infuriating and grossly demeaning, particularly as their desire to know the truth themselves has not in any way diminished and remains uppermost in their minds. In fact, they have resorted to goading me into singlehandedly confronting their mother. This, I believe is nothing less than cowardly. I feel extremely weary at the prospect of tackling Margaret and I am not prepared to consider the possibility of being subjected yet again to her wicked tongue and Paddy's volatile behaviour.

Whilst I am still considering my next move, my brothers' approach to my dilemma is nothing short of faint-hearted. Even since my own meeting with Theresa a year earlier, they have still refrained from broaching the subject of a sister with her. And despite John's albeit infrequent communications with his cousin Rosalyn – Theresa's daughter – she too remains oblivious to my existence.

Sadly, my brothers' reticence concerning my existence extends beyond the confines of their immediate family. Still ill at ease with the situation, they have avoided making any reference to me in their social circles. Visits to John and Helen's home have at times even precluded us from sitting in the garden, as John expressed his fear that neighbours might overhear our conversation and thereby draw their own conclusions.

John's reaction to his mother's life-long guarded secret has been extraordinary. From the outset he declined a plea from his brother Michael to join him and confront their mother together over this most unexpected discovery of a sister. Instead, he chose to leave his younger brother to suffer the terrifying ordeal alone. Since establishing a relationship with me, he has returned to Ireland only twice, each time during the Christmas period. On his first visit, six months after our initial meeting, he waited until his very last day before choosing to raise the highly contentious subject. His mother's seething reaction was to tell her eldest son that this was none of his concern. Compliant to her wishes, he duly reported the incident back to me, satisfied that he had indeed made every effort to assist me in my quest for the truth. During the year that followed he continued to avoid any reference to me when speaking to his mother on the telephone, waiting instead for her to instigate any conversation that related to me. His next trip home, a year later, was after both he and Helen had spent Christmas Day with us in Sevenoaks. Once again he spent several days under his parents' roof, loath to mention the numerous occasions he'd spent in the company of my family and me in recent times. However, Michael had kept his mother abreast of these episodes and it was only on the final morning of his stay when Margaret, clearly extremely intrigued by the regularity of John's visits to his sister over the past year, orchestrated time alone with her eldest son.

Paddy needed no encouragement to take a 'lie in' and Oliver

had been dispatched to purchase a newspaper. Bombarded with questions which all centred on me, John's reaction was to give only a guarded and limited response, thereby frustrating his mother even further. I struggle to understand John. He appears to revel in what for him seems no more than a game, as he eagerly awaits his mother's introduction of this highly sensitive subject, but nonetheless he is reluctant to voice his own opinions on the matter, if indeed he really has any.

Michael, too, has acted rather insensitively as he continues to accept the ridiculous behaviour and wishes of his mother. When his daughter's confirmation to the Catholic faith was imminent, he nervously broached the subject of my family attending the ceremony and celebrations. News that her chosen confirmation name was to be Rose, after my own daughter, appeared to be a gesture intended to cement our relationship further. However, he was quick to add that should we decide to attend, both Margaret and Paddy had made it quite clear that they would not. Sadly, this was never a genuine invitation but a reminder that almost two years on, I still have not been accepted into the Coleman family. Fortunately for Michael his predicament was short-lived. I declined his decidedly tentative invitation, paving the way for the entire Coleman clan to attend in force. Michael and Helena's decision to present their daughter for confirmation at a time when the family was shrouded in a shameful secret, seems amoral and highly hypocritical.

At this point I cannot exclude Oliver from my negative feelings. He has also been reluctant to show any true commitment. He may have difficulties in his life brought about by his parents, but he is a grown man, with ability for free thought if he chooses. Once out of reach of his mother's controlling behaviour, I have seen evidence of a brother able to voice opinions and make decisions for himself. Despite my belief that his October 2008 visit was a complete success, he has made no attempt to plan or even speak of any further trips to Sevenoaks. In fact, Oliver no longer mentions my name to either of his brothers. The relationship between Oliver and me is doomed. He is aware of not only a sister, but also of the existence of three additional nieces, all happy to make him part of their lives. Despite my efforts, I'm left feeling that Oliver, has through inaction, chosen to let time, people and life pass him by.

My brothers have allowed their mother to dominate their entire lives, for fear of incurring her wrath. Sadly, I feel their reluctance to put Margaret and Paddy under any pressure to give an accurate explanation of events almost fifty years ago only serves to condone her actions. This situation may well ensure an easier and more manageable, if not questionable, way of life for my brothers but it is totally unacceptable to me. I am left dumbfounded by their lack of action.

One recent event, in particular, was immensely upsetting. After extending our invitation to Rosemary's eighteenth birthday celebrations in March 2009, to my brothers, I was delighted to hear of Michael's intention to fly over with his family to spend the weekend with us. Joined by John and Helen, a very memorable time was had by all. Yet, just one month later, when Helen returned to Ireland alone for the Easter break to visit her family – a trip that included a lunch at Margaret and Paddy's home, where Michael and his family would also be present – John expressly forbade her to raise the subject of either me, or the recent family celebrations, whilst in the company of his parents. It was particularly distressing to hear Helen's account of her time in Thomastown, conversing in hushed tones with Michael and Helena on the subject of the recent weekend in Sevenoaks, but away from Margaret and Paddy's earshot. After all, Margaret had been fully aware of our family event, as she herself had purchased cards for both Rosemary and for my own imminent birthday on Oliver's behalf.

I felt Helen's decision to abide by John's wishes, thereby guaranteeing harmony all round, showed little regard for me. I feel let down by her. Since my initial communications with Helen, I had seen her as an ally. Although not a mother herself, the understanding and compassion she expressed towards me was one of true empathy. Highly critical and shocked by the behaviour of her mother-in-law, a woman with whom she'd had a close relationship with for some twenty-five years, I had hoped, perhaps naïvely, that Helen might feel compelled to champion my plight with Margaret herself. However, it wasn't to be. Despite her strength of feeling and the longstanding relationship with Margaret and Paddy, she too remains as reticent as each of my brothers. Instead she follows the example of both John and Michael and claims that it is my fault that I have been ineffectual in my efforts to tackle Margaret. She also believes that if I continue to expect my brothers to intervene, then I will certainly jeopardise my relationship with them. Since confronted by Helen's rather forthright and hurtful opinion, I have refrained from making any contact with either her or John. They too have abstained from communicating with me and have made no further effort to stay in touch.

I strongly resent the deluge of unfair criticism from them all. After having made such enormous efforts with Margaret, being accused of doing very little, shying away and reluctant to put Margaret and Paddy under any pressure leaves me feeling utterly despondent. I have done absolutely everything within my power to consider everybody throughout this recent time and done everything possible to handle everything most sensitively. My initial contact with Margaret and Paddy was extremely discreet and, despite the hostile reaction I received, I remained patient in the hope that a meeting with them would lead to the opportunity for them to talk openly and honestly with me. Regrettably they had a very different agenda, but even then I continued to give them the time and space they requested.

After realising that this was nothing more than some eternal delaying tactic in telling me what I was desperate to know, I approached John cautiously and thoughtfully. My family and I were eventually met with a very welcoming and positive response from each of my brothers in turn, and I was delighted to see my daughters begin to develop and establish their own individual relationships with their new-found uncles and their families. I also devised various events, which enabled us to experience some highly enjoyable and memorable times together. However, throughout this seemingly joyous time, I have been fully aware of my brothers' reluctance to reciprocate any of my various invitations. Ever conscious of their mother's reaction to the flourishing relationship with their sister, they have refrained from making any gesture that may appear to have been instigated by them. Their attitude to our relationship disappoints and saddens me. Whilst I know we have all benefited from this most unexpected union, I sense I am chasing something that can never be. Although I have discovered a very real feeling of belonging and connection, I fear that the relationship with my brothers is regrettably flawed. Given the unspoken constraints imposed upon them by their mother, they have never been able to completely embrace our relationship. I'm left feeling destined to remain very much an outsider. Perhaps it was the prospect of my writing a book that gave my brothers the excuse needed to begin to disassociate themselves from me.

The idea that I might produce a written account of my search was a strong possibility even before my first meeting with John. Initially, news of my project was well received, with him even suggesting how he too could incorporate his own story alongside mine. For both John and Michael, as time has passed, the likelihood has increased that something highly untoward lies behind the reason for my adoption. Fearful of what might lie ahead, as I set about exposing their mother's highly shocking and cruel behaviour to a wider audience, their interest in me has diminished and they have withdrawn. Indeed it has caused great unease amongst all the Coleman family. It was John who reported news of my book to his parents and it was no surprise to hear that Margaret and Paddy were incensed with rage. In fact, it brings me great satisfaction to know that (unlike their relationship with their sons), they are unable to exercise any control over their first-born.

At this point, any regular, light-hearted conversation with Michael has ceased. My determined approach unsettles him. As my book becomes a reality, Michael has cited his children as his main concern. I believe he should address these issues with his mother who should finally bear responsibility for her actions. Instead, he has reported to me his concern for his mother's well-being. The tension within the family has increased considerably and Margaret is now smoking significantly more than usual.

So I have witnessed another side to my brothers that disappoints me and I am astounded by their spineless approach to their mother. They have failed to fulfil my hopes and expectations. Their decision to remain compliant to their mother's wishes is in total conflict with my determination to uncover the truth. I will continue to pursue Margaret and dispute her very tenuous explanation for my adoption.

Faced with an entire family waiting in the wings for my next move, I feel very alone. I have reached the conclusion that a DNA test has to be my next step. With so many unanswered questions, I need confirmation that I am indeed the product of both Margaret and Paddy. I hardly imagine that either of my supposed parents would subject themselves to such a test, but a Siblingship Test with one of my brothers could confirm whether I am indeed a full sister. Unfortunately, at present the high cost and the strained relationship with Michael, who would be the most likely brother to perhaps agree to the test, prevents me from carrying out this test immediately. So, I have no alternative but to bide my time.

32. DNA

September 2009

'Are you sure that Margaret's your birth mother?' asked yet another interested individual, after hearing a brief résumé of the curious circumstances surrounding my birth and subsequent adoption.

This question had certainly occurred to me, long before I'd discovered the whereabouts of Margaret Coleman, the woman named on my birth certificate.

The search for my birth mother had indeed thrown up several inconsistencies, each posing a number of unanswered questions and all causing my mind to run wild with outrageous theories. However, after finally unearthing Margaret and Patrick, any thoughts that they were not who they seemed to be, were quickly dispelled. The first telephone conversation between Margaret and me, followed by a meeting with them both in Dublin, confirmed their authenticity. Patrick's display of emotion, as we sat together, was very tangible.

'Are you my father?' I'd asked, looking directly at him. Watching him bow his head and nod shamefacedly, whilst clutching my hand and dabbing his eyes with his handkerchief, could only confirm his kinship with me.

Two and a half years on, I am now certain beyond a doubt that they have not been honest with me. The reasons they first gave for my adoption were incomplete and evasive and have not sat comfortably in my mind. Although I have continued – unsuccessfully – to challenge their explanation, the discrepancies remain.

Both Margaret and Patrick's behaviour towards me and my family has been erratic to say the least. Warm invitations to visit Thomastown were followed by firm instructions to their sons not to mention my name in their presence and although we have all received cards and gifts from them in the early stages of our relationship, these have now ceased.

I am aware that it has been my persistent questioning and reluctance to accept their unsatisfactory version of events that has led to a very hostile relationship between us. Unfortunately this has also had an impact on the relationship between my newly discovered brothers and me. With both John and Michael, the reluctance to acknowledge and accept me openly amongst their family and friends has been distressing and disappointing after the initial joy of discovering their sister. I believe, following their parents' wishes, they now keep me at arm's length.

I'm convinced that there is something underlying, known only to Margaret and Patrick that will provide the answers I so desperately seek. I am determined to resolve the mystery. My continual nagging doubts and uncertainty, together with the recent deterioration in my relationship with my brothers, has left me no choice but to take other measures to obtain categorical proof of my parentage. Although up until now the cost has been a factor, a DNA Siblingship Test is now inevitable. My unanswered questions remain the same:

Why was I born in a private nursing home, if lack of money was the reason for my adoption? My adoptive parents were adamant that family money was involved in the arrangement, although Bernice and Peter did not provide any cash payments themselves. Why does a woman, recently married, declare her husband dead – unlawfully – on a birth certificate? Why did my adoption file contain such pitifully limited information? Why was there a court document, signed by Margaret, declaring me illegitimate? How could Jim Donovan be so certain that Margaret was never pregnant whilst living under his roof? Why, as a Catholic baby, was I not baptised within a couple of days of my birth? And why was I unnamed? Since our meetings, further questions have arisen:

How could Margaret not have remembered my precise date of birth? Why are Margaret and Patrick so reluctant to talk to their sons and me about the circumstances surrounding my adoption? Why was Margaret so adamant that her sons must never know of my existence? Why do Margaret and Patrick show such anger towards me? And just recently, I have learned from Michael, that Margaret claims although there is more information concerning my adoption - she will never disclose it? With all these questions in mind I have considered four possible theories.

Theory One: Margaret and Patrick are indeed both my parents.

They have both reassured me of this personally. Their names are on my birth certificate and they have confirmed to their sons that I am a full sibling. I have a picture of Margaret on her wedding day that shows a beaming, happy pose with her hand positioned low down on her abdomen and she admitted to being aware of her pregnancy on that day.

However, more than forty years on, I believe their hostility towards me is due to their feelings of shame and guilt. For Margaret, ten weeks pregnant on her wedding day, her deep, moral approach could not allow her to keep her baby. Despite her residing in the UK while her parents remained in Ireland, her main concern would have been about family shame. The pregnancy was hidden so as not to draw attention to the inevitable missing baby later. To avoid any awkward questions

312

as to why a married Roman Catholic couple would give away their first-born child, she announced her husband dead and in doing so drew sympathy and understanding from the Adoption Agency. Declaring her husband as dead also ensured that she alone would handle the paperwork, thereby avoiding any need for Patrick to find himself in a situation of self-doubt over his actions.

If this is the answer, the following questions remain unexplained. Jim Donovan claimed that Margaret loved children and was a tremendous help to his wife, Mary Donovan and their young family. How could such a 'good woman' who loved children give her own child away? If lack of money and no home of their own were the reasons given for my adoption, then why was I born in a private nursing home and why, three years later and still living in rented rooms, did they keep their second child, John? Their claim that I would go to a better home is weak. A baby handed over for adoption can be given to a family of any means. They were practising Roman Catholics and married in church. It is difficult to understand how they could act as they did. How did their Catholic principles allow me to be given away unnamed and unbaptised, particularly if the circumstances were purely financial?

Theory Two: Margaret is my mother but Patrick is not my father.

The County Court document, signed by Margaret and held in my adoption file, states that I am illegitimate. However, Margaret has denied all knowledge of this document. Perhaps Margaret was involved in another relationship and could not be certain that I was Patrick's child. Therefore, did Patrick give her an ultimatum? If this theory is correct then it raises the following questions. Why was Margaret so keen that Patrick and I talk on the telephone prior to our meeting? Why did Patrick behave in such an emotional way towards me in Dublin? Why did Patrick's name appear on my birth certificate? And finally, Paddy was alarmed not by the sight of his name on my birth certificate but the realisation that he had been pronounced dead. Even if I had been the result of an indiscretion, it was not necessary to disclose the name of the father when registering a birth. And how is it that there appears to be a strong family likeness that runs through my brothers, myself and even my daughters, which appears to stem from Patrick?

Theory Three: Neither Margaret nor Patrick are my natural parents.

Perhaps Margaret really was the kind, thoughtful girl that Jim Donovan had described? Was she protecting someone? If so, it could only be someone very close, like a sister perhaps? In the eyes of the Catholic Church for an unmarried woman in southern Ireland to become pregnant in the 60s would have been totally unacceptable. Many traumatic experiences have now come to light concerning the ill treatment of young single Catholic girls and their babies. Is it so far fetched to consider that I might never have been born of Margaret? In an effort to protect and assist an unmarried sister and prevent any shame falling on the family in Ireland, did Margaret, with the help and support of her parents concoct a plan to enable her sister to enter the nursing home using Margaret's identity, hence my sparse adoption file? Jim Donovan was adamant he had no recollection of Margaret's pregnancy. How could she have continued to work as a bus conductor throughout this time? This particular theory goes some way towards explaining the many discrepancies. Margaret has two younger sisters, Theresa and Catherine, but having spent several hours with Theresa and seeing her reaction to me, I can rule out any idea that she is my mother. It is Catherine that interests me. I couldn't forget Margaret's vehement reaction during our very first conversation, to my suggestion that Catherine could be my birth mother. Theresa, like Margaret was also adamant that Catherine should be left alone and not informed of my existence. Why does Catherine appear to be ostracised by her family? Did Margaret falsely give both her and Patrick's details on my birth certificate to ensure legitimacy? Did Catherine and Margaret's father, my grandfather, provide the money for the nursing home? An aunt may not have accurately retained my date of birth. And now, was it the fear of the potential legal implications that prevented Margaret and Patrick from disclosing information to me? Any resemblance I might have to Margaret comes from Catherine. Finally, there is the fact that I am left-handed and as far as I know there are no left-handed members of the Coleman or Hennessy families. With these thoughts in mind, I can't ignore Patrick's tears in Dublin. Were they solely for the sadness of my situation?

Theory Four: An idea most outlandish.

Was Catherine my mother and Patrick my father? A very sinister thought, but one I couldn't rule out. Would Margaret have been prepared to register a child born to her husband and her sister?

Taking into account my four possible scenarios, it had become imperative for me to find out once and for all whether my parents are indeed both Margaret and Paddy as they claim. Any contact with my eldest brother John had become non-existent, but a meeting with Michael in London presented the opportunity to carry out the DNA test. Although he was willing, it was with a somewhat blasé attitude that he provided the simple mouth swab, convinced of the outcome. He was quick to reject all of my bizarre theories, ridiculing them, adamant that the result would prove me to be a full sibling, reminding me of our strong facial likeness to Patrick. Whilst he was complacent, I was already prepared for a revelation.

One week later I telephoned him with the result. I had not been surprised by the outcome, but Michael I knew, would be devastated.

'Hi, do I need to pull over?' he asked flippantly, already convinced of the result.

'Yes, I think you'd better,' I replied.

'Ok I've stopped and . . . what does it say?' still in a light-hearted frame of mind.

'We share only one parent.'

I waited for him to break the momentary silence.

'I really hadn't expected that,' he said. His tone was suddenly very subdued.

Noticeably shocked and saddened, he listened as I explained the result in more detail. It gave a 97.7% chance that both Michael and I were half biological siblings. This ruled out most of my theories, including one that up until this point I had been loath even to consider – the unspoken and unimaginable idea of incest. With that eliminated, I continued to present the findings. I couldn't be Margaret's and Patrick's. Any idea that I might be Catherine's was also rejected, as although Margaret and her sister shared similar DNA, the percentage match to one parent, would not have been so high. This also dispelled the theory that I might be the product of both Patrick and Catherine. The result would have shown us sharing the same two parents. However, if my mother was indeed Margaret's sister, it would have given a lower than the expected percentage match if Michael and I had shared the same two parents. And any idea that I could be only Patrick's was immediately rejected. It would have been most unlikely that Margaret would have been the one to register me. Margaret had to be our shared parent. Michael's sudden alarm and the implications of this unexpected result prompted him to request that I refrain from disclosing his involvement in my findings to his mother. Yet again, I felt disappointed and exasperated by his lack of support even at this crucial stage.

I had no intention of telephoning Margaret immediately – I had my own feelings to consider. Foremost there was anger – she had continued to lie, not only to me but also to her sons. There was also a great sadness that my relationship with my three brothers suddenly felt diluted. They were only half-brothers. I feared that for them, the result was most fortuitous, giving them yet a further opportunity to distance themselves from me, thereby bringing them some relief and also easing the conflict between their loyalty towards their parents and any empathy they may have for me. The prospect of a close and fulfilling relationship with my siblings had been short-lived.

'I'm going to phone Margaret today from work and give her one final chance to come clean and tell you the truth,' announced Paul the following morning. A wave of relief came over me. I made no attempt to deter him.

'And I will be suggesting that she comes over here. She can come on her own, with Paddy or any of the boys, I don't care, the lies have gone on long enough,' he proclaimed emphatically. Paul's resilient approach made him far more able to tackle Margaret than I could at this stage. Inevitably, the relationship between her and me was fraught and painfully emotional.

'Hello Margaret, it's Paul,' he said resolutely. She needed no prompting as to the full identity of the caller and sensed immediately that this was not a courtesy call. He continued.

'Some irrefutable evidence has come to light, that proves that you have lied to Karen about her parentage,' he declared. Margaret did not respond.

'The lies and deceit have gone on long enough, Margaret, and now is your last chance to tell Karen the truth. I think the very least you should do is to fly over to Gatwick and meet with her.

What about this Sunday?'

'Oh, this is absolute nonsense,' she replied dismissively. 'Here, talk to Paddy,' she said, immediately passing the receiver to him and relinquishing any further involvement in the matter.

'What on earth is all this about, why must you keep bringing this up time and time again?' he asked, clearly tired and irritated by the continual reference to this highly charged subject.

'We've told you that we are both Karen's parents, what more do you want us to say?' said Paddy impatiently.

'But we have recently obtained information that confirms that you cannot both be Karen's parents,' advised Paul.

'Well I'm telling you it's wrong,' said Paddy adamantly. Although his tone was becoming more irate, Paul was undeterred.

'We know that Margaret has lied to Karen and now she just wants the truth.'

'This is nonsense.' he bellowed furiously. 'I'll send you a blood sample to prove it, oh, and some hair and Margaret will happily do the same and perhaps we can finally bring an end to this nonsense.' Although enraged, his offer appeared genuine. Paul was taken aback by Paddy's insistence to prove the impossible.

'I don't need a blood sample, Paddy, a simple mouth swab from each of you is all that's required for a DNA test,' he explained, determined not to let this opportunity slip by.

'Right, OK,' he barked.

'Are you sure that Margaret's happy to do the same?' he stressed, aware that Paddy had instigated the offer.

'Yes, yes, she's here with me and she agrees,' he insisted. Their reaction was most unexpected.

'OK, how about I fly over on Saturday (the day after tomorrow) and carry out the swab test?' suggested Paul, snatching the moment.

'Fine, you can come and have some lunch here with us,' came his somewhat unexpected response.

'I don't think that's appropriate under the circumstances,' said Paul, anticipating a difficult outcome to this whole affair.

'OK, we'll drive to Dublin and meet you there, it will save you hiring a car and driving to us,' said Paddy. Although Paddy appeared very accommodating, Paul had real concerns over their true commitment to this matter.

'Paddy, I'll check the flights this evening and I will call you before I go ahead and book.'

'OK that's fine,' he said.

Later that evening Paul made the call. He was surprised that even after several hours they still hadn't reneged on their decision. After seeking a final reassurance from Paddy, the flights were booked. However, a brief call from Margaret that same evening querying the procedure of a DNA test and asking for confirmation that Paul had no intention of poisoning her, were undoubtedly the words of a very anxious woman.

It was a call from Michael the next day that alerted me to the sudden change of plan. Paddy and Margaret had decided against meeting Paul in Dublin and Paddy, full of bluster, was intending to call Paul and tell him a thing or two. He tackled Michael to discover what, if any, had been his involvement in these recent developments, to which Michael admitted denying to them that he had provided any DNA sample. This avoidance of yet another opportunity to confront his parents and demand the truth irritated me immensely. Although there had indeed been a heated conversation with Paddy who stuck to his story, he remained adamant that both he and Margaret were my parents. However, in doing so he had of course inadvertently thrown doubt over Michael's parentage. If as they claimed they were both my parents then it was impossible for Paddy to be Michael's father.

Having been forewarned, Paul received a very unpleasant call from Paddy.

'We won't be coming to Dublin to meet you tomorrow,' said Paddy triumphantly.

'But Paddy you gave me your word.'

'Well, we've changed our minds. What business is it of yours to come over here demanding a DNA test?' asked Paddy angrily.

'You suggested it. You offered a blood test,' said Paul calmly.

'We're not doing it, it's got nothing to do with you.'

'It's got everything to do with me, I'm Karen's partner.'

'Why isn't she sending her husband over?' he asked vindictively. 'You ought to think about your own family, it's not all happy there, from what I understand. Get your own family in order', he added spitefully.

'My family has nothing to do with you, Paddy, so please don't even go there.'

Patrick was provoking Paul, but with Nancy sitting beside him hanging on his every word, it prevented him from retaliating.

'Paddy, are you saying, that you won't meet with me?'

'No we're not,' he said adamantly.

'But you gave me your word and a man who doesn't keep his word is not a man.'

'I don't care, we're not coming.'

'Then I shall come to you. I think we should talk.'

'If I see you, you'll have a spade across the back of your head,' yelled Paddy.

'Don't threaten me Paddy. I don't respond to threats and you certainly don't frighten me.'

Paddy's manner towards Paul became even more abusive. Throughout the call Paul had sensed his voice was being relayed on the telephone speaker and once again Margaret could be heard goading Paddy at every opportunity. Angered by the continual onslaught from both Margaret and Paddy, Paul decided to bring the heated conversation to a head.

'If you are still insisting that you are both Karen's parents – '

'Yes we are,' Paddy interrupted.

'Then Paddy, you leave me no choice but to tell you that you are not the father to all your sons.'

The line went dead. Paul was silent and moved the receiver away from his ear indicating the abrupt end of the call. After a moment he redialled the international number. Paddy answered and spoke immediately, full of fury.

'Of course I know the truth, do you think I'm stupid? I've always known the truth and yes I've lied to Karen.' Once again he abruptly ended the call.

Although tempted, Paul decided not to travel to Margaret and Paddy's home the following day. On a purely practical note, the time between the flights, there and back prevented such a journey.

Interestingly, I wonder what exactly Patrick was referring to? Did he really know all along that I wasn't his daughter or had Margaret deceived him too and was he just trying to save face, after perhaps hearing a confession from his wife? His reaction towards me in Dublin appeared to be that of sadness and regret, not pity.

Michael was particularly apprehensive at the prospect of visiting his parents over the weekend. However, much to his surprise, their behaviour was most unexpected. His father was remarkably chipper and Margaret was busy with her regular chores. Paddy effortlessly dismissed the events of the past couple of days and was still claiming that he was happy to undergo a DNA test, but not with any involvement from Paul. Much to my relief, Michael did concede to his involvement in the DNA test and although he met with tremendous fury from his parents they still remained adamant that the findings were incorrect, attributing the result to a possible mix-up at the nursing home where I was born. A most ridiculous and impossible theory.

Michael also reported back that Margaret was keen to talk to me, but that I needed to call her. I wondered what the reason might be. Was she stalling or was she finally prepared to bring an end to all the lies and deceit and speak the truth? There had been no communication between us for almost a year.

'Hello Margaret, it's Karen.'

'Ah, you just caught me nodding off in the chair. How are you?' she asked, as if our conversations were a regular occurrence.

'Margaret will you talk to me?' I asked. I had no intention of a cosy chat.

'Of course, what is it you want to know?' she asked calmly. Her personable tone unnerved me.

'I want the truth, I want answers to questions that I have been asking you for nearly three years.'

'OK, what are they?'

I sensed that she was just humouring me.

'Who are my parents?'

'Paddy and me, of course, I've told you that.'

'But that's not what the DNA test shows.' This was not going to be an easy call.

'Well, I don't know how that's happened,' she replied innocently.

Exasperated, I moved on to the next question.

'Why have I got a copy of a court document that says I'm illegitimate?'

'But you're not illegitimate, I keep telling you that,' she said in a most patronising tone.

'Margaret you are not answering my questions honestly,' I responded, trying hard not to lose my patience.

'But I am,' she insisted, with the same condescending tone. 'You've got to get yourself sorted out. I understand that you see a psychiatrist don't you?' she asked.

Her callous inquiry was incorrect. I did not see, nor have I ever seen a psychiatrist and the suggestion that I might be in need of one was offensive. She was referring to my visits to Maggie, my counsellor. I had told both Michael and John in confidence. Disappointed that they had chosen to share this with her, I battled on.

'Margaret, the DNA test shows that you cannot both be my parents and Michael's.'

'I don't understand, there must be a mistake.'

'I still have the swabs for the DNA tests for you and Paddy. If I send them to Michael would you be prepared to do them?'

'Yes, of course we would,' she stated calmly.

'Thank you, I'll put them in the post tomorrow and Margaret, if I'm wrong, I will be the first to apologise to you.'

How could she remain so adamant, even at this stage? Although it was beyond belief, at this point, the situation had reached bizarre proportions and I did indeed find myself considering any small error rate that exists with DNA testing.

A further week passed before I heard from Michael. He'd had an extremely traumatic week. At last the news that I was desperately waiting for arrived. Michael reported that, after finally admitting to an affair prior to her wedding day, Margaret had taken to her bed, refusing to reveal the name of my biological father. Any attempt to carry out the DNA test had been rejected by both her and Paddy. Paddy appeared highly distressed by recent events and once again, Margaret had made a harrowing threat of suicide, this time with the aid of the petrol can in the garden shed. Failing that, she was intent on retreating to a women's refuge. I found the idea hilarious. There was certainly no suggestion that Paddy had been violent towards her. I knew her well enough to understand these dramatic words were intended only to remove her from a life of deceit. At this point I felt little sympathy for the entire family. I had battled to discover the truth, while my brothers had resolutely continued to condone the actions of their parents. Nevertheless several other revelations had come to light.

To Michael's surprise, Paddy chose to disclose to his son that both he and Margaret had taken time-out early in the marriage. Unfortunately, true to form, Michael did not press Paddy for any details and neither did Paddy choose to elaborate. Another particularly surprising remark from Paddy was his indication to his son that a DNA test with John might be favourable. What was Paddy implying? Not surprisingly, John declined.

Michael telephoned to alert me to a call from Margaret – she was intending to contact me, but only when she felt up to it. I only had to wait two days.

'Well, hello Karen,' she said sharply, with no sign of remorse. 'So now you know. People have affairs and that's it. You have to understand this whole business has made me very ill. Now you can just put it all behind you and move on. I have no intention of talking any more about it. I'm worried about Michael and what effect all this is having on him. You've got to leave it all alone now.' Even with time to reflect she still had no intention of speaking openly and honestly to me.

'Margaret, are you going to give me a name?' I asked impatiently.

'No, I'm not,' she barked. 'It was nearly fifty years ago, what difference does it make? Anyway he's been dead for thirty years.'

'I need to know the name of my father,' I pleaded.

'Well I'm not telling you, I'll never tell you. Just put it all behind you and move on with your life. Think about Paul and your three daughters.'

'Margaret I need to know his name. You have lied to me for almost three years. I have given you so many opportunities to tell me the truth and you have chosen not to do so. I want to know about the private nursing home. It was my father who paid wasn't it?' I remembered the words of my adoptive mother that I'd so readily dismissed, '*The father had money.*'

324

'Oh, for goodness sake, how am I supposed to remember that? It's been nearly fifty years. I can't even remember how to make a cup of tea at the moment,' she exclaimed, disregarding the importance of my demand.

'If you could put it all behind you and move on with your life, I thought that I might come over next year and we could have a week's holiday together or something,' she announced.

I ignored her most inconceivable suggestion. It was utterly ludicrous.

'Margaret, I can't put it all behind me, I need to know.' My persistence was annoying her. Unlike her sons, she couldn't dictate to me.

'No, I'm not telling you and that's final, it doesn't matter,' she said callously before embarking on a venomous attack. 'I don't know what it must be like living in your house. You have refused to let this drop. It must be unbearable for the girls. I hear Rosemary has already left home (referring to Rosemary's recent and most contented move to London for her gap year) and Paddy says he's not surprised. He also thinks as soon as Annie's old enough she'll do the same,' she declared vindictively.

Even now she was incapable of any contrition. 'I don't want to talk about this any more, but I do want you to be happy. I do love you. I want you to put it all behind you. Give me a ring in a few weeks. God bless you.' The call was over.

Her words 'What does it matter?' were left ringing in my ears. It was the cruellest remark. I had no intention of wasting any more time on her. I also refrained from calling Michael immediately to disclose the nature of the call. Keeping the rest of her family informed of my communications with her had done little in the past to help me, other than to keep them abreast of my next move. No amount of lies or shocking behaviour on the part of their mother had driven them to truly act on my behalf.

When I did finally speak to Michael I was left utterly

disheartened. He dutifully reported to me a recent conversation with his parents. It was intended to finally provide the truth that I had been seeking, however I knew immediately it was yet another fabrication from Margaret and Paddy.

My conception was dismissed as the result of a girls' night out with a few too many glasses of wine and what followed next was just a chance liaison with an ex-boyfriend. Michael was keen to point out that there really was nothing more to it than that.

The explanation left me seething. It was a lie. I considered it highly unlikely that she would have been out on a girls' night in 1961 and it was also doubtful that she would have consumed wine at that time. And how did a supposedly reckless one night stand lead to her giving birth in a private nursing home? Why couldn't Michael see through the deception? Why, even at this stage, did he lack the power to challenge his parents?

I had another, far more pressing question. If I were to believe Margaret's claim that my father had been dead for thirty years, how was it she knew this? Having returned to Ireland in the early 70s, why and how did she manage to keep tabs on a man in England who had supposedly been a chance encounter?

Michael, as ever, was curious to know my next move. This time, however, I did not plan to share it with him.

33. The Final Chapter

December 2009

Undeterred by the Coleman family's behaviour, I turned my attention once again to St Margaret's nursing home, where I had arrived in this world. Despite Margaret's seemingly vague recollection of events at that time, I firmly believe that my father did provide the necessary funding for this privately run establishment. The building no longer exists and, unfortunately, whilst the various authorities acknowledge that it had once existed, there appear to be no records remaining. In an attempt to locate anyone who may have been connected to the nursing home back in the early 60's, I penned a letter to the Hackney Gazette, giving a brief résumé of the circumstances surrounding my birth, including the name of my birth mother. It gave me great satisfaction to see my letter published. No doubt in the unlikely event of Margaret reading the letter, it would certainly have brought on yet another suicide threat. Nonetheless, the pleasure was short lived, as sadly there was no response.

Disappointed and frustrated I sent a second letter, this time to the General Register Office for England and Wales explaining the facts surrounding the incorrect entry on my birth record and requesting an alteration. To support my request I enclosed copies of the various documents obtained over recent years, including my recent DNA result.

During an initial conversation with an employee at the

government department, I was delighted to find that they were prepared to investigate the revelation that Patrick Coleman was recorded incorrectly as dead by his wife Margaret. This was of particular interest to them, and not long afterwards, I received notification of a letter sent to Margaret requesting an explanation on this matter. The official request issued by the Home Office Identity & Passport Service would surely guarantee a true account of events. I also learned that only the person or persons who have registered a birth have the authority to amend it. Margaret could hardly fail to comply with an official demand from the British Government. As the authorities were also in possession of my extensive findings, this would ensure that any attempt by Margaret to be evasive would be challenged, leaving her no alternative but to finally divulge the truth.

I waited anxiously for news of further developments, even wondering if I might hear from Margaret herself, very probably livid at the lengths I am prepared to go to in order to unearth the truth. There was nothing. Eventually, unable to contain my curiosity any longer, I telephoned the department for news of her reply. To my utter amazement, I discovered that Margaret had not only chosen to ignore this request, but also a second follow-up letter had been ignored. Furthermore, I was devastated to learn that as this concerned events which happened almost fifty years ago, the authorities were unable to pursue the matter any further. I stressed the importance of my knowing the identity of my father, particularly as my birth mother had deliberately set out to record incorrect information, whilst being fully aware of the facts.

A Government worker was at pains to point out to me that because an adoption order supersedes an original birth certificate, there is no reason to amend a record that has been considered closed since January 1963.

This explanation is extremely unsatisfactory and I am

astonished that a birth record can be considered null and void, whatever the circumstances. How can this be? In common with every other UK citizen, whether adopted or not, I have only one birth record and if found to be incorrect, it should be amended at whatever stage of one's life this discovery is made. How can an adoption order, which is not a public document, take precedence over a birth record, an official document?

This question also raises a number of other issues facing adopted people. Under the current system at the General Register Office there is an incomplete public record of the life and death of adopted people. For anyone compiling a family tree, which involves an adopted person, it is almost impossible to trace the complete life and death and legal parentage of that adopted family member. A death is registered under the legal name or, in the case of a female, her subsequent married name. However, if adopted, the birth record of that person would be untraceable, as it remains under their original birth name. There is no public record showing the name of the legal parents of an adopted person, so it is practically impossible to trace back beyond a marriage, or indeed a death record, should that person remain single.

Remarkably, there is no public record in existence stating the legal names of both the mother and father of an adoptee. The marriage certificate of an adoptee is, in fact, the only public document which can provide a clue as to the legal family, stating as it does the legal name of the father. This information may help in the process of searching a family tree, but other than his name and occupation, no other information is provided. Without the mother's name it still remains a challenging exercise, particularly if the family name is a popular one. However, if an adoptee never marries then information linking him or her back to their legal parents is unobtainable.

Therefore, registered as I am under my birth name and

not under my subsequent legal name, it will be practically impossible for any future generations searching my family tree, to find anything beyond my marriage, as my marriage certificate states my maiden name as my adopted name. Although I was legally raised as Karen Gay, there is no birth record or similar to corroborate this name, nor any public document which actually states that both Bernice and Peter Gay are my legal parents. As the current situation stands, even in death, without a complete record, I will remain unidentifiable.

For most of my life I have struggled with my identity and today this struggle has become even more significant as I try to resolve what has turned out to be a highly complex issue. As I approach my 50th year, I have come to realise that the catalogue of names bestowed upon me to date have all failed to provide the comfort and recognition that I so desperately long for. Brazel is the married name I committed to for over twenty years and the name of my three daughters, but since the legal dissolution of my marriage, it now, inevitably, feels incongruous and inapt. Gay is my legal maiden name, but after my recent emotional journey it no longer feels right to revert to it, even after the change in my marital status. Coleman was my very first name, albeit briefly, and although no longer my legal name it nevertheless remains the one name under which my own beginning is logged in perpetuity – a highly distressing record, not only for its erroneous entry, but also for the extraordinary omission of a Christian name, something denied to few. Finally, even the prospect of a future marriage to Paul does not solve my lifelong torment. Whilst his name will unite us, my own internal turmoil concerning identity will remain.

The subject of identity is not the only issue to concern anyone adopted, particularly if it happened in the 60s, when babies were given up for adoption without any consideration for their future medical well-being. Whilst compassion was shown towards the many unmarried mothers fearful of any retribution, there was little justice for the countless number of babies involved. Medical intervention involving genetics had already begun. The first kidney transplant occurred as early as 1950 and the first transplant from a living donor took place in 1954, involving identical twins.

Regardless of these medical developments and their possible implications for the future, part of the adoption process was to immediately cut off all connections to blood relatives, leaving adoptees destined to inferior medical care for a lifetime. Unless an adopted person from my generation successfully locates their birth mother and father, they remain completely unaware of any hereditary conditions. Throughout my life, in the absence of any obvious reference to adoption on my medical records, I have been frequently asked for my medical history. This vital information should appear in a prominent place on my medical file, thereby reducing the pain and trauma that is generated each time I have been forced to remember my own lifelong flawed circumstances.

Sadly and somewhat perversely, even as I write this in 2011, it appears that the law that protects adopted people not only discriminates against us, but also differentiates us adversely from the majority of the population. Provoking and emphasising something that is so fundamental, it is destined to set us apart and deprive us of any true acknowledgement for our entire lifetime and beyond.

At this point, it is far easier to understand Margaret's initial and continued hostility towards me. For over forty years, her every effort has been to conceal the truth. This has ensured that there could never be any kind of relationship between us. Not unnaturally, I had always lived in the hope of a positive and deeply moving reunion with the woman who had felt compelled to give up her child, but sadly this was never to be. My sudden

331

and very unwelcome appearance evoked a period in her life, which had been deeply buried away, perhaps she hoped, forever. For her it was a reminder of the day of her marriage to Patrick Coleman, when she knowingly walked up the aisle of St Dominic's Roman Catholic Church, carrying another man's child. I remain convinced that sitting together in Dublin on that fateful day in April 2007, Patrick truly believed even after forty-five years, that I really was his daughter. I still don't understand why Margaret made the decision to include Patrick's name on my birth certificate. She has always known the identity of my father and it wasn't Patrick. Although she led Patrick to believe I was indeed his daughter, she convinced him unwittingly to agree to my adoption.

Regrettably the most recent revelations have had a consequential and immensely detrimental effect on what was left of any relationship with my three brothers. Although, initially, news of a sister was positively received and warmly embraced, our very new relationship was not strong enough to withstand the perils ahead. My sheer determination to delve further and uncover the truth was in direct conflict with my brothers' need to remain compliant and complacent and abide by their mother's familiar, tyrannical rule. Somehow, it was inevitable that without their mother's sanction, we were destined to falter. By playing safe and choosing to continue a lifetime habit of unquestioningly obeying their mother, unwilling to challenge the woman who allowed them all to believe that we were indeed full blood siblings, only serves to condone her immoral actions. While I remain steadfast in my search for the truth, my brothers prefer the easy way out and to settle back to a life of denial that precludes me – their sister. Any doubts they may have, as to the veracity of their mother's account of events, has perhaps left them fearful of what further surprises might still be lurking in relation to their own existence.

This sad outcome leaves me faced once again with abandonment and rejection, this time rejected not only by my birth mother, but also by my brothers, John, Michael and Oliver. All that remains is a sense of sadness for what might have been. The briefest of time with my brothers and their families provided Paul, my daughters and me with happy and enjoyable memories forever. It exposed my daughters to a way of life that they'd never truly experienced. To have regular, close contact with family members, who were all as keen to share our lives as we were to share theirs, brought a new dimension to our everyday existence.

My last communication with any of the Coleman family was with Michael shortly before Christmas 2009. The purpose was for him to relay some very worrying and unwelcome news. Margaret had been diagnosed with breast cancer and an operation to remove the tumour was to be carried out immediately. Although concerned to hear of Margaret's condition, I was furious to discover from Michael that Margaret had been insistent that under no circumstances should I be alerted to her illness. As already mentioned earlier in this chapter, without doubt medical history is one of the prime reasons for searching for a birth mother and her decision to deprive her three granddaughters and me of such knowledge seemed to be one of sheer malice. However, Michael's decision to go against his mother's wishes and show concern for our well-being was much appreciated. This was his last genuine display of kinship. A call from him following the surgery, reporting that all had gone well, was indeed our last conversation. Despite receiving a birthday card from Michael the following March, it lacked any sentiment. Unlike the cards I had received from him the previous two birthdays, on this occasion there was no reference to 'sister' or any kind words, just a very curt 'to' and 'from'.

Reflecting on the brief time that we all shared has provoked feelings of sadness. John and Helen's relatively close proximity to us had enabled frequent opportunities to get together and were always eagerly anticipated by everyone. Without children of their own, John's constant tomfoolery and boundless energy and Helen's caring nature made them instantly appealing to my daughters. It wasn't long before Annie had found the confidence to make her first solo visit to their home and travelled across London on public transport to spend a day in their company.

'I miss Helen the most,' said Nancy poignantly, remembering our hugely enjoyable girly shopping expeditions with Helen in Oxford Street.

Michael, undoubtedly, was the brother with whom I felt the greatest natural connection. Despite the miles separating us, I sensed something very special between us. His lifelong desire to have a sister was always guaranteed to accelerate our relationship. Rosemary too, soon formed a special bond with Michael. She bears an uncanny resemblance to him, looking more like his daughter than his own. Rosemary was delighted to fly alone to Ireland to spend a week looking after Michael's son and daughter during the summer of 2008. Although the intention had been for her to childmind, both Michael and Helena preferred instead to take much time off work to get to know their niece, and in doing so ensured a thoroughly enjoyable time for them all.

Sadly, it is Oliver for whom I have the most concern. Deprived of his independence he is doomed to a life of solitude. Living with his parents still, it was always going to make for a difficult relationship between us. If, as I understand it, the house where he lives with Margaret and Paddy is truly legally his, then he is compelled to live under his mother's strict regime until circumstances change. John and Michael's apparent inertia towards Oliver has been shocking. Allowing their mother's actions to go unchallenged and continuing to dictate their brother's every move is outrageous. His few unaccompanied trips to the

UK to visit John and Helen are missed opportunities to inject something more into Oliver's limited and mundane life. Away from the constraints of his mother, his attire and hairstyle could be revamped to something more befitting his age. Regrettably, nobody is prepared to oppose Margaret's autocratic reign. Oliver is very able. He has gardening skills, a driving licence and a very personable nature, but he needs the support of those closest to him in order to succeed. As I reflect on the limited but very positive time that Oliver spent with my family and me, I cherish the wonderful memories of a brother who in our company undoubtedly encountered the best experiences of his life. I miss his weekly texts, asking after the well-being of each one of us and ending with just a snippet of information regarding his mundane existence. I loved being addressed as his 'big beautiful sister.' It made me feel very special.

Margaret's misguided conduct towards her youngest son has been suffocating. Perhaps, as a Roman Catholic, Margaret's utter devotion to him is deemed to be her penance. Although nine years my junior, Oliver's birthday is remarkably close to mine. Maybe every stage of her fourth pregnancy served as a reminder of the one she had tried so hard to forget. After producing two very fit and healthy sons, each during the month of August, she had a difficult labour and bore a child susceptible to poor health. His feeble disposition caused her endless worry. By devoting her entire attention to Oliver, does she live in hope of finding redemption for her actions years before?

Oliver's needs are certainly far greater than mine. In witnessing John and Michael's reluctance to tackle Margaret in support of their brother, there is little hope of them ever supporting me.

Margaret has at last conceded that Patrick Coleman is not my father. However, I am immensely angry and resentful that she refuses unequivocally to reveal the identity of the man who indeed is my true biological parent. In view of the lengths she has gone

335

to in order to withhold this information from me, I realise that my chance of ever learning his true identity is extremely slim. I continue to live in hope though, that she may have documented these details, to be passed on to me on her death. Realistically, I fear she will take the secret to her grave. How tragic to be so close to the truth at long last and yet still perhaps never learn the identity of my own father, my daughters' grandfather, because of Margaret's selfishness. If what Margaret says is true, that he died over thirty years ago, I have wondered about the circumstances of his death. Was it simply old age, an accident, or perhaps a hereditary condition? I am curious to know something of the man responsible for half my genetic make-up. I suspect I would find him to be left-handed and tall in stature, but most of all I would love to learn something of his nature, possibly a warm, open and gregarious individual, qualities that I have yet to see in my birth mother.

I have come through some extremely turbulent years. Fortunately, I have had the total love, support and kindness of those closest to me, namely Paul, my three daughters and a handful of extremely valued friends. The comfort of others at such an emotional time has been heartfelt and I am glad to say that I now feel happier and more content than I have ever been. The decision to write my story has been an immensely challenging one. Although the writing process has been long and arduous, it has also been surprisingly enjoyable. Writing an account of my search and life as an adopted person has been extremely cathartic. I have grown in confidence and feel a more complete and balanced individual, having in the process also discovered what truly matters in life. It is for this reason that I have decided to write my story under the simple pseudonym Karen Lesley, the names given to me by my adopted parents and the only names that have remained truly mine throughout my life.

Despite the inconclusive outcome, I have absolutely no regrets over my decision to trace Margaret Coleman. Whilst I accept that Bernice and Peter are my parents, nothing can ever alter a true bloodline. After many years wondering and searching, I discovered only one of my birth parents and it is very unlikely I will ever discover the identity of my father. I did, however, make the bitter-sweet discovery of three brothers and enjoyed a brief and wonderful relationship with them. Prior to this mammoth undertaking, I had lived with a void in my life, never really feeling a sense of connection or belonging. In recent years my fraught and highly emotional journey has involved all aspects of my life and has indeed provided me with a greater sense of who I really am.

Karen, Annie, Rosemary, Nancy and Paul, 2011.